The Art of
Architectural
Daylighting

Mary Guzowski

The Art of Architectural Daylighting

Design + Technology

Mary Guzowski

Laurence King Publishing

DEDICATION

With love and appreciation to James Lindbeck,
and with gratitude to my teachers Joel Loveland
and Marietta Millet.

LAURENCE KING

Published in 2018
by Laurence King Publishing Ltd
361–373 City Road
London EC1V 1LR
Tel +44 20 7841 6900
Fax +44 20 7841 6910
enquiries@laurenceking.com
www.laurenceking.com

A catalogue record for this book is available from
the British Library

ISBN 978 1 78627 164 8

Design: Blok Graphic, London
Commissioning editor: Liz Faber
Senior editor: Gaynor Sermon

Printed in China

Picture credits

Cover images: The Chapel of St. Lawrence, Vantaa,
Finland; Avanto Architects.

Front cover photograph by Tuomas Uusheimo;
back cover photograph by Kuvio.

Inside cover: Concept studies for the Clyfford Still
Museum, Denver, USA; Allied Works Architecture.

Pages 2 and 5: Reid Building, Glasgow, Scotland, UK;
Steven Holl Architects. Photographs by Iwan Baan.

Contents

Introduction

DAYLIGHT AS PHENOMENON AND MATERIAL

Daylight is a dynamic environmental phenomenon and an ephemeral architectural material. It embodies the dimension of time as the movement of light and shadow reveal the changing diurnal and seasonal cycles. In a digital age that runs 24/7, daylight is an antidote to our increasing alienation from nature. Daylight and the changing environmental forces of sun, wind, and weather help us to know "where we are" and "who we are" by rooting us in the ecological phenomena of a particular place, in that climate, and on that site. When coupled with passive solar and bioclimatic design strategies, daylight can reduce energy consumption and provide environmental benefits while enhancing human comfort, health, and well-being.

Daylight is also an architectural medium and the most intangible of materials. In his discussion with Charlie Rose on the design of the Whitney Museum of American Art in New York City, Italian architect Renzo Piano suggested that "light is probably the most essential material for architecture. It is the least touchable, but probably the most important."[1] Light embodies the changing moods of the sky and qualities of place as it interacts with the building form, materials, surface textures, hues, and reflectivity. The varied and changing material and atmospheric effects of daylight can awaken the senses and further enhance our understanding of and relationship to the world in which we live.

THE ART OF DAYLIGHTING

The *Art of Architectural Daylighting* uses twelve "masters of light" case studies to explore how contemporary architects have bridged the poetic and practical potentials of daylighting. These masters of light artfully reconcile the objective attributes of site, climate, and program with the subjective qualities of beauty and human experience. Daylight shapes architecture at all scales— from site planning to building form; room configuration and finishes; and detailing of the structure and envelope. It informs the architectural vocabulary and aesthetic language of the building and is a primary force in defining the atmospheric qualities and program responses.

"In recent decades architecture has often been compared with science. ... But architecture is not a science. It is still the same great synthetic process, a conglomeration of thousands of significant human functions, and it will stay that way. Its essence can never become purely analytical. Architectural study always involves a moment of art and instinct. Its purpose is still to bring the world of matter into harmony with human life."[2]

Alvar Aalto, Architect

DAYLIGHTING DESIGN TRENDS

Several trends have influenced the evolution of daylighting design in contemporary architecture, including: 1) advances in the science of daylighting design; 2) the impacts of parametric façade design and digital fabrication; and 3) advances in digital design methods and tools.

Over the past decade, the "science of daylighting" has matured as practitioners and building-science researchers have continued to demonstrate measurable benefits of daylighting in the areas of energy savings, carbon and greenhouse gas reductions, increased human comfort, and improved productivity and health. Great improvements have also been made in digital rendering, analysis tools, and an ever-increasing number of daylight metrics, guidelines, and assessment methods. These developments have benefited architects and designers in more effectively integrating daylight with other design and performance issues.

Yet, with the promise of scientific and analytical advances, there also lies a risk of too narrowly framing the parameters of daylighting to those that are measurable and empirically defined. An analytical perspective on daylighting design needs to be balanced with a focus on the qualitative dimensions of natural light.

Architectural daylighting and its design processes are complex, multi-faceted, and oftentimes messy and unpredictable. Alvar Aalto suggested that architecture is a "synthetic process," which is a good reminder for today's daylighting designers: "... architecture has often been compared with science. ... But architecture is not a science. It is still the same great synthetic process. ... Its essence can never become purely analytical. Architectural study always involves a moment of art and instinct. Its purpose is still to bring the world of matter into harmony with human life."[3] The following daylighting case study profiles explore the balance between the practical and the poetic; the measurable and the immeasurable.

There has also been increasing interest in the use of parametric façade design and digital fabrication. In the best cases, innovations in parametric design, glazing, cladding, and construction technologies support and enhance the luminous program, daylight performance, aesthetic, and program goals. At times, however, the expressive opportunities and form-giving potential of parametric façade design have little to do with the interior luminous program and quality of light. In the most troubling cases, when the envelope design and program are not integrated, exterior window forms and resulting interior daylighting patterns can impede luminous goals and visual comfort. Advances in parametric design and digital fabrication methods have, in part, shifted the focus of daylighting design away from its inherent spatial qualities to the animation of the building façade and its relationship to the envelope surface. Consequently, there has been an emerging shift from daylighting "space" to daylighting "surface." Despite the rich potential of parametric design, the vital importance of daylight in creating meaningful spatial experiences should not be forgotten.

▷ The narrow urban house elegantly integrates daylighting, natural ventilation, and passive cooling in the double envelope, which includes "stacking green" exterior planting boxes, large interior glass walls with operable windows, and a multi-story light well. Stacking Green House, Ho Chi Minh City, Vietnam; Vo Trong Nghia Architects.

"Artificial light is a single tiny static moment in light and is the light of night and never can equal the nuances of mood created by the time of day and the wonder of the seasons. A great building, in my opinion, must begin with the unmeasurable, must go through measurable means when it is being designed and in the end must be unmeasurable." [4]

Louis Kahn, Architect

Louis Kahn underscored the programmatic and spatial significance of daylight: "One may say that architecture is the thoughtful making of spaces. ... It is the creating of spaces that evoke a feeling of appropriate use. To the musician a sheet of music is seeing from what he hears. A plan of a building should read like a harmony of spaces in light. Even a space intended to be dark should have just enough light from some mysterious opening to tell us how dark it really is. Each space must be defined by its structure and the character of its natural light." [5] The focus on the building façade and the surface of the envelope need not be at the expense of interior luminous and spatial qualities, experience, comfort, and performance. The challenge of contemporary daylighting design is to explore the full potential of design from the inside out and the outside in; to mediate space and surface; and to celebrate practical performance benefits as well as aesthetic, experiential, and ecological dimensions.

The processes and tools for daylighting design include places for both analog and digital design methods. The predominance of digital tools in contemporary practice can mistakenly bias designers toward digital methods. Simple physical models are still an essential design tool for studying and simulating the experience and atmosphere of natural light in space and time. The appropriate choice of design methods and tools depends upon daylighting aspirations, design issues, performance metrics, and phase of design. The scope and scale of daylighting analyses vary greatly from project to project—from simple intuitive explorations to in-depth analyses, using methods that include sketching, diagramming, physical models, computer simulations, energy and systems integration studies, and full-scale mock-ups and prototypes. The case studies reveal varied approaches, methods, and tools for thoughtfully integrating daylighting into the design process.

CASE STUDY PROFILES

The case studies were selected to illustrate a cross-section of daylighting design intentions, building types, scales, and geographic locations. The daylighting profiles are organized around six themes: 1) choreographed light, 2) atmospheric light, 3) sculpted light, 4) structured light, 5) material light, and 6) integrated light. The masters of light range from emerging architects to seasoned practitioners. They represent different design philosophies, priorities, methods, and approaches to natural light. Included are works by architects Tadao Ando, Brad Cloepfil (Allied Works), David Chipperfield, Mario Cucinella, Sverre Fehn, Steven Holl, Neil Gillespie (Reiach and Hall Architects), Vo Trong Nghia, Renzo Piano, Anu Puustinen and Ville Hara (Avanto Architects), Cristián Undurraga, and Peter Zumthor.

They all approach daylight as an environmental phenomenon and a dynamic "building material" with evocative site, form-giving, programmatic, material, and experiential design potential. Each chapter explores a daylighting theme through the lens of two case studies to address related design intentions, climate and geographic implications, program considerations, and architectural strategies.

Chapter 1: Choreographed Light considers how daylight can be used to create a sequence of spatial and luminous events to celebrate the experience of place, climate, and program. Whether intentionally meandering or tightly composed, light can be scripted much like the choreography of music and theater.

Chapter 2: Atmospheric Light celebrates the qualities and moods of light particular to a geographic location and latitude for a given program. The desired atmospheric qualities of light and darkness are intimately related to design intentions, experiential concepts, and practical program goals.

Chapter 3: Sculpted Light explores how architectural form can be shaped to support daylighting program and performance goals. The building massing, section, spatial organization, envelope, and window detailing are inseparable from the quality, quantity, distribution, effectiveness, and ecological benefits of natural light.

Chapter 4: Structured Light considers the relationships between light and structure as it expresses design intentions and desired atmospheric qualities. The choice of daylighting strategies, form, and detailing are inseparable from a selected structural system and material palette.

Chapter 5: Material Light explores natural light as a dynamic and ephemeral building material that interacts with architectural space and material surfaces to influence the resulting luminous quality of space in time.

Chapter 6: Integrated Light explores opportunities to couple daylighting with architectural form, passive design, and innovative technological systems to integrate program, aesthetics, performance, energy, and sustainable design goals.

MASTERS OF LIGHT

Daylighting has both quantitative and qualitative dimensions. On the one hand, light is tangible, measurable, and predictable. The apparent movement of the sun can be precisely determined, and luminous attributes can be measured using standardized metrics such as lux, footcandles, daylight factors, and candelas per square meter. Yet, there is also a dimension of natural light that is unpredictable and immeasurable. There is a necessary element of intuition and experimentation required to discover the oftentimes unanticipated and emergent qualities of natural light as it interacts in time with changing site forces and sky conditions, architectural form, and material properties. The processes of discovery, experimentation, and serendipity are inherent to the art of daylighting design.

Daylighting masterpieces of exceptional beauty and architectural clarity form a body of seminal works that shape and inspire succeeding generations of designers. The legacy of the modern masters of light such as Alvar Aalto, Louis Kahn, Carlo Scarpa, and Luis Barragán continue to influence architects and daylighting designers to this day. It is hoped that the clarity, innovation, and elegance of the following contemporary projects will inform and inspire design practitioners, educators, and students in their own daylighting explorations. May this book be of benefit to all those who seek to integrate the rich potential of daylighting into contemporary architectural design.

HOW TO USE THIS BOOK

Each chapter topic is illustrated by two contemporary case study profiles that include narrative descriptions, photographs, architectural illustrations, concept diagrams, and qualitative and quantitative daylighting assessments. The narrative profiles provide insight into the comparative daylighting design intentions, strategies, and methods. Daylight diagrams provide a graphic summary of the design strategies, structural systems, materials, and underlying concepts. Varied types of daylighting analyses illustrate the estimated illuminance levels (lux or footcandles), luminance ratios (candela per square meter), and light distributions (three-dimensional shape of light). Perspective renderings capture the experiential character and quality of light in the space.

Each project profile reveals distinct design intentions and strategies from the architects and design teams in response to the particular lighting goals, program activities, environmental forces, site conditions, and other design parameters. The related daylight design representations, diagrams, and analyses therefore vary in scope, method, and media. Daylight analyses were conducted by the architectural firms or were developed by the author and student research assistants at the School of Architecture at the University of Minnesota. Quantitative assessments provided by firms were conducted using varied types and scales of physical models as well as computer modeling programs including Radiance, Ecotect, and Maxwell Render (as noted in each case study profile). Analyses by the author were developed using Velux Daylight Visualizer: they are intended only to provide insight into daylight strategies and quality of light, and to allow relative comparisons between projects. As computer simulations, the estimated illuminance levels and contrast ratios are not intended to illustrate the actual luminous effects and richness of daylighting in the built works, but rather to help visualize an approximate quality and distribution of light. Whenever possible, interviews were conducted with the principal architects, project architects, daylighting consultants, and/or engineers to provide insight into the design processes and assessment methods.

DAYLIGHT ANALYSES

As the projects have varied geographic locations, climates, and program types, the parameters and types of daylighting analyses and representations also vary to reveal their particular story of light. With four of the twelve projects, the daylight analyses were provided by the architectural and consulting firms. Although varying in approach and scope, these analyses typically focus on the illuminance levels and light distribution on vertical surfaces or on the horizontal workplane to support program activities and to meet target illuminance levels (in lux or footcandles). For the remaining eight projects, the daylight analyses were conducted by the author and research assistants, with three types of assessments provided: 1) seasonal and diurnal illuminance studies in plan or section (isolux contours); 2) perspective renderings with corresponding luminance studies (in candela per square meter); and 3) seasonal and diurnal time-lapse renderings (experiential quality and movement of light patterns through time).

Seasonal and diurnal illuminance studies in plan or section, using isolux contours, illustrate the estimated light distribution through time for typical local sky conditions. Depending on the locale, the selected sky condition for analysis might include clear, overcast, and/or intermittent (clear and overcast skies). Like a topographic map, isolux contours illustrate the "shape of light," the distribution of light and darkness in space, and the estimated illuminance levels (in lux or footcandles) relative to the desired atmosphere, program, and lighting goals.

Perspective renderings and corresponding luminance studies (using false-color renderings in candela per square meter) illustrate strategic perspectives as perceived when walking through the building or selected spaces. The paired perspectives and luminance studies help elucidate the experience of daylight and corresponding contrast ratios, potential sources of glare, and luminous effects of material finishes and surface reflectance. Qualitative seasonal time-lapse renderings, at select times of day and year, help the observer visualize the changing phenomena and atmospheric conditions of light and darkness in space and time for the specific geographic location and latitude.

The project profiles can be used in various ways: from providing insights into the strategies and lessons of a single project, to comparing profiles across projects through different means and media, including descriptive narratives, photographs and drawings, conceptual diagrams, and qualitative and quantitative analyses.

---

1 Charlie Rose, "Renzo Piano: Architecture About 'Fighting Against Gravity,'" YouTube video, 33:06, May 28, 2015, https://charlierose.com/videos/28141.

2 Goran Schildt, *Alvar Aalto: The Mature Years*, New York: Rizzoli, 1989, 272.

3 ibid.

4 Robert Twombly, *Louis Kahn: Essential Texts*, New York: W. W. Norton & Company, 2003, 68.

5 Robert Twombly, *Louis Kahn: Essential Texts*, 68.

Chapter 1

Choreographed Light

1.1 Chapel of St. Lawrence
1.2 Reid Building, Glasgow School of Art

"Due to its power to seduce and attract, light has always played a pivotal role in successions of space that are rewarding and memorable. It is not single isolated moments or views that are important for the moving eye, but a continuous flow of human perceptions." [1]

Henry Plummer, *The Architecture of Natural Light*

How does the choreography of daylight support the broader vision of a project, a program, and the desired qualities of light? How is time architectural and how might daylight be used to express the diurnal and seasonal cycles? How do the movements of the body and the movements of time and light correspond? As with dance, music, or cinema, architecture can be orchestrated as a sequence of spatial, luminous, and experiential progressions.

To choreograph light is to create intentional relationships between the desired luminous qualities and other architectural design variables such as spatial sequence, activities, materials and structure, and context. Daylight can enrich a design as the moods and colors of light and changing sky conditions interact with space,

▷ Night view of the west-entry courtyards and copper-clad façades of the chapels in winter. Chapel of St. Lawrence, Vantaa, Finland; Avanto Architects.

▷ Skylight and south-facing monitor within a "driven void of light." Cuts within the void provide views through the adjacent circulation spaces and studios. Reid Building, Glasgow, Scotland, UK; Steven Holl Architects.

form, and surface. The dimension of time, although predictable in the apparent movement of the sun during the course of the day and the year, introduces an oftentimes unpredictable and transient beauty, which is embodied in dynamic, fleeting, and momentarily luminous phenomena.

In *Ritual House*, architect Ralph Knowles discusses the importance of designing architecture to support daily rituals that connect us to the cycles of nature: "Our rituals are often a celebration of nature's rhythms—a joyous response to the recurring changes around us. Ritual imparts special meaning to alternations of time and season, setting up rhythms in our own lives that attach us to the places we occupy ... a time-rich environment offers a complex potential for ritual." [2]

In the following studies of works by Avanto Architects and Steven Holl Architects, daylight is choreographed to support design intentions and program goals while enhancing the unique phenomena of light in place. First is the funerary Chapel of St. Lawrence in Vantaa, Finland, by Ville Hara and Anu Puustinen, of Avanto Architects, where daylight is used to create a calm and comforting environment for mourners and funerary rituals. Puustinen and Hara studied and experienced the mourning process from the perspective of the families, friends, and staff by attending funerals and working intimately with the clients and users. The Chapel of St. Lawrence is a "feeling architecture," designed from the inside out. Light is choreographed as a sequence of experiences that move from the landscape through a courtyard, into the building entry, chapel, and back out to the cemetery. The symbolic meanings and luminous qualities are inseparable from the physical journey, with carefully framed views, varied degrees of privacy, movement, and stillness, and changing spatial and luminous qualities—from low and dim to high and bright. The skillful integration of daylight, simplicity of form, and elegant material palette (including plastered

"The vista along this narrow street in Siena is closed by brighter fragments of the buildings that stand at the edge of the Piazza del Campo . ... And the character of light suggests—but only suggests—that an open expanse lies ahead to the right. If this view withholds so much of itself from us, why do we find it interesting? 'Withholds' is the key: ... The partly revealed, partly hidden fragments that close the vista urge exploration, which we expect will reveal more about the multiplicity of material that holds our attention and our interest."[3]

Grant Hildebrand, *Origins of Architectural Pleasure*

masonry walls, oak, slate, and patinated copper) support the program goals while celebrating Finland's seasonal extremes and dramatic northern climate.

Next is the Reid Building at the Glasgow School of Art, in Scotland, by Steven Holl Architects, which places natural light and the movement of the human body at the center of the architectural and spatial choreography. Movement along circulation pathways provides varied qualities of space, light, and view to foster interactions between students and faculty from diverse design disciplines. The building envelope, light shafts, circulation paths, spatial volumes, and structure encourage informal connections, afford rich interior and exterior views, create distinct atmospheric qualities, and define a "new language of light" in relation to Charles Rennie Mackintosh's historic 1909 Mackintosh Building. The building form was studied and sculpted to reveal how space can be shaped by light and how light can be shaped by space.

Architecture is a three-dimensional experience of the body in space, brought to life by the fourth dimension of time through the changing rhythms of day and night and the cycles of the seasons. Light can be used to encourage wandering, to gently guide, or to draw people through architecture and space. Avanto Architects and Steven Holl Architects reveal that luminous experiences can be choreographed as architectural journeys that engage the body, awaken the senses, and foster relationships between people and the built and natural environments.

▷ The ephemeral glass façades of the Reid Building merge with the night sky to contrast with the masonry walls of the historic Assembly Building and adjacent Mackintosh Building to the south. Reid Building, Glasgow, UK; Steve Holl Architects.

△ Whitewashed masonry walls of the
west entry and bell tower merge with
the winter landscape.

Case study 1.1

Chapel of St. Lawrence
(Pyhän Laurin Kappeli)

Vantaa, Finland

Anu Puustinen and Ville Hara, Avanto Architects

"The theme of the proposal, 'polku' or 'path,' portrays man's journey from mortality to eternity. ... Giving peace and dignity to the funeral ceremony has been of primary importance in the planning of the building, and movement from one room to another is highlighted with a change of lighting and spatial characteristics." [4]

Anu Puustinen, Avanto Architects

△ Large portals in the west façade open into exterior courtyards that lead to the adjacent lobbies of the two chapels.

LIGHT AND THE QUALITY OF PLACE

Vantaa, Finland
Sited adjacent to the medieval stone Church of St. Lawrence in Vantaa, Finland (ca. 1450), the new Chapel of St. Lawrence has a quiet presence designed to support funerary activities and religious events in the community. Ville Hara and Anu Puustinen of Avanto Architects thoughtfully considered the scale, form, materials, and detailing of the chapel to create a respectful architectural conversation with the beloved historic church and cemetery.

Finnish Light and Climate
Vantaa has a humid continental climate with mild summers and relatively severe winters. It is 14 kilometers (9 miles) northeast of Helsinki, within the greater metropolitan region, and is designated as a culturally significant area. At 60.2° north latitude, just south of the Arctic Circle (66.5° north latitude), it is a place of seasonal extremes. Daylight changes dramatically as the length of day varies from roughly 6 to 19 hours on the winter and summer solstices. The long summer days are known as "white nights," when the sun dips below the horizon only briefly and twilight is experienced throughout the night. During the winter months, there are extended periods of darkness. The noon solar altitude varies from a low of 6.3° to a high of 53.3° from winter to summer.

Author Barry Lopez describes the experience of the sun in northern latitudes: "In a far northern winter, the sun surfaces slowly in the south and then disappears at nearly the same spot, like a whale rolling over. The idea that the sun 'rises in the east and sets in the west' simply does not apply. The thought that a 'day' consists of a morning and a forenoon, an afternoon and an evening, is a convention. ... The pattern is not the same here." [5] In addition to dramatic seasonal change, this location experiences the Aurora Borealis, or "northern lights," with extraordinary fields of colored light visible in clear night skies from September through March.

△ (Top) Sunlight animates the copper-mesh shading and glazed entries of the south façade and native wildflower gardens in summer.

△ (Bottom) Soft diffuse light and snow within an entry courtyard in winter.

The weather in Vantaa can vary as greatly as the length of day. Precipitation is typical from October through April, in the form of fog, drizzle, rain, and snow. Springtime and summer are often clear and sunny, while overcast skies are more common in fall and winter. Average temperatures range from −6°C (21.2°F) in February to 17.5°C (63.5°F) in July, with average lows of −9°C (15.8°F) and average highs of 22°C (71.6°F). [6] Winds are variable throughout the year, with prevailing southerly to southwesterly winds shifting to the west and north. Weather conditions can be volatile, with rapid changes in temperature, humidity, and precipitation resulting in dramatic atmospheric effects as the changing light interacts with snow, rain, and wind.

LIGHT AND THE DESIGN INTENTIONS

Path and Program

Architects Anu Puustinen and Ville Hara used the concept of "polku," or path, to shape the design intentions and spatial organization of the Chapel of St. Lawrence. The new facility needed to accommodate two very different types of funerary programming: the first to comfort mourners and support related rituals; the second to facilitate behind-the-scenes preparations of the deceased and attendant activities. The chapel is also used for other types of ritual and

◁ Site plan of building with historic
church and cemetery to the south.

▽ Floor plan illustrating the nested layers
of space and choreographed pathways
through the west-entry courtyards,
lobbies, chapels, and south gardens.

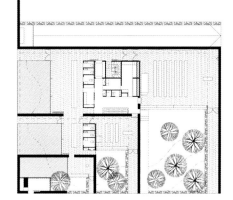

West–east section

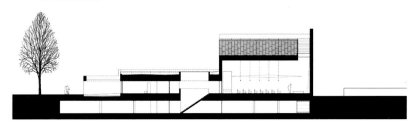

North–south section

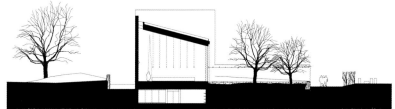

celebratory occasions such as weddings, baptisms, and community gatherings. The design challenge was to embody poetic symbols, rituals, and atmospheric experiences of the "human path" and life journey, while supporting the practical needs of the staff. Puustinen and Hara gained insights by attending funeral services, shadowing the staff, and engaging other collaborators (clients, artists, and architectural, engineering, and construction consultants) in the design and construction process. Puustinen explains: "We thought very carefully how it feels to be in this space and go through the ritual ceremony. We empathize with people in making spaces where they feel as good as possible in a demanding situation. The daylight along the way always has symbolic meaning. We are trying to help people to go on and underline this feeling of life after death … it might relieve somebody.[7] The design solution lies in carefully choreographed public paths and service paths that are spatially separated to ensure acoustic and visual privacy.

Ritual Space and Form
Sited to the northeast of the historic stone church and cemetery, the chapel's rectilinear plan is organized as nested spaces of decreasing size and intimacy and includes two lobbies, two chapels, an urn-receiving room, and three south gardens. The inner spaces are entered through two courtyards that lie behind

◁ West–east site/building section
reveals the layering of spaces in the
landscape, courtyards, and chapel.
A central skylight provides daylight
to the lower level.

△ North–south site/building section
illustrates the relationship between the
main chapel, garden, and adjacent
cemetery.

large portals in the west façade, which is a whitewashed masonry wall that extends outward from the chapel to shelter from view the parking and service areas to the north. The southwest corner of the chapel is anchored by a slender bell tower. On the interior, two parallel lobbies allow for concurrent services while maintaining physical separation and visual and acoustic privacy. Three ritual spaces—the large chapel, small chapel, and urn room—each exit to the adjacent cemetery on the south through their own native wildflower gardens. Staff spaces and a service stair are clustered between the lobbies and chapels to provide acoustic separation and access to the lower-level support spaces and private viewing area. Strict technical requirements for the mortuary spaces led to the acoustic isolation of mechanical systems. With Helsinki airport only 8 kilometers (5 miles) to the northwest, the spatial organization and wall construction are also designed to provide sound isolation between interior spaces and the site.

LIGHT AND THE DESIGN STRATEGIES

A Journey of Light and Shadow

Choreographed as a sequence of quiet luminous and acoustic exterior and interior spaces, the atmosphere of the chapel creates a calm and comforting journey. Puustinen explained how daylight is used to create the symbolic qualities and desired atmosphere: "[You] enter the building through the courtyards with a pool of water, a kind of place for quiet before entering. It's an in-between space to take a breath before entering the chapel itself. ... In summer, the water reflects and mirrors the daylight everywhere around. It's a special light. All the way during the ritual path to the chapel there is a skylight leading you, with a symbolic meaning of God who leads you through a way of life; a path of life. The skylight is always following a massive wall, which is leading you forward in the building." [8]

On arrival, visitors walk a gravel pathway beside the rectory garden and a long, whitewashed masonry wall to enter one of two courtyards. The northern entry path leads through a larger courtyard to the main chapel hall, while the smaller courtyard provides entry to a lobby shared by the center chapel and urn-receiving room. Each courtyard is framed by a portal in the whitewashed wall, with a circulation path leading along an exterior wall and a water garden that mirrors the sky and responds to the wind and changing weather. Light reflected from the surface of the water casts dancing patterns onto the adjacent ceiling and wall surfaces. After passing through glass doors, the visitor is enclosed in a serene lobby with a low patinated copper ceiling, slate floor, whitewashed masonry wall, and white oak surfaces and furnishings. This quiet lobby overlooks the courtyards and water gardens, which provide a backdrop for changing views of the landscape.

△ (Above left) A sheltered pathway passes along the masonry wall of the west entry courtyard animated by direct sunlight and the reflected play of light on water.

△ (Above right) Lobby view of the dynamic sunlight from the west courtyard and soft reflected light along the whitewashed north wall leading to the main chapel.

▷ Entry details reveal the play of light on the whitewashed masonry wall, contrasted by the color and textures of the patinated copper ceiling, slate floor, and white-oak door. A brilliant play of sunlight animates artist Pekka Jylhä's glass sculpture entitled "Soul."

▷ In the main chapel, sunlight is filtered through interior and exterior copper-mesh shading on the south façade while the north and east masonry walls are washed with soft diffuse toplighting. Artist Pertti Kukkonen's sculpture "Way of the Cross" integrates as vertical and horizontal elements within the masonry walls.

Puustinen explained the transition between outside and inside: "The lobby areas are dimly lit, with not so much light coming from the west or northwest. We wanted to make it dim, cozy, and homelike, with low ceilings so that it feels safe."[9] Sliding wood doors between the two lobbies can be opened or closed, depending on the desired level of privacy. A linear skylight softly illuminates the pathway along the north masonry wall and through a series of subtly glazed thresholds into the spacious volume of the main chapel.

A strong contrast of light and shadow supports the symbolic goals of the chapel, as Puustinen explains: "In the [main] chapel, there is more light, with a much higher ceiling. We have emphasized the outer wall also by using a much larger skylight there. Light is strong on the outer wall. The symbolic meaning is that you are called toward the light and going toward the light."[10]

Grazing light from the skylight emphasizes the textures of the whitewashed brick surface at the chapel entry and leads the eye around the north boundary to the eastern focal wall behind the informal altar. Skylights illuminate artist Pertti Kukkonen's *Way of the Cross*, a horizontal and vertical sculptural element structurally integrated into the north and east walls. Floor-to-ceiling glazing on the south is screened on the interior and exterior by patinated copper mesh to filter direct views into a sheltered native wildflower garden. The copper mesh layers also mediate direct sunlight and solar gains. In contrast to the white plastered walls, the ceiling and west walls are clad in solemn perforated copper panels. The custom-designed white oak furnishings and organ housing

provide a feeling of warmth at the scale of the human body. After a service, mourners follow the pathway to exit along the east wall into the garden and cemetery beyond.

The smaller chapel, located in the center of the complex, is an intimate volume with low levels of illumination. Light and shadow from a skylight wash over a masonry wall on the east and an

▽ Diffuse toplighting illuminates the center chapel. Pertti Kukkonen's three-dimensional cross is sculpted within the brickwork of the east masonry wall.

▽ Mid-day sunlight animates the east wall of the urn receiving room. South glazing and patinated copper shading provide views into an adjacent garden in contrast with the deep shaded recesses of the urn niches in the north wall.

▽ (Bottom) Play of reflected sunlight on the whitewashed masonry walls and pool of water within a west courtyard.

abstract three-dimensional cross within the masonry surface, also by artist Pertti Kukkonen. Repeated from the large chapel, yet smaller in size, is a glazed wall on the south, with copper mesh and adjacent garden. The urn-receiving room is an even smaller and more intimate space, with niches for urns in the north wall forming an irregular pattern that captures shadows and emphasizes mass and depth, contrasting with the transparency of the south wall and the solid east wall that is gently grazed by daylight from a linear skylight. Copper screening shields the south glazing, which opens into an intimate garden. Even the support spaces are thoughtfully considered in terms of the quality of light, with staff areas illuminated by skylights. The quietly restrained daylighting, form, materials, and detailing have enabled the architects to achieve a serene, comforting atmosphere for both visitors and staff.

Light and Art

Early in the design process, a competition was held for the integration of art in the building, which ensured a thoughtful collaboration between the architects and the artists Pertti Kukkonen and Pekka Jylhä, winners of the competition. Artworks are located in the corridor, chapel hall, stairway, and private viewing room in the lower level. In addition to the masonry sculptures for the *Way of the Cross* in the two chapels, Pertti Kukkonen has installed sculptural elements entitled *Spirits* in the north corridor. These luminous crosses are constructed of light-transmitting concrete within the masonry wall, behind which a void containing fiber-optic cables provides illumination from projectors in the lower level. At night and during the short winter days, the cross-shaped forms of the *Spirits* are revealed in the darkness of the corridor. Adjacent to the north wall, a skylight illuminates the sculptural concrete stairway and a glass sculpture entitled *Soul*, by Pekka Jylhä. In the lower-level private viewing room, these organic glass forms are repeated in a second sculpture by Jylhä entitled *Sorrow*. Electric lighting and daylighting were

▽ Soft diffuse daylight combines with intimate candle light to provide a quiet space of reflection within the private viewing room on the lower level.

△ Detail of artist Pekka Jylhä's glass sculpture entitled "Soul," located in the stair to the lower level.

△ (Middle and right) Artist Pertti Kukkonen's sculptures entitled "Spirits," located in the north corridor, are constructed of light-transmitting concrete within the masonry wall. Projectors in the lower level illuminate fiber-optic cables within the sculptural void.

designed to illuminate the art installations under changing diurnal and seasonal conditions, using on-site electric lighting mock-ups and custom fixtures that were tested by the lighting designers and architects.

LIGHT AND THE ART OF MAKING

Window Form and View

A restrained palette of window forms, skylights, and interior apertures is employed to achieve a quiet quality of light, with visual connections to the site through the seasons. In the courtyards, views of the rectory garden and sky to the west are framed by an overhead beam and portals in the sheltering wall. Once inside, large windows on the west and south façades frame dynamic views of the weather, cycles of nature, and phase changes of water, ice, and snow. Sidelighting is repeated on the south façade, with copper mesh screens softening and filtering the view of the cemetery and walled gardens. A large skylight illuminates the path into and through the main chapel hall, while other discreet skylights illuminate objects and spaces within. Interior glazing is strategically located to frame discreet views while ensuring privacy. A unified luminous theme is achieved through repetition and variations of the window sizes, forms, materials, and detailing. Within this restrained architectural vocabulary, the seasons and weather create ever-changing moods and qualities of light, shadow, and views of nature.

▷ Autumn view through the west courtyard overlooks the changing foliage and forested landscape.

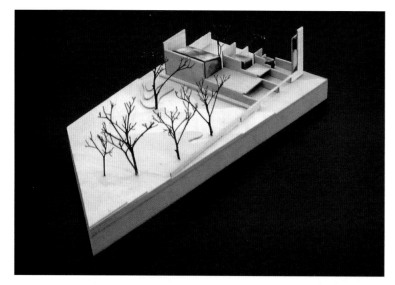

Light, Materials, and the Design Process

The chapel has received praise for its exquisite craftsmanship and construction, including awards and recognition for the architectural design as well as the concrete work, copper detailing, and electric lighting designs. On the exterior of the building, the stacked-stone walls and hand-patinated copper roof reference the material palette of the adjacent historic church and cemetery. In the interior, the clean lines of the architectural forms and restrained material palette create a serene yet welcoming atmosphere. Simplicity and quality craftsmanship are found throughout, from the plastered masonry walls and copper ceilings, cast-in-place white concrete interior walls, and slate floor, to the interior finishes of custom white oak furnishings and steel accessories.

Prototypes, on-site mock-ups, and physical and digital modeling assisted the architects in the integration of materials, construction, and daylighting. Puustinen emphasizes that aspects of the daylighting design had to be tested on-site during the construction phase: "For the mesh screens, the only way to test was using real mesh while under construction. We put mesh where it would be in the end and tried several thicknesses outside and inside. We tested what is enough and what is too much. On-site testing was the only way."[11] Prototypes of many sorts were tested on-site during

△ Process images of design and daylight studies, including site-massing model, physical daylight model, computer renderings, and daylight patterns on the east wall in the main chapel.

construction, including mock-ups of the stone floor to determine the correct shade of black grout, as well as refinements of interior finishes, furnishings, ritual artifacts, and electric lighting.

Performance analyses were conducted to evaluate energy consumption and to refine the systems integration and envelope design for the masonry construction, solar shading, and triple glazing. Building material life-cycle analyses were also conducted to assess sustainability goals, as Puustinen explained in an interview with Chris Hodson for *Architectural Review*: "[We] aim to create architecture that is long-lasting, durable and environmentally friendly. Of course, climate change is taken into consideration and our buildings are well-insulated and use recyclable materials. Certainly, the chapel is built to last, with a limited palette of extremely durable materials, including copper used extensively both internally and externally. We set a goal of a 200-year lifetime and a life cycle simulator was used during the design to check this."[12]

Daylighting and electric lighting are coordinated by control systems with preprogrammed lighting scenarios to adjust illumination for different activities. Electric lighting fixtures are integrated quietly into the architectural design, often with hidden light sources and discreet wallwashing, downlights, and task lighting, while elegant pendant fixtures provide ambient illumination in the two chapels.

LIGHT INSPIRATIONS

The Chapel of St. Lawrence uses daylight to enrich the human experience, foster a relationship to place and nature, and to reveal the beauty and craft of materials and construction. Ville Hara and Anu Puustinen explain the firm's design approach: "Avanto means 'a hole in the ice for bathing in winter'—a popular hobby in Finland—which symbolizes our design philosophy. We want to 'open up' the environment to people with architecture that evokes emotions."[13]

In filmmaker Antti Seppänen's video documentation of the chapel, Puustinen and Hara use descriptive words to explore the relationship between choreographed "path" and the emotional qualities of space: "Path...time, mirror of water, gleam of water, dim, low, intimate, looking back, safe, light...shrouded view...turning point, valediction, farewell, transition, procession, garden of paradise."[14]

The design concept "polku," or path, informed poetic and practical issues, with daylight used as a primary strategy to express the symbolic journey and physical path from the landscape into the chapel and back out to the cemetery. A restrained palette of daylighting strategies is varied subtly to capture the desired emotional and atmospheric qualities of different spaces and activities. Daylight is at the heart of Avanto's work and is central in revealing the experience, beauty, and character of Finnish light. Hara and Puustinen honor the legacy of Finnish architect Alvar Aalto in their celebration of daylight in architecture, while creating their own strong and confident language of light.

DESIGN PROFILE

1. Building Profile
Project: Chapel of St. Lawrence (Pyhän Laurin Kappeli)
Location: Pappilankuja 3, Vantaa, Finland
Architect: Avanto Architects Ltd.
Client: Vantaa Parish Union
Building Type: Chapel
Square Footage: 1,879 sq m (20,225 sq ft)
Estimated Cost: €10m
Competition: Open architecture competition, 1st prize, 2003
Completion: 2010

2. Professional Team
Architects: Ville Hara and Anu Puustinen (principal designer), Architects SAFA
Assistants: Felix Laitinen, student of architecture; Tommi Tuokkola, Architect SAFA; Jonna Käppi, Architect ARB, SAFA; Piotr Gniewek, student of architecture; Asami Naito, student of architecture
Interior Designer: Avanto Architects Ltd.: Kai Korhonen, Architect SAFA
Landscape Architects: Landscape Architects Byman Ruokonen Ltd.: Eva Byman, Niina Strengell
Structural Design: R J Heiskanen Engineers Ltd.: Kari Toitturi, Helena Lomperi
HVAC Design: Leo Maaskola Engineers Ltd.: Jukka Sainio, Esa Leino
Electric Design: Veikko Vahvaselkä Engineers Ltd.: Rauno Nyblom, Lassi Jalava
Lighting Design: Tülay Schakir
Acoustic Design: Akukon Ltd: Olli Salmensaari
Textile Design: Avanto Architects Ltd.
General Contractor: Rakennuspartio Ltd.
Electric Contractor: Lassila & Tikanoja Ltd.: Building Services/ Electric Services
HVAC Contractor: Sähköpeko Etelä-Suomi Ltd.
Timber Furniture Contractor: Wooden Ltd.
Metal Furniture Contractor: Selki-Asema Ltd.
Metal Mesh Contractor: Inlook Ltd.
Artists: Pertti Kukkonen, Pekka Jylhä
Organ Constructor: Urkurakentamo Veikko Virtanen Ltd.
Landscape Contractor: Lemminkäinen Ltd. and Suomen Graniittikeskus Ltd.

3. Climate Profile
Climate (Köppen-Geiger Climate Classification System): Dfb: humid continental climate; hemiboreal
Latitude: 60.2° north latitude
Solar Angles: Noon
June 21: 53.3°
March/September 21: 29.8°
December 21: 6.3°
Length of Day: Approximate Hours of Daylight from Sunrise to Sunset
June 21: 18h 58m
March/September 21: 12h 15m
December 21: 5h 56m
Heating Degree Days: 4129 heating degree days °C (7641 heating degree days °F) (18°C and 65°F base temperature)[15]
Cooling Degree Days: 64 cooling degree days °C (103 cooling degree days °F) (18°C and 65°F base temperature)[16]

4. Design Strategies
Daylighting Strategies:
1) Sidelighting: Floor-to-ceiling glazing on west and south façades; interior and exterior patinated copper mesh shading on south façade; clear glazing on west façade, and 2) Toplighting: Linear skylight along north and east walls in main chapel; toplight wallwasher in small chapel, urn-receiving room, and lower-level private viewing area; toplighting in staff areas.
Sustainable Design and High-Performance Strategies:
Daylighting throughout; high-performance envelope and triple glazing; and energy-efficient HVAC systems, electric lighting, and control systems.
Renewable Energy Strategies:
None.

Avanto: Structure and Materials

The exploded diagram illustrates the nesting of spaces created by the L-shaped masonry walls. Courtyards with water features and gardens are located adjacent to the floor-to-ceiling glazing on the west and south façades. Copper-mesh screens filter direct sunlight and views to the south. Skylights are located adjacent to the north and east masonry walls.

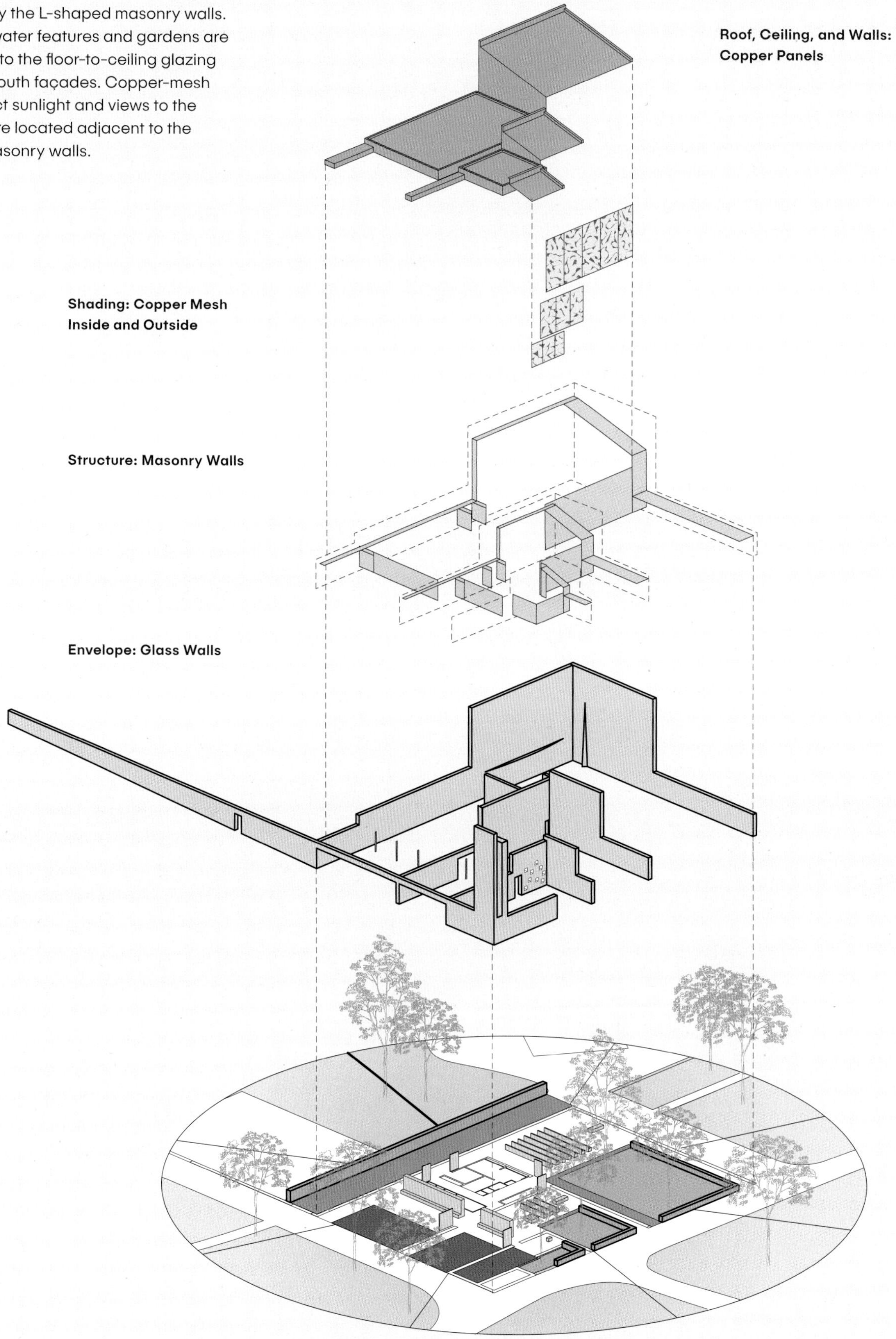

Roof, Ceiling, and Walls: Copper Panels

Shading: Copper Mesh Inside and Outside

Structure: Masonry Walls

Envelope: Glass Walls

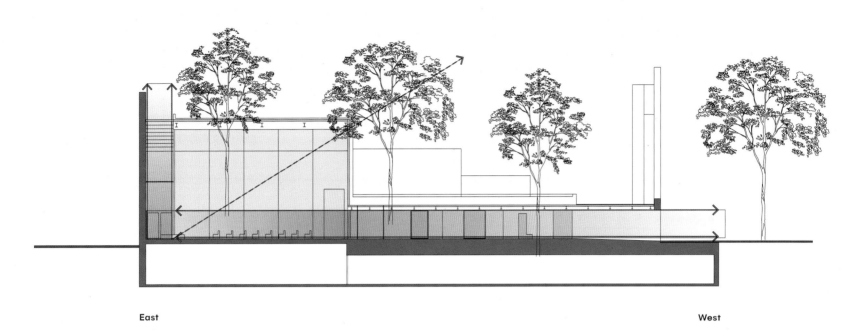

East   West

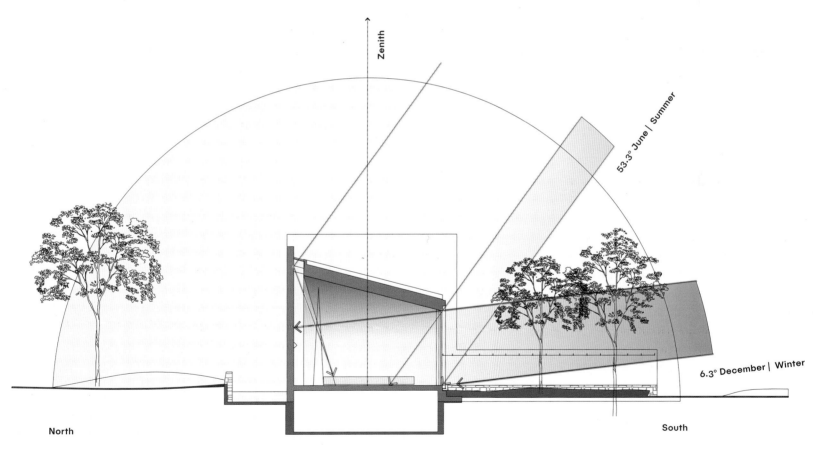

Zenith

53.3° June | Summer

6.3° December | Winter

North   South

The upper east–west section illustrates the direct views to the landscape through the west courtyards. In the main chapel, the south glazing and copper-mesh shading provide filtered views to the gardens and cemetery, while skylights allow glimpses of the sky. The lower north–south section illustrates the seasonal sun angles. During the winter months, low sunlight filters through the copper-mesh shading and south glazing. During the long days of summer, high sunlight reflects from the north masonry wall and filters through the south façade.

Program and Circulation

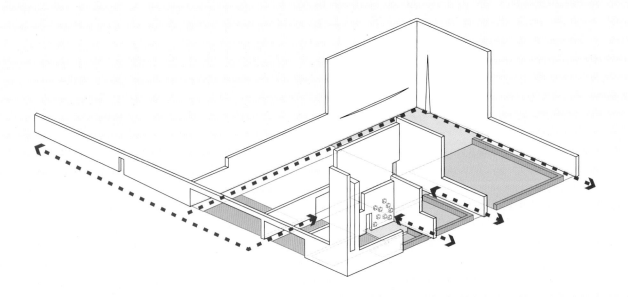

Water and Gardens

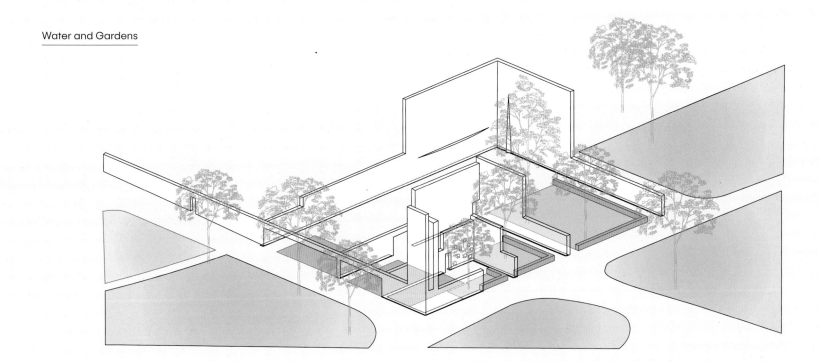

The upper diagram illustrates the circulation
paths through the two courtyards located on the
west façade. The northern path leads to the main
chapel, while the southern path leads to the smaller
chapel and urn receiving room. The lower diagram
illustrates the physical and visual connections to
the water features on the west and the wildflower
gardens on the south.

Skylights and Sidelighting

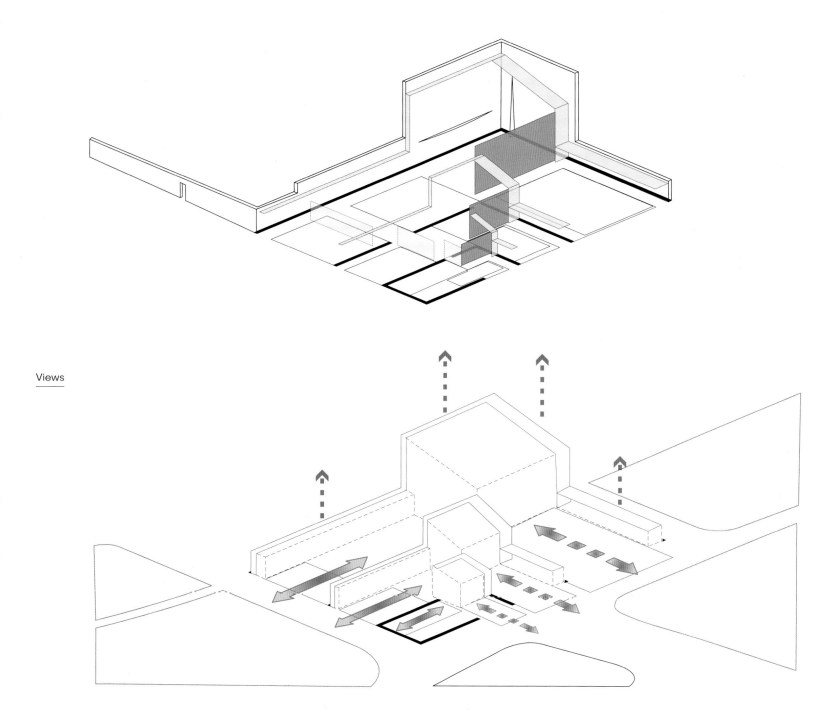

Views

The upper diagram illustrates the locations of skylights and vertical glazing on the west and south façades. The lower diagram illustrates the location of direct views to the water features and courtyards to the west, filtered views of the garden and cemetery to the south, and glimpses of the sky through the skylights.

Daylight Analysis
Seasonal Plans_Main Chapel

Illuminance studies (in lux) illustrate the effect of seasonal and diurnal sun angles on the amount and distribution of daylight. During the winter months, when sun angles are low and the length of days are brief, there is a relatively even distribution of daylight. In summer, illuminance levels increase along the south façade and through reflected light at the north and east masonry walls.

Sunny Sky
Illuminance (Lux)

———	500
———	438
·········	375
———	313
———	250
———	188
———	126
———	63

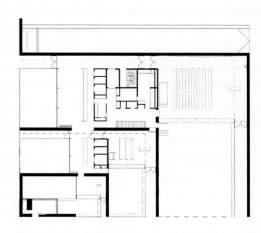

N

December 21	March/September 21	June 21

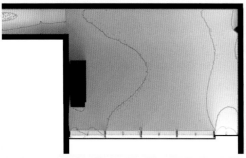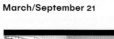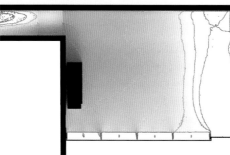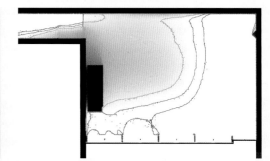

10:30 am

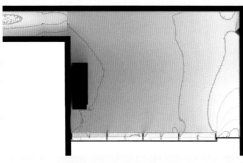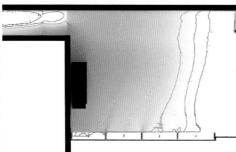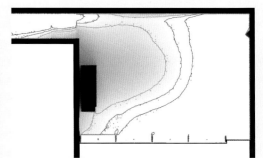

12:00 pm

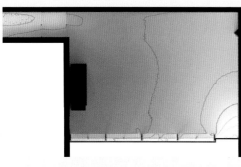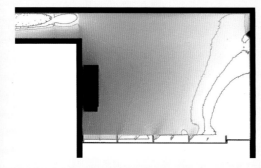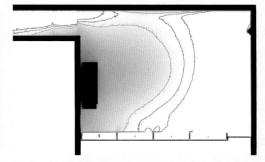

1:30 pm

Equinox Walk-Through_Main Chapel

View A: March/September 21 at 12:00 pm

View A: March/September 21 at 12:00 pm

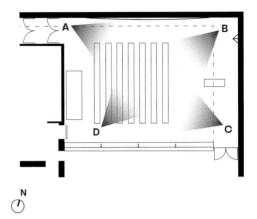

View B: March/September 21 at 12:00 pm

View B: March/September 21 at 12:00 pm

Perspective renderings and luminance studies (in candela/square meter; cd/m2) illustrate the visual quality of daylight and contrast ratios from four view locations within the main chapel during the fall equinox (September 21 at noon). The diurnal and seasonal changes enhance awareness of nature, impermanence, and the cycles of life.

**Sunny Sky
Luminance** (Cd/m²)

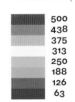

	500
	438
	375
	313
	250
	188
	126
	63

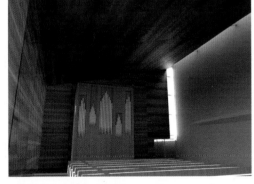

View C: March/September 21 at 12:00 pm

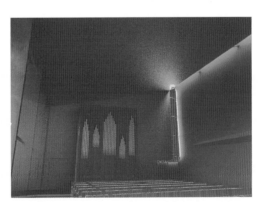

View C: March/September 21 at 12:00 pm

View D: March/September 21 at 12:00 pm

View D: March/September 21 at 12:00 pm

Seasonal Perspectives_Looking East

Seasonal and diurnal perspective renderings illustrate changes in daylight throughout the year. Time-lapse renderings looking east reveal the dynamic patterns of sunlight and reflected light from the white masonry walls.

The view to the west entry illustrates the visual and luminous effect of the darker patinated copper-mesh screens and ceiling in absorbing and filtering direct sunlight.

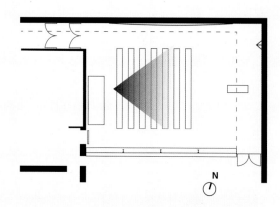

N

December 21

March/September 21

June 21

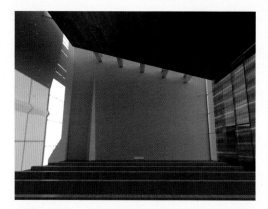
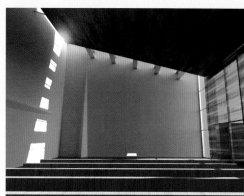

10:30 am

12:00 pm

1:30 pm

Seasonal Perspectives_Looking West

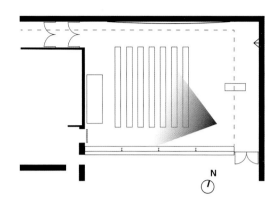

December 21	March/September 21	June 21

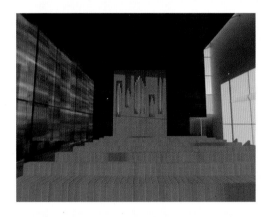  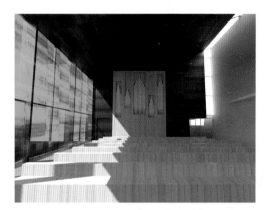

10:30 am

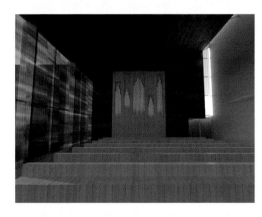 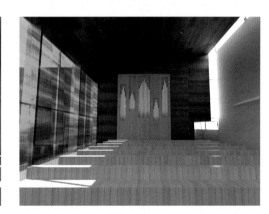

12:00 pm

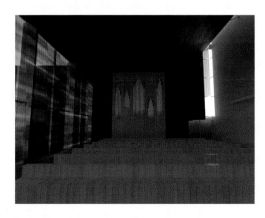 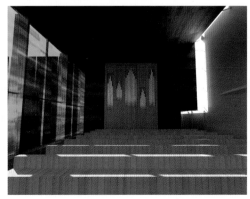 

1:30 pm

Seasonal Timelapse_Looking East

Time-lapse renderings of the main chapel illustrate seasonal and diurnal changes in the quality and distribution of daylight throughout the year given the high geographic latitude (62.2° north latitude) and varying length of day (18h 56m on June 21 and 5h 56m on December 21).

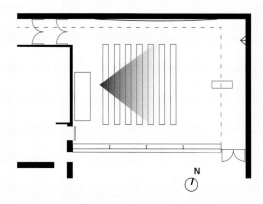

N

February 21   April 21   June 21

8:00 am

10:00 am

12:00 pm

2:00 pm

4:00 pm

August 21

October 21

December 21

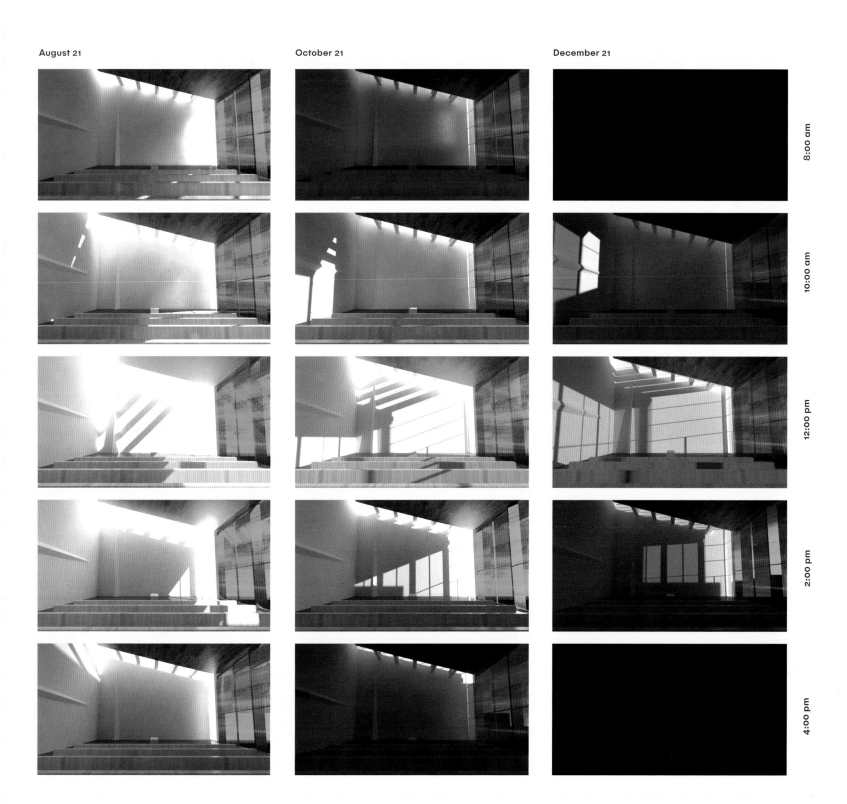

8:00 am

10:00 am

12:00 pm

2:00 pm

4:00 pm

Case study 1.2

Reid Building, Glasgow School of Art

Glasgow, Scotland, UK

Steven Holl Architects

◁ △ View of the south façade and glass rainscreen that captures the changing sky conditions and lighting qualities of the day and seasons. Layers of translucent and clear glass combine with opaque walls to express varied degrees of transparency from day into night.

"'Driven voids of light' allow for the integration of structure, spatial modulation and light. The 'driven void' light shafts deliver natural light through the depth of the building providing direct connectivity with the outside world through the changing intensity and color of the sky. In addition, they provide vertical circulation through the building, eliminating the need for air conditioning. ... A 'Circuit of Connection' throughout the new Reid Building encourages the 'creative abrasion' across and between departments that is central to the workings of the school."[17]

Steven Holl Architects

LIGHT AND THE QUALITY OF PLACE

Glasgow School of Art

Internationally renowned as a preeminent school for the study of fine arts, architecture, and design, the Glasgow School of Art (GSA)'s recent expansion reinvigorates the historic urban campus and fosters an animated conversation between Charles Rennie Mackintosh's 1909 architectural masterpiece, the Mackintosh Building, and Steven Holl's contemporary Reid Building. Located in the downtown core of Glasgow, the GSA is a center of creative activity within an international arts community. Steven Holl Architects (SHA), in collaboration with JM Architects and Arup, were responsible for developing GSA's new Garnethill Campus masterplan and the phase-one design and construction of the Reid Building.

As a precursor to the modern movement, Mackintosh's innovative use of natural light, simplicity of form, design restraint, and honest expression of materials were considered unprecedented for their time. SHA approached the Reid Building with the same spirit of innovation and a desire to define a "new language of light," which expresses the material and construction technologies of the day while remaining mindful of Mackintosh's historic legacy.

Chris McVoy, design architect at SHA, explains: "We began with studying the Mackintosh Building; in particular, the quality of light. There are twenty-five ways light comes into the spaces. ... Mackintosh elaborated on the basic typologies of light: skylights, clerestories, figural diffuse light, sidelighting, direct lighting. We studied daylight deeply."[18]

McVoy goes on to clarify that there were five organizing ideas for the School of Art: 1) create well-proportioned and flexible studios; 2) define a new "language of light" in relation to Mackintosh; 3) use materiality as a "complementary contrast" between the Mackintosh and Reid Buildings; 4) use circulation as a "circuit of creative abrasion" to encourage interaction; and 5) foster ecological innovation.[19]

Site, Climate, and Light

Glasgow is located at 55.9° north latitude, with seasonal extremes of light and darkness, relatively low sun angles, and short winter days that contrast with persistent summer daylight. All of these factors shape Glasgow's unique qualities of light and related architectural opportunities. During the winter solstice, there are just seven hours of daylight and the noon sun altitude is only 10.6° above the horizon. During the summer solstice, the sun rises to a noon altitude of 57.6°, daylight lasts for 17 hours, and twilight persists throughout the night. The Reid Building, sited across the street and north of the historic Mackintosh Building, is oriented on an east–west axis, affording optimal solar access on a seasonal basis.

Glasgow has a maritime temperate climate of cool winters and mild summers, with an average low of 0.5°C (33°F) in December and an average high of 19.4°C (67°F) in August. [20] High humidity and frequent precipitation are experienced throughout the year, resulting in a soft and misty quality of light as it is refracted and scattered by moisture in the air. The cloudiest month is typically January, while the sunniest months are May through July. Gray skies and overcast conditions dominate in the winter, yet clear and partly overcast skies can result in dramatic lighting qualities and cloudscapes throughout the year. Occasional snow is experienced from January to April, and prevailing winds are from the southwest and west. Despite the overcast climate, daylight and natural ventilation are effectively coupled with high-performance construction to optimize energy performance and comfort throughout the year.

▽ Site plan of the historic Mackintosh Building and Reid Building reveals the intimate relationship between the north and south façades of the two buildings and the related scales and massing.

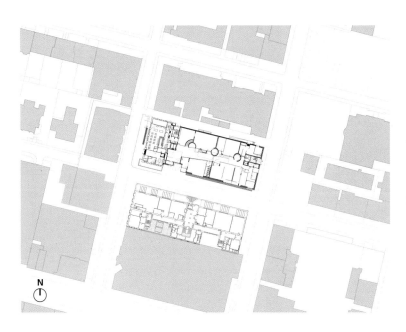

▷ South view of the entry lobby with glass and steel screen by artist Martin Boyce. Constructed of steel frames with horizontal glass leaves, the sculpture casts dynamic patterns of colored light onto the room surfaces as the sunlight moves through time.

LIGHT AND THE DESIGN INTENTIONS

Design Program

The GSA challenged the architects to reconsider the nature of design schools in the 21st century and to explore how the architecture could foster collaborations between the disciplines, was former GSA Director Seona Reid explains: "The chance meetings, the chance conversations, the chance opportunities to see somebody else's work doesn't happen as much as it should. These opportunistic meetings are often the spark of ideas of working relationships and partnerships." [21]

While the design studios are the heart of the GSA, virtually all spaces, including common spaces such as the entry, exhibition room, café and refectory, workshops, seminar rooms, and lecture hall, were designed to foster collaboration and support the creative process. The architects used "circuits of connection" (circulation ramps and stairs), "eddies of interaction" (niches and subspaces), "driven voids of light" (light shafts with openings), and interior views to encourage such informal exchanges and collaborations.

Choreographed Light

Daylight shapes the Reid Building from both the inside and the outside, with the movements of occupants and daylight carefully choreographed in space and time. Although straightforward in organization, the building section, spatial variety, and atmospheric qualities of light are complex, as Holl explains: "If you look at our building in plan it looks very simple: a rectangle and three circles in a square. You can't get anything out of the plan, which I really like, because I think that's the essence of architecture. It's spatial; it's three-dimensional." [22]

Holl explains how the historic masterpiece by Mackintosh inspired his approach to the Reid Building: "I studied all the ways that light comes in the Mackintosh Building and discovered many different interesting things, and one in particular is in the library where [there are] three story elements in glass—we call them 'driven voids of light'—and we transferred that into this idea of concrete 'driven voids.'" [23]

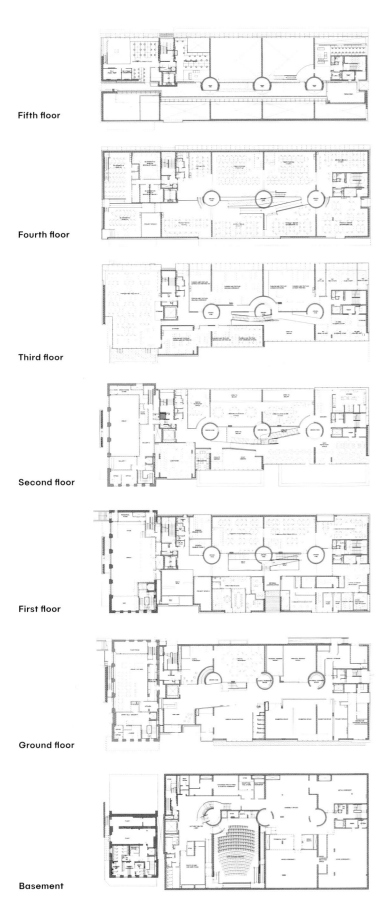

Fifth floor

Fourth floor

Third floor

Second floor

First floor

Ground floor

Basement

△ Floor plans reveal the visual and physical interconnections between the three "driven voids of light" (light shafts), "circuits of circulation," and north and south sides of the building.

The Reid Building is organized by "circuits of connection" (circulation paths) that intersect three "driven voids" (light shafts) to create south and north zones with distinct daylight qualities and program activities. As Craig Tait, project architect with JM Architects, explains: "There are rich and varied spaces with niches within. People occupy the spaces in many ways; the building makes people gather in different ways. It's a joy to see how people react to space. The 'circuit' [circulation] doesn't have a prescribed function—people are influenced by the space." [24]

Three "voids," inserted into the rectilinear plan, are created by concrete cylinders tilted 12 degrees to the south to capture the low sun angles and often gray "Glaswegian" light. McVoy explains that the interior openings, which were subtracted from the surface of the Euclidean cylinders, created "incredible curves and shapes" with unexpectedly complex forms and patterns of light as daylight enters the volumes and is borrowed by adjacent spaces. [25] The circulation paths, ramps, and stairs move through and around the voids to create rich spatial qualities, changing views, dynamic lighting qualities, and varied gathering opportunities.

▽ Circulation paths and stairs pass through and around "driven voids of light" to foster visual and physical connections while admitting light and air.

The studio spaces also express a fresh interpretation of daylighting, as Henry McKeown, design director with JM Architects, explains: "It's not just the traditional north light of an art school. It's an idea of different kinds of light blending and working with each other to create all sorts of atmospheres and ambiances within the space itself."[26]

Direct sunlight is admitted to the south zone of the building, while the diffuse northern light in the design studios is complemented by borrowed light from the voids and circulation paths. This dynamic meeting of warm south light and cool north light creates varied daylight patterns and atmospheric qualities that change with the time and seasons. Glimpses through openings in the "voids" and movement along the "circulation circuits" provide changing perspectives on the studios and shared spaces. Exterior views are provided on all levels, with the third-floor terrace and refectory framing a new perspective on the Mackintosh Building, the city, and surrounding hills. The roof, a fifth façade, includes skylights to admit diffuse north daylight to the upper-level south studio and clear skylights at the top of the "driven voids," which open to the south and zenith.

△ (Left and top) Circulation paths, gathering spaces, and view openings interact with the light shafts to foster informal connections between students and faculty.

△ (Above) A northern view of the sky contrasts with direct sunlight from south-facing clerestory windows in the fourth-floor studio. Operable windows in both orientations facilitate cross ventilation.

△ Large south-facing windows in the student refectory frame views of the historic Mackintosh Building. An exterior garden with a green roof and water feature captures rainwater while providing outside access and views to the city beyond.

◁ The south-facing fourth-floor studio combines sidelighting with north-facing skylights. Operable windows facilitate ventilation.

LIGHT AND THE DESIGN STRATEGIES

Language of Light

Holl's "new language of light" is revealed in his concept for the envelope and structure, which he characterizes as "complementary contrast." He describes the heavy stone cladding and steel frame of the Mackintosh Building as "thick skin and thin bones," while the Reid Building's delicate glass envelope and concrete structure are expressed as "thin skin and thick bones." The "new language" emerges from the luminous effects of the translucent glass rainscreen and custom "ghost fittings" (which are subtly visible through the glass); a palette of transparent, translucent, and opaque materials; and aesthetically minimal details for windows, skylights, glass railings, and doors. In contrast to the underlying grid and uniform industrial windows of the Mackintosh Building, the seemingly idiosyncratic façades of the Reid Building are animated by windows of varied sizes, two- and three-dimensional forms, and differing degrees of translucency and transparency.

On the interior, the Reid Building's three "driven voids" define a new precedent for interior light shafts by skillfully combining functions for illumination, ventilation, circulation, views, and structure. The robust sculptural geometry of the voids and the openings, with windows of varying size, proportion, and shape, affords differing views through the building of ever-changing patterns and qualities of light.

The studio sections are designed to combine borrowed light from the toplit voids with sidelighting from north clerestory windows. The upper-floor studio windows tilt upward to increase the view of the sky to the north and optimize indirect daylight, while the fourth-floor studio employs a three-dimensional north window with a glass sill to admit borrowed light to the third-floor studio window below. Lower-level studios and seminar rooms are illuminated either with sidelighting from the north or bilaterally with a combination of light from the east or west. At the lowest levels, the metal workshop takes advantage of indirect light from the "void" and north toplighting, while the basement woodshop on the south borrows light and a connection to the street above from glazed pavers in the ceiling.

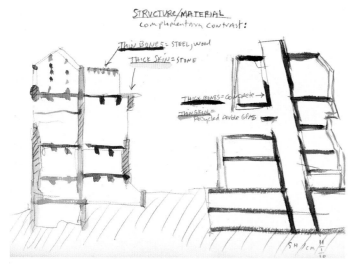

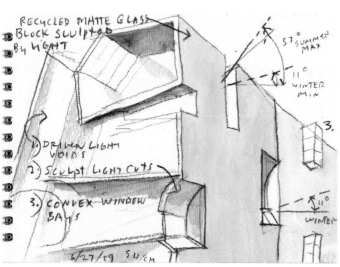

△ Early watercolors by Steven Holl explore how the building is shaped by daylight in section and massing.

▷ View openings in the "driven voids of light" foster interconnections between the design studios and circulation paths.

△ Detail of a "driven void of light" reveals the large south-facing skylight with operable windows that admit light and exhaust air.

◁ Large north-facing windows in the third-floor studio have horizontal glass sills to admit daylight to the studios below.

◁ Details of the northeastern façade reveal the various configurations of translucent and clear glass and opaque walls combined in the façades.

▽ The south-facing student refectory brings together the adjacent "driven voids of light" and circulation spaces, while providing views of the Mackintosh Building and city beyond.

Atmospheric Light

The Reid Building's ephemeral translucent rainscreen captures the varied moods and colors of the sky and seasons. During an overcast day, the glass has a soft and misty quality, while the surfaces are animated on a sunny day with a play of light, shadow, and subtle color variations as the sun is reflected from translucent and clear surfaces. The character of the envelope transforms at night to reveal a translucent enclosure surrounding opaque walls with windows of different size and form that open to activities within. Direct daylight is admitted through clear glass windows while three types of glass create diffuse conditions: clear glass behind the translucent rainscreen, translucent glass behind the rainscreen, and a glass cavity with an inner layer of translucent paint flush with the rainscreen. [27]

McVoy stresses that natural light—including direct sunlight—is essential in even the most light-sensitive building types and programs: "We don't see a distinction between the analytic and functional, pragmatic aspects of light and the poetics of light. We |see that natural light creates an atmosphere through time and through movement, and that a good space for every kind of activity benefits from generous natural light." [28]

He emphasizes the importance of "dynamic light," in which the intensity, distribution, mood, and patterns of indirect daylight and direct sunlight are celebrated and appropriately considered: "Our favorite building material is light. We believe in dynamic light, ... which registers the time of day and seasons and weather. A variation in daylight intensity is important. It's a good thing ... light is by its nature poetic and how you bring it into space through openings is the nature of architecture." [29]

Reflecting on the ancient domes and oculi of the Neolithic architecture of the region, McVoy suggests that a "fundamental connection to light is a vertical connection through a vertical space that pivots around the movement of the sun," with the experience of the daylight connecting the "subjective time" of the body moving through space with the "universal time" of light moving through the building. [30] In this spirit, the Reid Building's white walls, concrete floors, and interior detailing of wood, steel, and glass create visually quiet environments that act as neutral canvases for the ever-changing atmospheric qualities of daylight captured through the façades and within the "driven voids" that receive and redistribute light down and through the building section.

LIGHT AND THE ART OF MAKING

Light and Integrated Design

Key to the integration of aesthetic and practical design concerns throughout the building interior and exterior are the "driven voids," which Holl states "were designed to do everything," by providing structural support, daylight, and ventilation while creating rich spatial and atmospheric experiences. [31] Passive strategies for light and air are integrated into the voids, as McVoy explains: "[The void] acts as a natural solar stack, with hot air rising and driving air up through it to draw air through studio windows. The building is completely naturally ventilated; there is no air conditioning. When interior sensors get too warm they open up windows at the top of the 'driven voids of light.'" [32]

The building envelope applies other innovative materials and construction detailing. The rainscreen is a "thin shroud" of acid-etched laminated glass with translucent interlayers that are held 300 millimeters (11.8 inches) from the structural wall. To create a shroud effect, in which the brackets were not visible, SHA and JM Architects worked with Arup to design and test "ghost brackets," custom glass fittings that enabled the team to create a subtle luminous and homogeneous envelope. The balance of aesthetic and practical considerations was paramount, as Henry McKeown of JM Architects explains: "The technical resolution of this skin is inseparable from the aesthetic concept. ... The thinness and lightness of a glass skin ... [and] the way this concept was interpreted in aesthetic terms was a quest to find a glass-based material that would resemble an alabaster finish, a mute material that could be capable of holding the light and color of the sky through all weathers and seasons, in such a way that it would be animated by the environmental and climatic conditions of any given day." [33]

The designers even went to the extent of studying the reflectivity of the rainscreen to ensure that light did not inadvertently reflect onto the Mackintosh Building façade.

▽ Full scale mock-up details of the "ghost brackets," rainscreen, and "driven voids of light" were tested on-site in Glasgow.

The collaboration with Arup also included design and analysis of the energy and sustainability features. A radiant heating system is integrated into the concrete floor topping, while the additional mass mediates thermal comfort on a seasonal basis. Passive strategies for daylight, natural ventilation, and cooling are coordinated with active mechanical, lighting, and ventilation controls. Ecological site strategies include a second-floor terrace and green roof with native landscaping and a water feature, while a stormwater system on the north roof harvests rainwater for the sinks and lavatories. A shared biomass plant heats the Mackintosh, Reid, and nearby Bourdon Buildings. The integrated design strategies allow the building to meet the BREEAM Excellent standard and provide a reduction in energy consumption of 30 percent over current regulations—with an estimated annual energy consumption at 100kWh/sq m (31.7kBtu/sq ft) and carbon emissions at 40kg CO_2/sq m (430kg CO_2/sq ft). [34]

Design Testing

To realize the high degree of innovation and integration at the Reid Building, rigorous design mock-ups and assessments were developed in collaboration with a team of experts, as Craig Tait of JM Architects explains: "Façade specialists were involved from the very start, as well as specialist manufacturers and subcontractors. ... We did mock-ups of the correct balance of technical performance and aesthetic quality." [35]

General contractor Sir Robert McAlpine and JM Architects developed full-scale mock-ups of the rainscreen and "voids" during the early phases of construction to assess the aesthetic qualities, experiment and test various materials and finishes, and verify the construction process. The "voids" were also mocked up to evaluate the construction methodology and sequencing, to study how daylight would be reflected down the volume, and to assess the reflectivity of the smooth concrete surface. Tait explains the importance of mock-ups and analysis to resolve aesthetic and practical issues: "The mock-up studies of the glass were tested in different light conditions, to experience flat and animated light, and how the building acts as a receptor for light that constantly reacts to and reflects the seasons. Building modeling software was

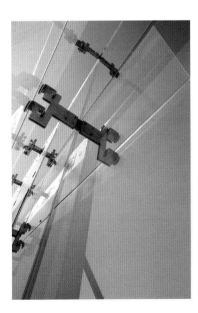

SUSTAINABLE DESIGN FOR GLASGOW SCHOOL OF ART NEW BUILDING

BREEAM EXCELLENT
Energy consumption: 100 kwh/m² per year
Carbon emissions: 40 kg co²/m² per year
30% reduction over current regulations

NEW "CARBON NEUTRAL" BIOMASS PLANT
Centralized facility to serve new building, Mackintosh and Bourdon

GREEN LANDSCAPE
Used as public terrace and bio-diverse landscape

STORM WATER
Rainwater retention collection and reuse

NATURAL VENTILATION
Driven voids utilize solar stack for natural ventilation of all above-ground spaces

Rainwater harvesting tank feeds sinks and lavatories

Building lighting control system to respond to use and daylight demands

Optimized glass performance with integrated thermal and solar control

Radiant heating integrated into concrete topping slab

Thermal mass of exposed concrete structure used to moderate heating and cooling loads

Decarbonized heating supply to the Mackintosh Building

Bourdon Building

Central Biomass Plant

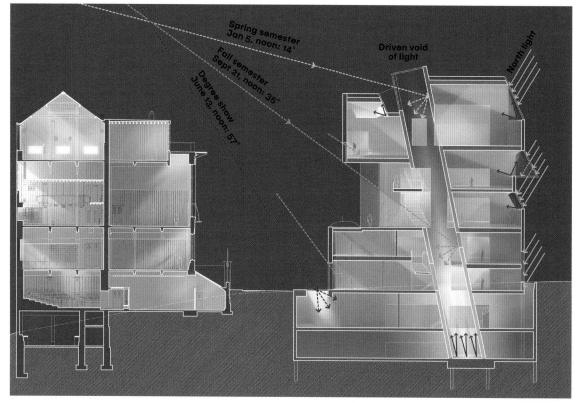

Spring semester
Jan 5, noon: 14°

Fall semester
Sept 21, noon: 35°

Degree show
June 13, noon: 57°

Driven void of light

North light

△ Daylighting design integrates with a host of sustainable design strategies, including natural ventilation, electric lighting, and high-performance glazing, control, and mechanical systems. Other features include a new biomass plant, green roof, and storm water system.

◁ The building section and envelope respond to seasonal sun angles and changing qualities of daylight in each orientation.

△ The relationship between direct sunlight, indirect north light, and soft diffuse borrowed light studied in a physical daylight model of a fourth-floor design studio.

also used to analyze the lighting, but the client didn't dictate a set lighting [criterion], just that it was suitable for the arts. Design is not approached in a purely scientific way, but also in the creative and human aspects." [36]

LIGHT INSPIRATIONS

Daylight is a design driver at the Reid Building, as McVoy explains: "It's the idea that architecture can shape a volume of light; that it can contain the most ethereal material there is and give it a volume presence. In the case of the Mackintosh, light is pushing into the library and pushing out of the façade. And in the case of our building, it's driven right down through the heart of it, right down through the five stories and the social space and alongside studios. ... We have a whole language of light along the perimeter and different ways of bringing light in. ... You can particularly see this in the section." [37]

The Reid Building skillfully relates to the scale, proportions, and sectional qualities of the Mackintosh Building while introducing a new language of light, materials, and structure. Atmospheric qualities of light are choreographed with practical and pragmatic considerations such as solar control, glare, and light distribution to ensure effective and beautiful luminous experiences that support the program and aesthetic vision.

As the GSA requested, the Reid Building acts as a source of inspiration and as a three-dimensional canvas for the design and exhibition of creative work. The variety of spatial and atmospheric qualities successfully fosters the desired interactions and creative collaborations across the disciplines and with the broader art community of Glasgow. Respectful of the legacy of Mackintosh, the Reid Building confidently embodies a fresh architectural language with a new and ecologically creative vision for the GSA.

DESIGN PROFILE

1. Building Profile
Project: Reid Building, Glasgow School of Art
Location: Glasgow, Scotland, UK
Architect: Steven Holl Architects
Client: The Glasgow School of Art
Building Type: Education
Square Footage: 11,250 sq m (121,094 sq ft)
Estimated Cost: £30m
Completion: 2014

2. Professional Team
Design Architects: Steven Holl and Chris McVoy
Partners in Charge: Chris McVoy, Noah Yaffe
Project Architect: Dominik Sigg
Assistant Project Architect: Dimitra Tsachrelia
Project Team: Rychiee Espinosa, Scott Fredricks, JongSeo Lee, Jackie Luk, Fiorenza Matteoni, Ebbie Wisecarver
Competition Team: Dominik Sigg, Peter Adams, Rychiee Espinosa
Associate Architects: JM Architects
Design Director: Henry McKeown
Project Architect: Craig Tait
Architects: Paul Twynam, Vicky Batters
Design Director, Competition Stage: Ian Alexander
Project Manager: Turner & Townsend
General Contractor: Sir Robert McAlpine
Engineer: Ove Arup & Partners
Quantity Surveyor: Turner & Townsend
Landscape Architect: Michael Van Valkenburgh and Associates
Planning: Turley Associates

3. Climate Profile
Climate (Köppen-Geiger Climate Classification System): Cfb: maritime temperate climate
Latitude: 55.9° north latitude
Solar Angles: Noon
June 21: 57.6°
March/September 21: 34.1°
December 21: 10.6°
Length of Day: Approximate Hours of Daylight from Sunrise to Sunset
June 21: 17h 35m
March/September 21: 12h 15m
December 21: 6h 59m
Heating Degree Days: 3320 heating degree days °C (6191 heating degree days °F) (18°C and 65°F base temperature) [38]

Cooling Degree Days: 16 cooling degree days °C (24 cooling degree days °F) (18°C and 65°F base temperature) [39]

4. Design Strategies
Daylighting Strategies:
1) Sidelighting: throughout building with clear and translucent glazing; daylight zoning with access to direct sunlight on the south and indirect daylight on the north, and
2) Toplighting: driven void (light shafts), clerestories in north studios, and skylight in top-floor south studio.

Sustainable Design and High-Performance Strategies:
Daylighting and natural ventilation; high-performance envelope, mechanical systems, and electric lighting; mechanical, lighting, and ventilation controls; radiant heating system integrated into the concrete floor topping with additional mass for thermal storage; biomass plant; green roof with native landscaping; stormwater system to harvest rainwater for sinks and lavatories.

Renewable Energy Strategies:
None.

Energy: 100kWh/sq m (31.7kBtu/sq ft).
Carbon: 40kg CO_2/sq m (430kg CO_2/sq ft).
BREEAM Excellent Rating: 30 percent reduction over current regulations.

Holl: Structure and Materials

The exploded diagram illustrates the structural
and material logic of the building. The "thin
skin and thick bones" of the Reid Building
are expressed through the ephemeral glass
envelope in contrast to the heavy concrete
"driven voids" (light shafts), floors, and roof.

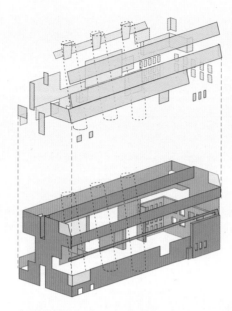

Envelope: Glass Walls, Windows, and Skylights

Envelope: Translucent Rainscreen

Structure: Concrete Light Shafts

Structure: Concrete Floor

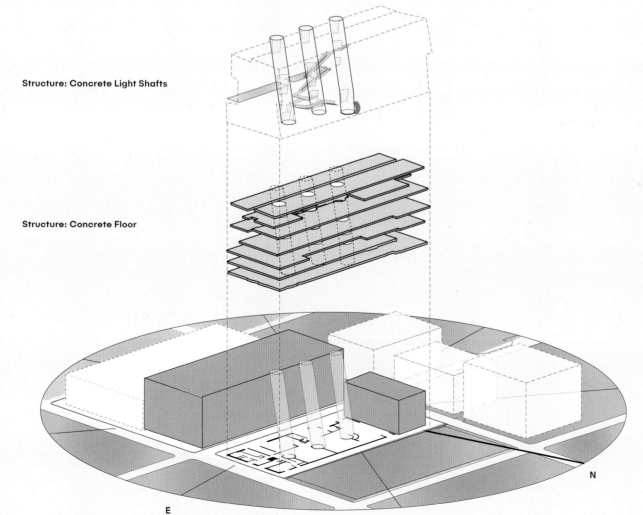

N

E

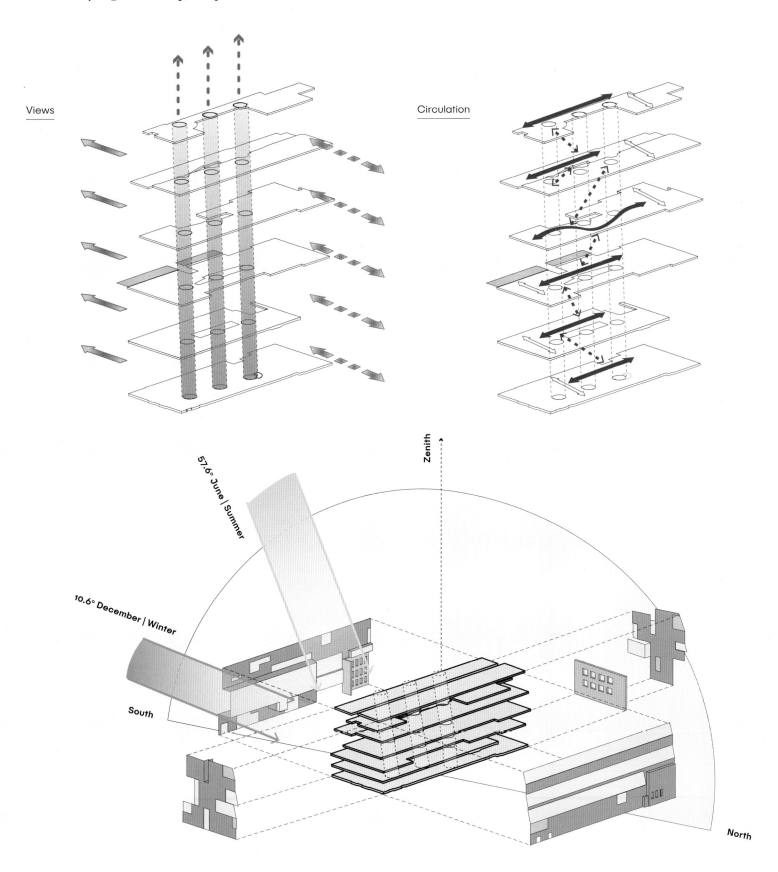

Views

Circulation

Zenith

57.6° June | Summer

10.6° December | Winter

South

North

The upper diagrams illustrate the primary views and circulation pathways. South windows celebrate direct views to the historic Mackintosh Building, while the sky is viewed through the north-facing clerestories and skylight in the light shafts. The lower diagram illustrates the changing seasonal sun angles. Light shafts admit high summer sunlight that reflects from white walls to lower-level floors. Translucent and clear glazing on the south façade admits low winter daylight while light shafts bring diffuse and reflected light to the heart of the building.

Equinox Walk-Through_All Floors

Perspective renderings and luminance studies (in cd/m2) illustrate the visual quality of daylight and contrast ratios from eight view locations during the fall equinox. Given the proximity of adjacent buildings, light levels increase from the lower to upper floors. The overall distribution of light and surface brightness is relatively even, with the greatest contrast occurring in direct sunlight and at the window wall.

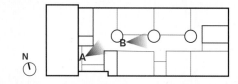

Ground floor

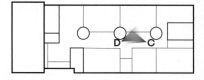

First floor

March/September 21 at 12:00 pm_Sunny

March/September 21 at 12:00 pm_Overcast

March/September 21 at 12:00 pm_Overcast

View A: Entry looking northeast

View A: Entry looking northeast

View A: Entry looking northeast

View B: Ground-level stair looking east

View B: Ground-level stair looking east

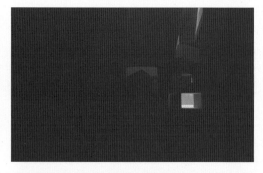

View B: Ground-level stair looking east

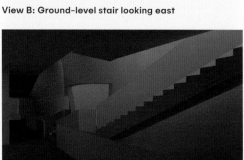

View C: First-level stair looking northwest

View C: First-level stair looking northwest

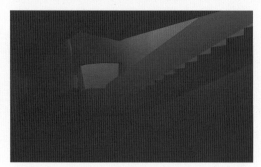

View C: First-level stair looking northwest

View D: First level, center void looking east

View D: First level, center void looking east

View D: First level, center void looking east

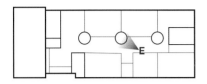

Second floor

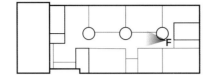

Third floor

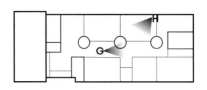

Fourth floor

Overcast Sky Luminance (Cd/m²)

250
219
188
157
126
94
63
32

March/September 21 at 12:00 pm_Sunny

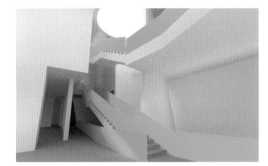

View E: Second-level café looking northwest

March/September 21 at 12:00 pm_Overcast

View E: Second-level café looking northwest

March/September 21 at 12:00_Overcast

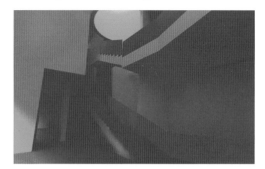

View E: Second-level café looking northwest

View F: Third-level bridge looking west

View F: Third-level bridge looking west

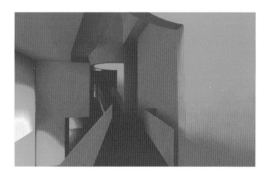

View F: Third-level bridge looking west

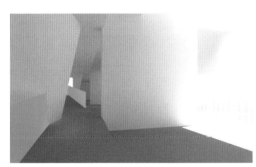

View G: Fourth-level studio looking east

View G: Fourth-level studio looking east

View G: Fourth-level studio looking east

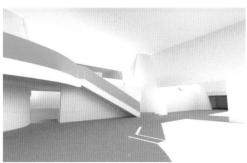

View H: Fourth-level studio looking southwest

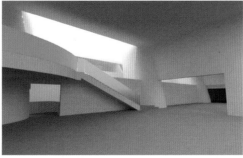

View H: Fourth-level studio looking southwest

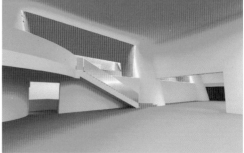

View H: Fourth-level studio looking southwest

Seasonal Timelapse_Driven Void (East)

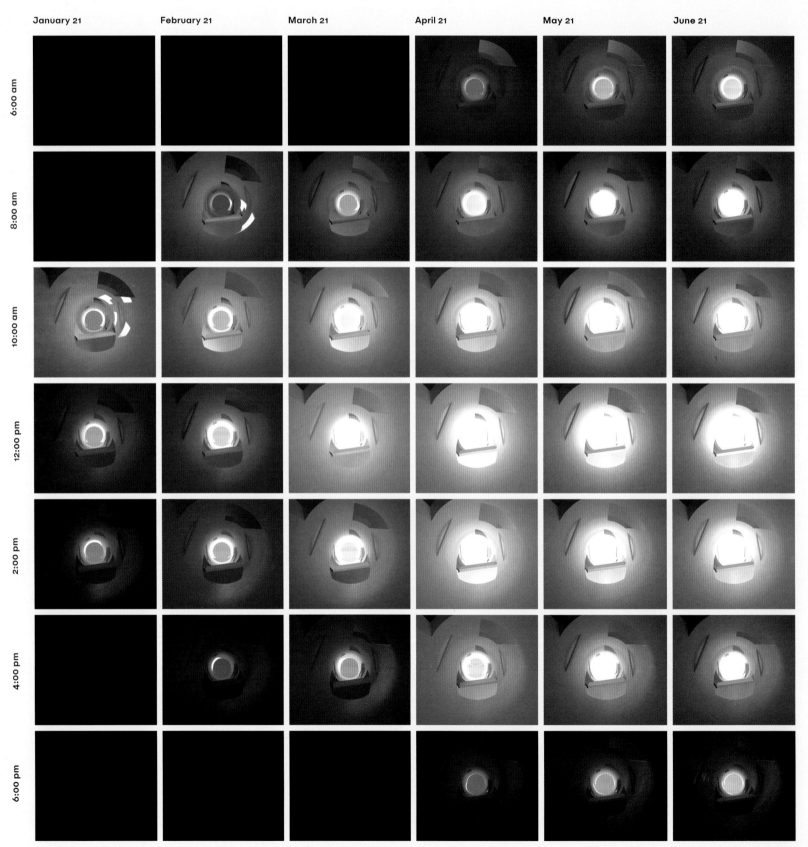

Time-lapse renderings of the east "driven void" illustrate the dramatic seasonal and diurnal changes in the quality and distribution of daylight throughout the year, given the geographic latitude (55.9° north latitude) and varying length of day (17h 35m on June 21 and 6h 59m on December 21).

July 21	August 21	September 21	October 21	November 21	December 21

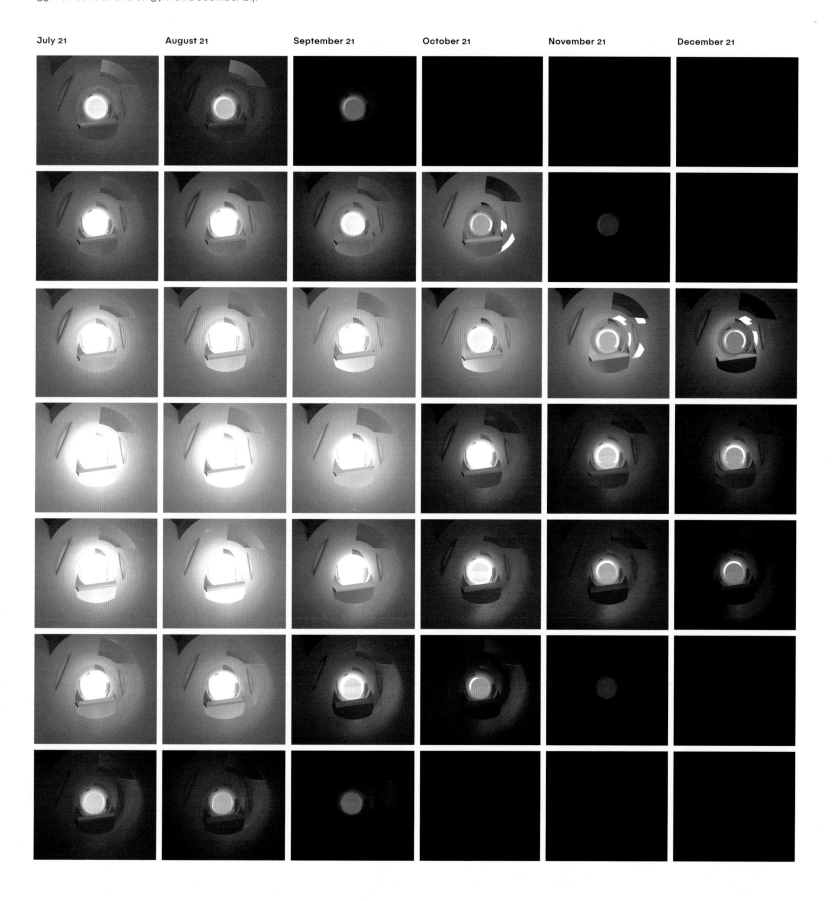

Daylight Analysis: Seasonal Plans_All Floors

Illuminance studies (in lux) illustrate the increase in daylight from the ground level to the upper floors resulting from the urban context and adjacent buildings. The north and south façades admit sidelighting, while the "driven voids" admit toplighting to the heart of the building.

Sunny and Overcast Sky Illuminance (Lux)

———	500
———	438
———	375
	313
	250
———	188
———	126
———	63

March/September at 12.00 pm

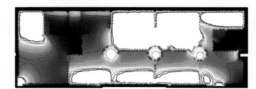

Fourth Floor_Sunny

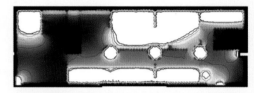

Fourth Floor_Overcast

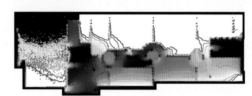

Third Floor_Sunny

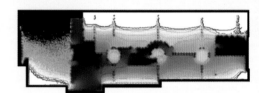

Third Floor_Overcast

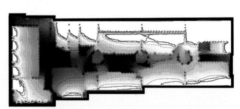

Second Floor_Sunny

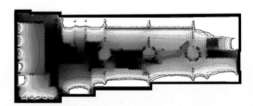

Second Floor_Overcast

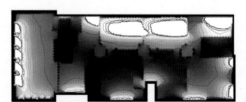

First Floor_Sunny

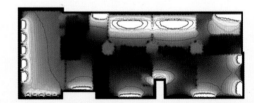

First Floor_Overcast

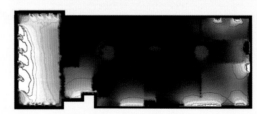

Ground Floor_Sunny

Ground Floor_Overcast

N

Chapter 1: endnotes

Introduction

1 Henry Plummer, *The Architecture of Natural Light*, New York: The Monacelli Press, 2009, 54.

2 Ralph Knowles, *Ritual House*, Washington: Island Press, 2006, 16–20.

3 Grant Hildebrand, *Origins of Architectural Pleasure*, Berkeley: University of California Press, 1999, 51–52.

Chapter 1.1

4 Anu Puustinen and Ville Hara, *Chapel of St. Lawrence Project Profile*, Helsinki: Avanto Architects, 2010.

5 Barry Lopez, *Arctic Dreams: Imagination and Desire in a Northern Landscape*, Toronto: Bantam Books, 1987, 17.

6 "Average Weather for Vantaa, Finland," WeatherSpark.com, https://weatherspark.com/averages/28671/Vantaa-Uusimaa-Finland.

7 Anu Puustinen, Architect, Avanto Architects, telephone interview with author, recorded October 5, 2015.

8 Ibid.

9 Ibid.

10 Ibid.

11 Ibid.

12 Chris Hodson, "Copper Awards: Winner, Chapel of St. Lawrence, Vantaa, Finland, Avanto Arkkitehdit," *Architectural Review*, November 1, 2011, http://www.architectural-review.com/copper-awards-winner/8621684.article.

13 "Office," Avanto Architects, http://www.avan.to/Frameset.htm.

14 Antti T. Seppänen – Oiva-Filmi, "AVANTO: Chapel of St. Lawrence," Vimeo video, 0:17, https://vimeo.com/33339110.

15 "Degree Days: Energy Data for Professionals," Degreedays.net: Weather Underground, http://www.degreedays.net/#generate.

16 Ibid.

Chapter 1.2

17 "The Reid Building, Glasgow School of Art," Steven Holl Architects, http://www.stevenholl.com/project-detail.php?id=140.

18 Chris McVoy, Architect and Senior Partner, Steven Holl Architects, telephone interview with author, recorded September 15, 2015.

19 Ibid.

20 "Average Weather for Glasgow, United Kingdom," WeatherSpark.com, https://weatherspark.com/averages/28752/Glasgow-Scotland-United-Kingdom.

21 "Future of GSA," *The Flow*, no. 14 (2011): 8–9, accessed January 13, 2016, http://www.gsa.ac.uk/media/455325/gsa_flowissue14_a4.pdf.

22 Spirit of Space, "Reid Building at the Glasgow School of Art, a Conversation with Steven Holl & Chris McVoy," New York: Steven Holl Architects, Vimeo video, 1:12, posted by "Steven Holl Architects," July 22, 2014, http://www.stevenholl.com/videos/101410201.

23 Ibid., 0:43.

24 Craig Tait, Architect, JM Architects, telephone interview with author, recorded January 15, 2016.

25 Chris McVoy.

26 Henry McKeown, "Glasgow School of Art," Glasgow School of Art Research Excellence Framework 2014, Glasgow: Mackintosh School of Architecture (2014), 9, http://radar.gsa.ac.uk/3148/14/McKeown131115JR.pdf.

27 Chris McVoy.

28 Ibid.

29 Ibid.

30 Ibid.

31 Spirit of Space, "Reid Building at the Glasgow School of Art," 1:07.

32 Chris McVoy.

33 Henry McKeown, "Glasgow School of Art," 6.

34 "Green Sheet: Seona Reid Building, Glasgow School of Art," Steven Holl Architects.

35 Craig Tait.

36 Ibid.

37 Chris McVoy.

38 "Degree Days: Energy Data for Professionals," Degreedays.net: Weather Underground, http://www.degreedays.net/#generate.

39 Ibid.

Chapter 2
Atmospheric Light

2.1 ANDO MUSEUM

2.2 2011 Serpentine Pavilion

"Atmosphere. … This singular density and mood, this feeling of presence, well-being, harmony, beauty … under whose spell I experience what I otherwise would not experience in precisely this way."[1]

Peter Zumthor, Atelier Peter Zumthor

Architectural atmosphere is inherently ephemeral, transient, and qualitative. Related ideas include ambiance, mood, feeling, character, and presence of space. In his 2003 lecture on the topic "Atmospheres. Architectural Environments. Surrounding Objects," architect Peter Zumthor described atmosphere as an emotional response to the environment: "Quality architecture to me is when a building manages to move me. … One word for it is atmosphere. … We perceive atmosphere through our emotional sensibilities – a form of perception that works incredibly quickly. … We are capable of immediate appreciation, of a spontaneous emotional response, of rejecting things in a flash. This is very different from linear thought, which we are equally capable of, and which I love, too."[2]

Atmosphere is experienced through feelings that have emotive qualities such as "calm," "safe," "contemplative," "playful," and "festive." Atmosphere is also connected to the haptic, kinesthetic, and synesthetic human sensory experiences. Finnish architect and professor Juhani Pallasmaa emphasizes the role of the bodily senses in relationship to atmosphere: "I am thinking of tactility in an existential sense, as an experience of one's being and sense of self. This is why the tactile, or haptic, experience becomes the integration of all the sense modalities, and that is why I regard it as the most important of our senses. It is this haptic sense of being in the world, and in a specific place and moment, the actuality of existence, that is the essence of atmosphere."[3]

An atmospheric approach to design places the user at the center of a dialogue between the qualitative and quantitative aspects of architecture. The human experience, along with program needs, guides the development of desired qualities, tones, and moods in a space or sequence of spaces. In his essay on atmosphere, Gernot Böhme emphasizes the importance of the user's proprioception of space and movement: "Architecture always has produced atmosphere, for instance atmosphere of holiness and power. But architecture beyond modernity rediscovers the perspective of the user. It is not only about the building as such, but it is dealing with felt space, mindful bodily presence."[4]

▷ The northern gallery of the museum reveals the juxtaposition of contemporary exhibition spaces enclosed by concrete walls and placed within a reconstructed traditional Japanese house of timber, plaster, and stone. Direct sunlight, admitted from a south-facing skylight, slips over a concrete wall to illuminate the upper portion of a traditional timber-frame and plaster wall. A low linear window with translucent glazing illuminates the horizontal surface of an exhibition. ANDO MUSEUM, Naoshima, Kagawa, Japan; Tadao Ando, Tadao Ando Architects.

"The ultimate meaning of any building is beyond architecture; it directs our consciousness back to the world and towards our own sense of self and being. Profound architecture makes us experience ourselves as complete embodied and spiritual beings. In fact, this is the great function of all meaningful art. In the experience of art, a peculiar exchange takes place; I lend my emotions and associations to the space and the space lends me its atmosphere, which entices and emancipates my perceptions and thoughts. ... An architectural work is not experienced as a series of isolated retinal pictures, but in its full and integrated material, embodied and spiritual essence." [5]

Juhani Pallasmaa, Architect and Professor

Whether from a poetic or a practical perspective, the essential concerns of human shelter and comfort are inseparable from beauty, aesthetics, and the atmospheric quality of space: How does the desired character of light support the design intentions and program activities? How does the quality change with time and seasons? What are the roles of flexibility and user interaction in defining and varying the character of light? How does the atmosphere of daylight relate to electric lighting and visual and thermal comfort? What are the needs of the users?

In the following studies of works by Tadao Ando Architects & Associates and Atelier Peter Zumthor, the question of architectural atmosphere is developed through varied perspectives, including programmatic needs and activities; emotional, symbolic, and metaphoric concepts; material choices and construction systems; and formal and spatial qualities. Light, which is essential in developing desired atmospheric qualities, embodies a richness of characteristics such as "diffuse," "direct," "dappled," "reflected," "refracted," and "dynamic." These qualities are not static; rather they are continuously transformed by time, season, climate, place, and changing sky conditions and as light interacts with room materials and surfaces. Atmosphere comprises the immeasurable and qualitative dimensions of architecture, yet it is through tangible strategies of form, structure, and materials that the intangible atmospheric and luminous qualities of space are defined.

In the first project, the ANDO MUSEUM in Naoshima, Japan, by Tadao Ando Architects & Associates, the atmosphere is defined by the journey through light and shadow in a sequence of nested spaces within a traditional Japanese house. The museum is designed as a series of transitions—from outside to inside and from inside to underground; from traditional to contemporary in materials and construction techniques; from light to darkness; and from the site to the intimate, inwardly focused spaces. The transitions unfold as incremental variations of light and darkness that are revealed only through movement. Ando's interest lies in the qualities of space that result from his rigorous attention to form,

construction, and detailing, as spatial experiences are brought to life by nature, light, and time.

The relationships between nature, atmosphere, materials, and users were of particular importance to Swedish architect Peter Zumthor in the next study, the 2011 Serpentine Pavilion at Kensington Gardens in London, England. Zumthor reflects on the focus of his work: "Maybe the core of what I'm trying to do in my buildings [is] to come up with the right materials to create the right emotions. Maybe what I like to do is create emotional spaces ... they have to do something with the use." [6] The elements of atmosphere are particularly shaped by the selection of materials, which Zumthor sees as comprising a "body of architecture," in which he "imagines how the materials and spaces create the sensual effect of a bodily mass, covered by a membrane, a fabric, a skin." [7] Zumthor also defines "material compatibility" as an important aspect of atmosphere, with each material considered from multiple perspectives, including how it is fabricated, its tactile qualities, and its weight. [8] Daylight, or the "light on things," is among other variables described by Zumthor as contributing to atmospheric quality. While atmosphere is intangible, it is the very tangible architectural elements—such as spatial definition, envelope design, material properties, response to climate, and the dynamic play of natural light—that give rise to particular atmospheric qualities. At the 2011 Serpentine Pavilion, we find precisely these elements shaped to de-emphasize the architecture and to frame a fresh experience of the garden and our relationship to nature.

Daylight, as it interacts with architecture, is a primary vehicle used to develop a desired atmosphere. The richness of daylight and its myriad qualities are transformed by time, season, climate, place, and the changing sky and weather conditions. Atmosphere embodies the immeasurable and qualitative dimensions of architecture as well as the quantitative and measurable. However, Ando and Zumthor reveal that it is through tangible architectural strategies of form, structure, materials, and light that the intangible qualities of space are defined.

△ Entry portals within the minimal black façade mark the threshold through space, darkness, and light, leading to a hidden inner garden. 2011 Serpentine Pavilion, Kensington Gardens, Hyde Park, London, UK; Peter Zumthor, Peter Zumthor Atelier.

△ ▷ Street view of the entry gate and reconstructed traditional Japanese house and new museum. The minimal garden, conical skylight, and horizontal window quietly suggest the contrast between traditional and contemporary structure, materials, and daylight found within the museum.

Case study 2.1

ANDO MUSEUM

Naoshima, Kagawa, Japan

Tadao Ando, Tadao Ando Architects & Associates

"I have always had a tendency to imagine architectural space as being enclosed and cave-like. It seems to me that clues to the origins of architecture are to be found below ground. Beneath the earth's surface, light is reduced, the sense of depth increases, and darkness is born. I have long imagined space as something into which one descends, until light is gradually reduced and one is wrapped in an atmosphere of cool tranquility." [9]

Tadao Ando, Tadao Ando Architects & Associates

LIGHT AND THE QUALITY OF PLACE

The Benesse Art Site

During the past thirty years, the island of Naoshima in the Seto Inland Sea of Japan has become an art and architecture destination for visitors from around the world. The original idea for the Benesse Art Site Naoshima was initiated at a meeting in 1985 between Tetsuhiko Fukutake, the president and founder of Fukutake Publishing, and Chikatsugu Miyake, the mayor of Naoshima. The vision was realized by Fukutake's son, Soichiro Fukutake. Over the decades, this quiet island, together with neighboring Teshima and Inujima islands, has been transformed by new museums, architecture, and art installations by renowned international artists and Japanese architects to celebrate the beauty of art and nature. Tadao Ando has been involved from the onset of the planning, and has designed numerous projects, including the Naoshima International Camp, Benesse House, Art House Project "Minamidera," Chichu Art Museum, Lee Ufan Museum, and the recent ANDO MUSEUM.

Naoshima is nested within the protective shelter of the main islands of Japan, with panoramic views of the surrounding water, mountains, and islands. The humid subtropical climate is predominantly clear, with the exception of the rainy season in summer, which typically lasts from June to mid-July. Temperatures are relatively mild, with cool winters averaging a low of 0.7°C (33°F) in January and a high of 31.5°C (89°F) in August. [10] Located at 33.6° north latitude, the island experiences relatively long hours of daylight throughout the year, ranging from approximately 10 to 14 hours on the winter and summer equinoxes respectively, when the noon-sun altitude varies from a seasonal low of 32.9° to a high of 79.9°. The quality of daylight is soft and indirect during the rainy season, when diffuse daylight enters the building from multiple orientations, while clear skies bring the sunlight's high contrast, rich colors, and warm solar rays.

Honmura and Naoshima

Located in the historic town of Honmura, the ANDO MUSEUM is contained within a reconstructed one-hundred-year-old *minka*

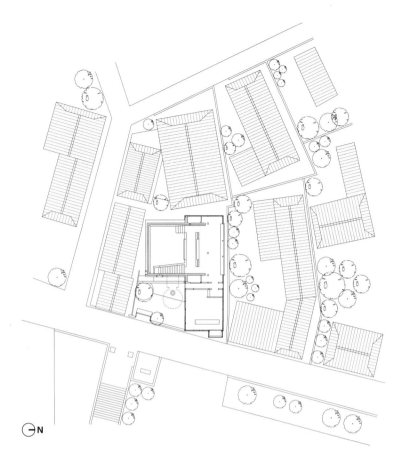

N

△ The site plan reveals the historic neighborhood context, proximity of neighbors, and narrow streets. Toplighting and sidelighting are strategically located in the building envelope to optimize solar access and to work within the constraints of the site context.

(traditional Japanese house), into which Ando inserted a series of contemporary concrete exhibition spaces. Visitors move from the historic streetscape through an entry and into the traditional house to discover a sequence of daylit galleries that culminate in a quiet underground meditation chamber. The small scale and intimate qualities of the site heighten the juxtaposition of the old and new, with spaces progressively transforming from traditional to contemporary in the experience of space, structure, and light.

Ando explains that he sees light as an expression of nature that helps us understand our place within a greater whole: "I think architecture is a place where one can affirm one's existence. ... Even in Naoshima, where daylight enters the building from all directions, I want to express how we all live with nature."[11]

Although visitors are separated visually from the site as they progress more deeply into the museum, the presence of nature is introduced through the dynamic play of light and shadow in space and upon room surfaces as the visitor moves from above to below ground through increasingly more enclosed spaces. With the exception of the entry area, the ANDO MUSEUM relies exclusively on natural light for illumination, with the galleries and meditation chamber brought to life through the changing moods, colors, and movements of daylight.

LIGHT AND THE DESIGN INTENTIONS

Light and Program

The architecture of the ANDO MUSEUM is in itself an exhibition that features the beauty and craft of traditional and contemporary Japanese architecture, while housing the drawings, models, and photos of Ando's varied projects at the Benesse Art Site Naoshima and elsewhere in Japan, as well as presenting the history of the island. Tadao Ando describes the underlying theme of "invisibility" in the ANDO MUSEUM, where the traditional house is a vessel that contains his contemporary interventions of space, structure, materials, and light: "I responded to the program to design a museum for my own architecture with an idea to create a building that would be focused on the spatial experience itself. ... The ANDO MUSEUM is also an 'invisible building' in which the new architectural elements are implanted within the existent *minka* and the earth. When a building cannot be seen, the quality of its space becomes the only matter of importance. I will be pleased if visitors are able to perceive within this modest building the essence of what I believe to be architecture."[12]

The elements of surprise and discovery are essential to the visitor's experience of the ANDO MUSEUM. It is not until the visitor is deep inside the museum that the new interventions are fully revealed with a dramatic contrast of space and light defined by concrete surfaces and volumes tucked within the traditional timber-frame house.

Light and Geometry

A geometric clarity and spatial order underlie the organization of the museum. While Ando is renowned for his exquisite craftsmanship, quality of construction, and refined detailing; he describes his work as a focus on space that is "born of light and geometry": "My limited use of materials—steel, glass and concrete— and the minimalist character of their detailing are also open to interpretation as signs of a preoccupation with materiality. ... [What] I am attempting to create through the honing of form is the space that appears when air flows through and light enters that structure. ... Reducing the elements of architecture and restoring it to its most primary form is nothing more than a way of creating an archetypical space, that is, a space possessing purity and power."[13]

The site is divided into four quadrants, with the entry and garden in the southeast, museum entrance in the northeast, main galleries occupying the west half of the site, and the underground meditation chamber beneath the garden. In section, the museum reveals a sequence of nested spaces, with the concrete surfaces and volumes of the new galleries tucked within the traditional timber-frame house. Visitors move through a choreography of spaces that transform from outside to inside, old to new, above to below, and from light to darkness.

LIGHT AND THE DESIGN STRATEGIES

Atmospheric Journey

In the journey from the street into the galleries and underground meditation chamber, visitors transition from connections with the outside neighborhood to progressively more inwardly focused

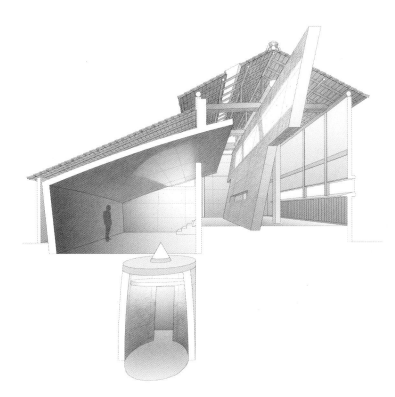

△ ▽ The section perspective illustrates the nesting of galleries and underground meditation space within the reconstructed traditional timber-frame house. A low translucent window and borrowed light illuminate the north gallery. A skylight in the south-facing roof admits daylight to the central gallery, while thin vertical and triangular windows provide direct sunlight in the south gallery. A conical skylight, hidden above a hovering ceiling plane, indirectly illuminates the walls of the underground meditation space.

contemplative spaces. The museum is surrounded by historic houses and a narrow pedestrian streetscape. On entry, the visitor passes through a traditional wooden gate that is screened by a *noren* (fabric divider) to mark the presence of the museum. A minimal garden is enclosed by the rammed earth wall and traditional burned-cedar cladding of the house. A gravel ground plane is punctured by the solitary conical skylight from a hidden meditation chamber below the garden. Within the museum entry, traditional construction materials are expressed in the *tsuchikabe* (mud-plaster) walls and *araidashi* (exposed stone aggregate) floors. Diffuse sidelighting is admitted through frosted windows and doors. A wooden screen affords a glimpse of a narrow wood-clad passageway to the galleries.

The first view into the museum frames a dramatic vertical space created by the traditional plaster wall to the north and a canted concrete wall to the south. A sequence of three gallery spaces is defined, from the north to south, by sloping and freestanding concrete walls and volumes tucked beneath the traditional timber-frame construction. The northern gallery is illuminated by a horizontal translucent window within the exterior timber and plaster north wall. Overhead, the traditional timber-frame construction is preserved and a long skylight is inserted over the central gallery to bring toplighting to the spaces below. The central gallery is framed to the north by a canted concrete wall and a partial concrete wall to the south. Daylight is reflected between room and ceiling surfaces to spill over the freestanding concrete walls and through low horizontal slots to adjacent galleries.

◁ Direct and reflected light wash the walls of the central gallery. Horizontal slots provide views and borrowed light to the adjacent north and south galleries. The warm timber structure of the traditional roof contrasts with the smooth surfaces of the contemporary concrete galleries.

The nesting of space is fully revealed in the southern gallery, which descends several steps and floats free of the traditional timber and plaster house to be completely enclosed by concrete planes on the east, south, and west, while the vaulted concrete ceiling rises toward the north. The northern and eastern boundaries of the south gallery are framed by partial concrete walls with horizontal slots to afford glimpses to the adjacent galleries and stairwell. Two narrow vertical windows in the outermost eastern wall, along with small triangular clerestory windows on the east and west, admit grazing light to illuminate the smooth concrete ceiling. Each gallery has a unique luminous quality, with a calm diffuse light in the northern gallery punctuated by abundant illumination in the toplit central gallery, which is contrasted by the quiet shadows and darkness of the southern gallery.

The meditation chamber, accessed through a stairway in the central gallery, is the most intimate, contained, and introspective experience of the journey, as Ando explains: "A slightly tilted concrete cylinder ... is buried in the ground as an independent

◁ A sliver of direct sunlight washes the north partition wall of the south gallery. Horizontal slots, partial walls, and nested rooms create spatial depth and layered ambient illumination.

▷ Triangular clerestory windows and vertical slots on the east wall admit direct sunlight to the south gallery. Horizontal slots in partition walls provide glimpses to the stairwell and adjacent toplit central gallery.

element set apart from the existent building. It contains a space for meditation that is composed solely from the texture of the light that falls into it from above." [14]

Ando also described his fascination with underground spaces in Werner Blaser's book on sunken courts: "It is precisely with an underground space that light becomes the theme. As one goes down deeper, the air, which had been active above ground, becomes thinner, and the still darkness becomes more profound. The moment light enters from above and falls on the walls shaping that darkness, space appears." [15]

The meditation chamber is constructed of a concrete cylinder with canted walls that are illuminated indirectly through the conical skylight. Beneath the skylight floats a steel ceiling with a thin gap along the perimeter to block direct views of the sky and to reveal the walls and volume of space in reflected light and gradated shadow.

Light and View
Views to the outside and within the museum are carefully controlled, with an increased sense of separation from the site as

◁ The conical skylight above the underground meditation space is hidden from view by a floating ceiling plane. A narrow gap between the ceiling plane and the walls enhance the luminous contrast and sense of mystery. A hidden structural frame anchors the "hovering" concrete ceiling to a roof structure above the ceiling.

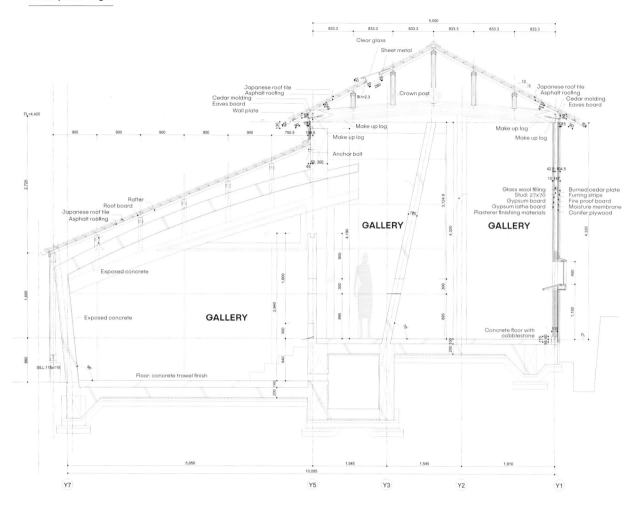

◁ A construction section looking west reveals the nested concrete galleries within the reconstructed traditional timber-frame house. Triangular clerestory windows are located in the south gallery, a linear skylight above the central gallery, and a low translucent horizontal window in the north gallery. Not shown in the section are thin vertical and horizontal windows on the east that provide borrowed daylight to the galleries through the stairwell that leads to the underground meditation space.

spaces progress from the garden into the entry, galleries, and subterranean meditation space. The only direct view to the garden is provided at the entry door, while discreet views of the sky are found in the central and south galleries. Translucent windows and indirect and reflected daylight foster a sense of mystery within a quiet, contemplative atmosphere. The sequence of spaces is organized along a circulation path with ninety-degree turns that create views to alternating cardinal directions, while the partial walls and interior apertures provide glimpses to and beyond adjacent spaces. Strategic interior views create spatial depth and interconnections between galleries that are animated by differing qualities of light and shadow.

In Michael Blackwood's documentary film on his early work, Ando describes the activity of "light watching," in which the movement of light and shadow is the focus of space: "If one lets light into architecture in many different and subtle ways one can enjoy light watching." [16]

Such is the case at the ANDO MUSEUM, where varied window forms, daylight strategies, and choreographed views create an experience of changing atmospheric qualities and patterns of light that can be considered an exhibition in its own right.

LIGHT AND THE ART OF MAKING

Light and Darkness

Ando is as fascinated with darkness and shadow as he is with light, as he explains: "You are able to see the light because of the darkness. Because of the darkness you felt the strong presence of light. Shadows and darkness contribute to serenity and calmness. In my opinion, the darkness creates the opportunity to think and contemplate." [17]

The beauty of both light and shadow are found in the changing atmospheric qualities of the ANDO MUSEUM. Depending on the season and sky conditions, the light varies dramatically from a soft, subdued, indirect, and diffuse illumination of overcast skies to dynamic patterns of sunlight animating space and surfaces on a sunny day. Gentle indirect light emanating through frosted glass windows and surface reflections is contrasted with direct daylight or sunlight from skylights, vertical slots, and triangular windows. Contrasting qualities of indirect and direct light engage and enliven the warmth of the traditional timber ceiling and post-and-beam structure as well as revealing the beauty and craft of the smooth surfaces of the contemporary concrete walls and volumes.

Structured and Material Light

Ando translates the exquisite craft of traditional Japanese architecture into his contemporary use of concrete, glass, and steel. Renowned for the fine finish and silky quality of concrete in his buildings, Ando's exacting attention to detail, collaboration with skilled carpenters, and use of quality formwork have enabled him to imbue concrete with the subtle qualities of traditional materials. As he explained in an interview with Michael

Blackwood: "My attitude towards concrete is to look for a kind of concrete that is closer in feeling to wood and paper. To find a beautiful and sensuous concrete." [18]

Ando's interests lie in translating the best qualities and values of traditional architecture: "I think that Japanese contemporary architecture has not incorporated the good qualities of traditional Japanese culture. ... I'm not talking about external things, such as form or material, but a way of thinking. What interests me most is to find a way to continue these traditional Japanese concepts and values and thereby pass them on to the next generation." [19]

At the ANDO MUSEUM, the juxtaposition of traditional timber frame and contemporary concrete construction heighten the beauty of both the old and new, as Ando explains: "My aim was to create a space that has a rich sense of depth despite its small size, where oppositional elements such as the past and present, wood and concrete, and light and dark clash intensely as they are superimposed against each other." [20] Spatial, material, and luminous contrast are further fostered by the separation between the timber-frame and plaster walls of the *minka* and the freestanding concrete structure. The exceptional craft and material qualities of each construction tradition are independently expressed, yet remain within an intimate spatial relationship.

LIGHT INSPIRATIONS

Although the site and the ANDO MUSEUM are small in scale, Ando skillfully choreographs a rich conversation between the spatial, material, and luminous qualities of the old and new. Ando's focus is on creating meaningful experiences, in which architecture is not an object, but rather a means of defining space. In an interview with Edan Corkill for the *Japan Times*, Ando explains his focus on space-making: "I think Japan's contribution has been the idea that architecture is not a 'thing'—it's not a solid object. It's like Kakuzo Okakura wrote in his 'Book of Tea' in 1906: Architecture is never a shape, it is the space enclosed by the shape, by the walls and ceiling." [21]

While the ANDO MUSEUM embodies a clarity and simplicity of form, structure, and materials, these tangible architectural elements are used to create a dynamic spatial and visual experience and to express the beauty of light and nature. In discussing his early work in Michael Blackwood's documentary, Ando explains light as an embodiment and expression of nature: "Beauty is felt in traditional Japanese architecture when spaces are illuminated by small rays of light. ... Nature is embodied in my architecture in the form of light ... [it is] the movement of nature through space that defines architecture." [22]

The ANDO MUSEUM is brought to life by light and the juxtaposition of atmospheric and spatial qualities. Ando uses the elements of structure, materials, and spatial composition to choreograph a luminous journey of discovery from the outer physical world to an inner contemplative space.

DESIGN PROFILE

1. Building Profile
Project: ANDO MUSEUM
Location: Naoshima, Kagawa, Japan
Architect: Tadao Ando Architects & Associates
Client: Naoshima Fukutake Art Museum Foundation
Building Type: Museum
Square Footage: Site area: 190.5 sq m (2,051 sq ft); building area: 114.5 sq m (1,232 sq ft); floor area: 125.8 sq m (1,354 sq ft)
Estimated Cost: Not available
Completion: 2013

2. Professional Team
Architect: Tadao Ando
General Contractor: Kajima Corporation
Structural Engineer: COREe structure design
Mechanical and Electrical Engineers: Kajima Corporation, Tonets Corporation, and Toko Electrical Construction Co., Ltd.

3. Climate Profile
Climate (Köppen-Geiger Climate Classification System): Cfa: humid subtropical climate
Latitude: 33.6° north latitude
Solar Angles: Noon
June 21: 79.9°
March/September 21: 56.4°
December 21: 32.9°
Length of Day: Approximate Hours of Daylight from Sunrise to Sunset
June 21: 14h 27m
March/September 21: 12h 12m
December 21: 9h 51m
Heating Degree Days (Okayama, Japan; 23.5km/14.6 miles north of Naoshima): 2072 heating degree days °C (3763 heating degree days °F) (18°C and 65°F base temperature) [23]
Cooling Degree Days (Okayama, Japan; 23.5km/14.6 miles north of Naoshima): 646 cooling degree days °C (1195 cooling degree days °F) (18°C and 65°F base temperature) [24]

4. Design Strategies
Daylighting Strategies:
   1) Sidelighting: frosted glass, clear glass, diffusing glass, and open windows, and 2) Toplighting: linear skylight over central gallery and conical skylight with ceiling reflector in meditation space.
Sustainable Design and High-Performance Strategies: Daylighting throughout museum with electric lighting only in the entry gallery.
Renewable Energy Strategies: None.

Ando: Structure and Materials

The exploded diagram illustrates the material, structural, and spatial relationships between the traditional timber-frame house and the new concrete art galleries and meditation space, which are placed within the reconstructed house.

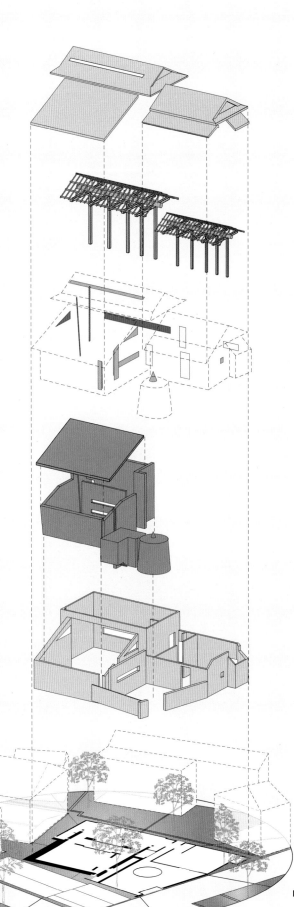

Roof: Tile

Structure: Timber Frame

Envelope: Glass Skylight and Translucent and Clear Glass Windows

Interior: Concrete Walls, Floor, and Ceiling

Envelope: Wood Cladding and Interior Plaster Walls

Floor: Concrete and Exposed Stone Aggregate

S

E

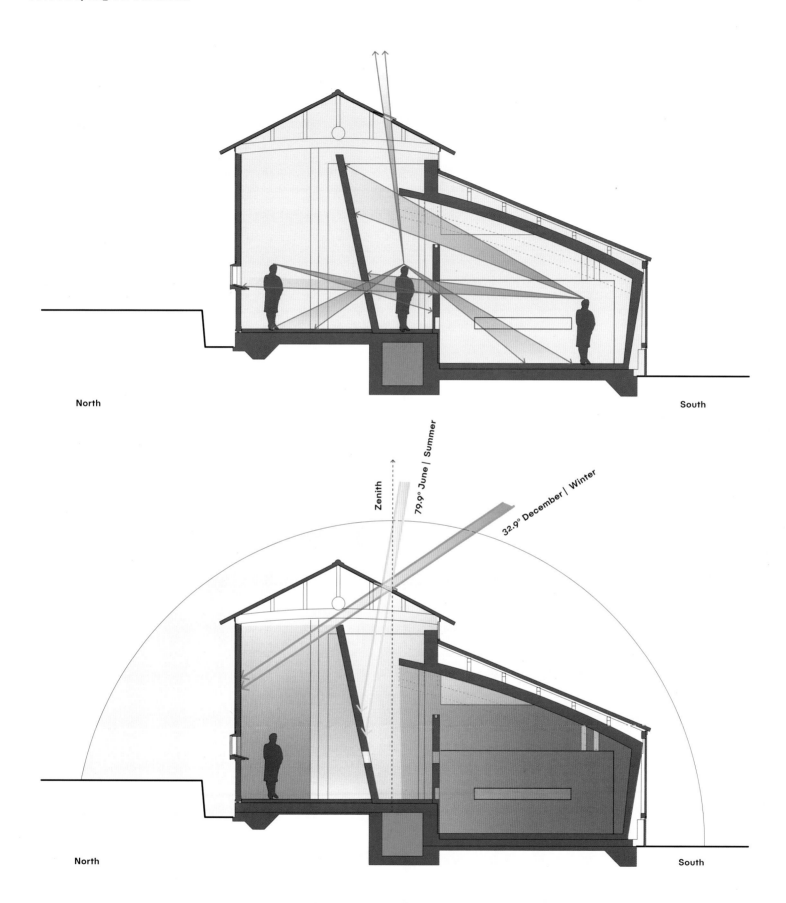

The upper north–south section illustrates the views between spaces, around partition walls, and through window apertures. The lower section illustrates the seasonal effect of sun angles on the admission of daylight into the galleries. Low winter sunlight slips over the top of the central gallery partition wall to reflect into the north gallery. High summer sunlight reflects from walls in the central gallery to adjacent spaces.

Equinox Walk-Through

Perspective renderings and luminance studies (in candela/square meter; cd/m2) illustrate the visual quality of daylight and contrast ratios from four view locations within the museum during the fall equinox (September 21 at noon). There is a decrease in light levels and an increase in contrast moving from the north to the south gallery. The highest contrast ratios occur at window openings in partitions and exterior walls. High contrast and a progression from light to darkness enhances the experience of mystery and discovery.

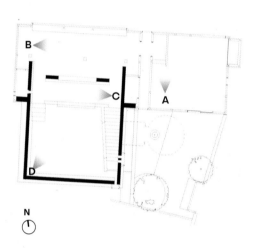

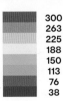

N

Overcast Sky Luminance (Cd/m²)

300
263
225
188
150
113
76
38

View A: March/September 21 at 12:00 pm

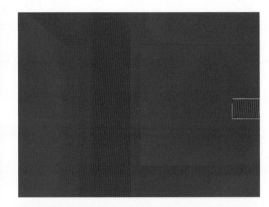

View A: March/September 21 at 12:00 pm

View B: March/September 21 at 12:00 pm

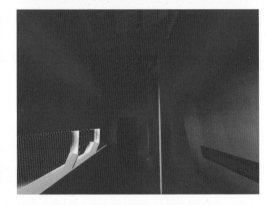

View B: March/September 21 at 12:00 pm

View C: March/September 21 at 12:00 pm

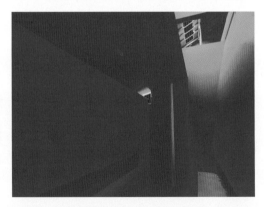

View C: March/September 21 at 12:00 pm

View D: March/September 21 at 12:00 pm

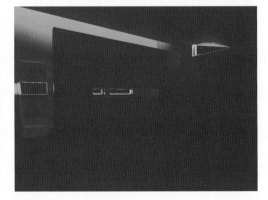

View D: March/September 21 at 12:00 pm

Seasonal Perspectives_Central Gallery

Time-lapse renderings of the central gallery illustrate the dramatic seasonal and diurnal changes in the quality and distribution of daylight throughout the year given the geographic latitude (33.6° north latitude) and varying length of day (14h 27m on June 21 and 9h 51m on December 21). During the winter months, daylight passes over the top of the partition wall to the north gallery. In the summer months, direct sunlight reflects between the two walls of the central gallery to adjacent spaces.

N

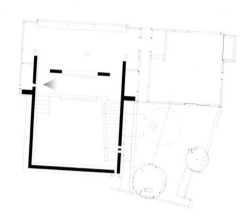

December 21	March/September 21	June 21
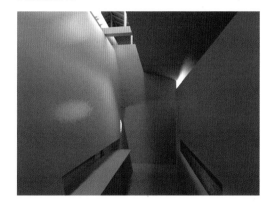		

9:00 am

12:00 pm

3:00 pm

Daylight Analysis:
Seasonal Plans_December

Illuminance studies (in lux) illustrate the progression from light to darkness moving from the entry through the galleries to the underground meditation space. Sectional studies illustrate the changing illuminance levels from the skylight and windows in winter and summer. High summer sun angles admit direct sunlight to the central gallery, with light borrowed by adjacent galleries.

Sunny Skies
Illuminance (Lux)

	150
	131
	113
	94
	76
	57
	38
	20

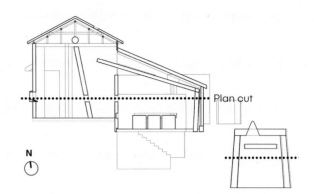

Plan cut

N

December 21

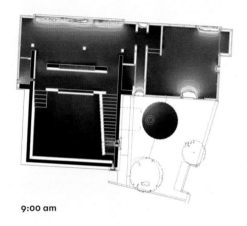

9:00 am

March/September 21

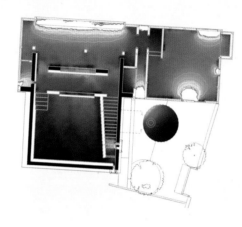

June 21

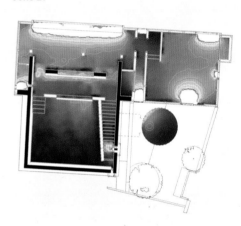

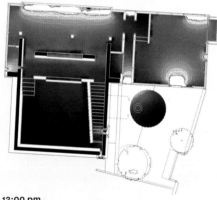

12:00 pm

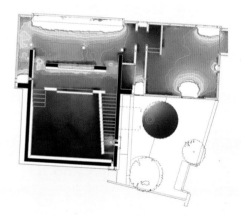

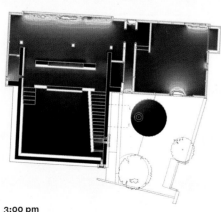

3:00 pm

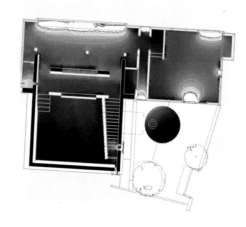

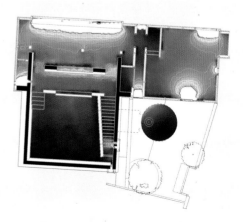

Daylight Analysis:
Seasonal Sections

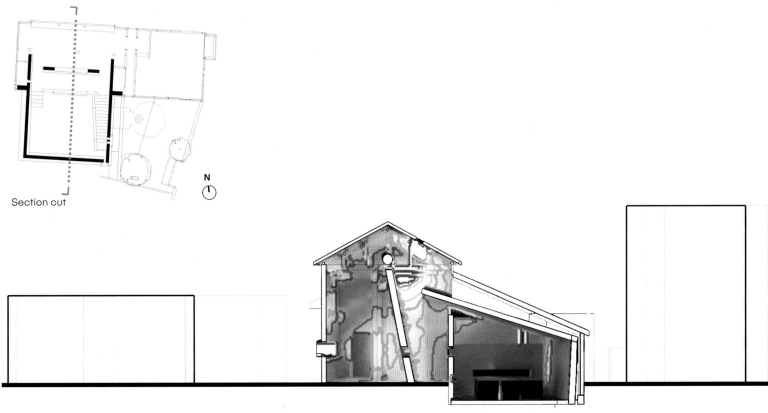

Section cut

N

December at 12:00 pm

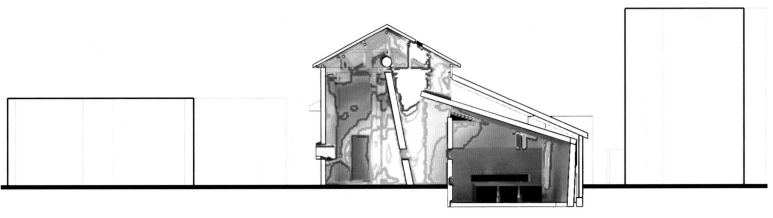

June at 12.00 pm

Sunny Skies
Illuminance (Lux)

——— 150
——— 131
——— 113
·········· 94
——— 76
——— 57
——— 38
——— 20

△ ▷ A sculptural electric lighting fixture playfully illuminated the pathways and northwest entries to the pavilion at sunset. Electric lighting pendants created pools of light and shadow in the tall vertical circulation corridor that led to the inner garden. The quiet simplicity of the monolithic black façade enhanced the sense of mystery and discovery.

Case study 2.2

2011 Serpentine Pavilion

Kensington Gardens, Hyde Park, London, UK

Peter Zumthor, Atelier Peter Zumthor (architecture)
and Piet Oudolf (garden design)

"Thinking about daylight and artificial light I have to admit that daylight, the light on things, is so moving to me that I feel it almost as a spiritual quality. When the sun comes up in the morning—which I always find so marvelous, absolutely fantastic the way it comes back every morning—and casts its light on things, it doesn't feel as if it quite belongs in this world. I don't understand light. It gives me the feeling there's something beyond me, something beyond all understanding. And I am very glad, very grateful that there is such a thing. ... For an architect that light is a thousand times better than artificial light." [25]

Peter Zumthor, Atelier Peter Zumthor

LIGHT AND THE QUALITY OF PLACE

Serpentine Pavilion

The Serpentine Pavilion is an annual commission, initiated in 2000, by the Serpentine Gallery Museum. Each year, a renowned architect is invited to design a temporary pavilion in Kensington Gardens, one of eight royal gardens in London, England. Sited on the lawn adjacent to the Serpentine Gallery Museum, the pavilion is designed within a six-month period and is open to the public, free of admission, during the months of July through October. This installation has fostered experimentation and innovation from a diverse group of architects, including the inaugural pavilion by Zaha Hadid, to works by Toyo Ito, Alvaro Siza, Rem Koolhaas, Jean Nouvel, and Frank Gehry, among others. The 2011 Serpentine Pavilion was designed by the Swiss architect Peter Zumthor, Atelier Peter Zumthor (APZ), and Dutch garden designer Piet Oudolf.

Kensington Gardens

Zumthor describes the pavilion as an instrument to frame the inner garden and sky, and imagined that the structure could be deconstructed and located in different sites and climates. As such, the architecture of the pavilion is not designed to respond to the particular conditions of the context but rather to act as a frame for the garden, as Zumthor explained: "It's not a contextual piece, but an instrument; if it were a contextual piece it would have entrances and things reacting to the surrounding. But since we said 'no'—it's a tool to be with the plants and to look at the plants. We knew the building had to be a building type in its own right." [26]

Yet, Zumthor clarifies that the pavilion does respond to the movement of the sun in this geographic location: "The orientation of the building is made so that I have the most sun here, on the ground, in the garden." [27] Although the pavilion could be reassembled in different locations, for its inauguration it was sited in Kensington Gardens; as such, it captured and interacted with the particular experience of London's maritime climate, with its characteristic mild, overcast, and oftentimes rainy weather.

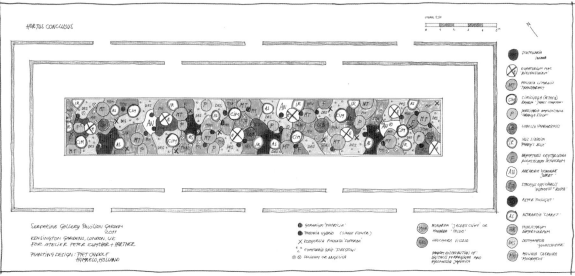

△ Garden designer Piet Oudolf's "nearly wild" garden installation included native plants to attract pollinators, birds, and wildlife during the four-month period of July to October. The garden celebrated the natural cycles of time, growth, and decay.

▷ Dramatic darkness in the perimeter corridor alternately punctuated by brilliant pools of daylight from the exterior site and interior garden. Pendant electric fixtures cast warm pools of light to the lower boundaries of the vertical space.

▷▷ A small channel at the edge of the ceiling gathered rain into a vertical screen of water as it flowed from the steeply-pitched roof into the gardens.

During the months of July through October, the period of the installation, the temperatures range from an average high of 23.3°C (74°F) in August and an average low of 8.3°C (47°F) in mid-October. [28] Sky conditions during the summer through fall have a median cloud cover of 70 percent in August to a high of 85 percent in October. Direct sunlight is periodic during this time, with clear to mostly clear skies 33 percent of the daylight hours. Located at 51.28° north latitude, there are approximately 8 to 16.5 hours of daylight on the winter and summer solstices, when the noon sun altitude rises above the horizon 15.2° and 62.2° respectively. During the months of the pavilion installation, the highest noon sun altitude varied from 61° in early July to 24° in late October.

LIGHT AND THE DESIGN INTENTIONS

A Garden Program

The program brief asked that the pavilion provide a multi-purpose space that was flexible in accommodating a variety of social and art gatherings during the day and night, including concerts, performances, films, presentations, debates, and other events. Zumthor's approach to the program was to create a contemplative garden—a garden within Kensington Gardens—where visitors could engage with nature and each other. For the inauguration of the

pavilion, Zumthor discussed his design intentions and reflected on his garden concept: "To be with the plants, where the plants are in the center and not the people ... to make something which would work like a looking glass. That you would have an object in the park and in the object again, plants. And then they would have a different scale, they would be intimate. You would not see it as a big configuration like the park outside, but a more intimate relationship to the plants. This was then the idea." [29]

To realize his vision of the garden pavilion, Zumthor invited the collaboration of garden designer Piet Oudolf. Renowned for his innovative and naturalistic garden designs, Oudolf makes the distinction of describing the Serpentine garden as an "installation," which needed to perform immediately and for a four-month period. As a dramatic and "nearly wild" counterpoint to the traditional English garden, Oudolf invited a piece of wildness into the heart of Kensington Gardens.

Garden within a Garden

Zumthor describes the pavilion as a *"hortus conclusus,"* with an inner garden enclosed within the boundaries of the architecture. He also used the descriptors "instrument," "frame," and "stage" to illustrate his concept, as he explains: "It would be great to do something in the landscape where you would not look at the landscape, but that the landscape would look at you. ... I thought maybe I could go on with this theme of garden and nature ... to be with nature, to be with the plants. Plants are the center and not the people." [30]

In contrast to previous pavilions, Zumthor shifted the attention from the architecture to nature. The modest black pavilion receded into the shadows of Kensington Gardens, yet quietly invited visitors to discover and explore the secret garden within. Zumthor created an intimate refuge for Piet Oudolf's garden design, which he described as: "Nature, a little bit designed. This is eighty-percent nature. ... Piet is painting with plants." [31]

◁▷ Despite the small scale of the pavilion, a dramatic journey of light and space was created through spatial layering and luminous contrast. Daylight entering alternating doorways on the inside and outside illuminated the tall vertical passageway. At the interior of the pavilion, a sitting space and ambulatory path, sheltered by a low protective roof, framed a view of the sky and garden.

Reminiscent of a medieval cloister, the garden was wrapped by a sheltering enclosure, seating, and ambulatory space. The layered walls and steeply pitched roof created a protective boundary to mediate sound and frame the changing sky.

Dark and light enhanced the journey of discovery and surprise. The black exterior and interior envelopes were separated by a tall, dark space with offset doorways to create an alternating rhythm of light and shadow, while eliminating direct views into the pavilion. On passage through the exterior wall, dark corridor, and inner wall, visitors were greeted with the light-filled garden and an explosion of living colour from native plants of varied hues, textures, heights, and forms. On the interior, views to the surrounding site were restricted, with only the sky and treetops framed by the steeply sloped roof and sheltering overhang. Simple sidelighting and pendant electric lights provided illumination within the dark corridor, while toplighting illuminated the inner garden.

Light and Atmosphere

The search for a desired atmospheric quality and emotional response are at the heart of Zumthor's work. Atmosphere is revealed through "real" sense experiences, as Zumthor explained in his 2003 lecture and subsequent book on *Atmospheres*: "We perceive atmosphere through our emotional sensibilities. … So what moved me? Everything. The things themselves, the people, the air, noises, sound, colours, material presences, textures, forms too. … The real has its own magic." [32]

At the Serpentine Pavilion, the mysterious, intimate, and quiet qualities of light and space are achieved through simple, tangible design strategies. The stark contrast between outside and inside and the dark pathway through which visitors pass heightens the experience of discovery. Contrast was emphasized between the inside and outside, extreme light and dark, and crisp rectilinear architecture and soft organic garden. Ed Clark, collaborator and engineer at Arup London, described the experience of contrast in the corridor between the outside and inside: "On a bright sunny day, the adjustment of your eyes into the dark corridor was so great … but the actual light levels were okay. It's intentional that you went from the daylight and then you're plunged into this comparatively dark corridor and let out again into the garden. There's a slight disorientation that arises in that you don't have time to adjust. I think that was part of it." [33] Zumthor employs both light and darkness to create a sense of discovery, while carefully balancing desired atmospheric qualities with illuminance and egress requirements.

In his interview with Christine Murray, editor of *Architects' Journal*, Zumthor emphasized the ordinary, everyday qualities of the pavilion: "The atmosphere is one that everybody recognises somehow; an enclosed garden at the centre, with people collected

The stark simplicity of the pavilion helped visitors to see the sky, garden, and changing weather from a new perspective and to rediscover nature.

LIGHT AND THE DESIGN STRATEGIES

Journey of Darkness and Light

The installation transitioned from the busy street life of London into the relative quiet of Kensington Gardens and through the exterior and interior layers of the pavilion to the inner garden. From the exterior, the stark black structure revealed little of the inner sanctuary. Sited on the east lawn of the Serpentine Gallery Museum, the long rectilinear pavilion was oriented on a northeast to southwest axis. The simple black mass, at 5.3 meters (17.4 feet) in height, and 12 by 33 meters (39.4 by 108.3 feet) in width and length, had a calm, humble presence. The sheltering double walls of the structure created a zone of transition between the "outer" Kensington Gardens and the "inner" contemplative garden. The exterior and interior of the black structure absorbed light and minimized its presence. Six entries, three each on the east and west façades, led visitors from the outer Kensington Gardens into a tall dark transition zone in which four inner thresholds opened onto the protected inner garden. Intentionally thin in plan, the narrow space fostered an intimate connection across the garden space.

around it. We're not there to pray – I designed some tables and chairs, you can have a drink and something to eat, and it's nice for us to be there and have a chat. It's not holy, not a sacred place, but I hope it will be intimate. I hope you go there and think, I have to come back with my friend. That's what I want." [34]

Zumthor described the space as a "looking glass" that mirrored and reflected the quality and mood of the activities as well as the changing garden, sky conditions, sun, and weather. The architecture seemingly disappeared; a shadowy frame for the sky and a quiet container for the secret garden.

LIGHT AND THE ART OF MAKING

Light, Time, and Impermanence

As a vessel for light, plants, and people, the pavilion captured the shifting sky conditions and sun angles from July through mid-October. Over the months, the sun altitude and azimuth slowly shifted toward the south each day, with lower sun angles, lengthening shadows, and shorter hours of daylight. From rain and sunshine to varied temperatures and humidity, the pavilion celebrated the unique qualities of each day. Zumthor's stark geometric architecture heightened the contrast with Oudolf's nearly wild garden. With the thin pavilion oriented on the northeast–southwest axis, Oudolf selected plants in response to solar conditions that would perform throughout the seasons under partial to full shade. Growth, decay, and impermanence were inherent to the experience of the garden installation, as Oudolf explains: "Plants are for me the ideal tools to create depth, emotion, dynamism. To create the sense that you feel the time going on and changing. ... We want to make gardens that are working through the seasons. You can see them come and grow and perform and die. And even decay is a big aspect in the way we work. ... If you look at this sort of planting, it's dynamic, ephemeral, it comes and goes quickly. It's emotional and changes much." [35]

Cultivated and native species such as bee balm, aster, anemone, liatris, and cow parsley transformed in color, texture, and form over the months while attracting bees, butterflies, and garden fauna. The pavilion framed a brief season in time to awaken the senses and to witness nature's cycle of growth, blooming, and decay.

Material Light and Material Shadow

Emotional and atmospheric quality is integral to the material and construction choices, as Zumthor explained: "So out of what material is this thing made? ... Is it wood? Is it brick? Natural stone? Precast concrete? We went through these things, always trying to image the place and the plants. ... So this is maybe for me the most important work ... to come up with the right materials to create the right emotions." [36]

Ed Clark, of Arup, worked closely with Peter Zumthor and Anna Page, the project architect, to explore and develop the choice of structure and materials. While brick was explored in depth, in the end, a timber system was chosen for time, constructability, and material qualities, among other issues. Clark described the timber structure as "a more ambiguous solution that was monolithic black and like a hollow violin structure." [37]

Anna Page, in an interview with Amanda Birch for *Building Design Online*, described the transient quality of the structure: "Peter [Zumthor] chose timber because he wanted a simple, honest material that reflected the temporality of the pavilions. ... He wanted something appropriate to the site and programme that would still hold a poetic resonance, and timber did all this." [38]

To achieve Zumthor's desired section and spatial quality, the deep roof overhang needed to be structurally stabilized to prevent overturning, as Clark clarified: "The front wall is thicker closest to [the] garden. The form of the floor work as an upside-down 'T' and the joints between that wall and floor are robust. The section that forms the bench became a solid plate of timber to reinforce that

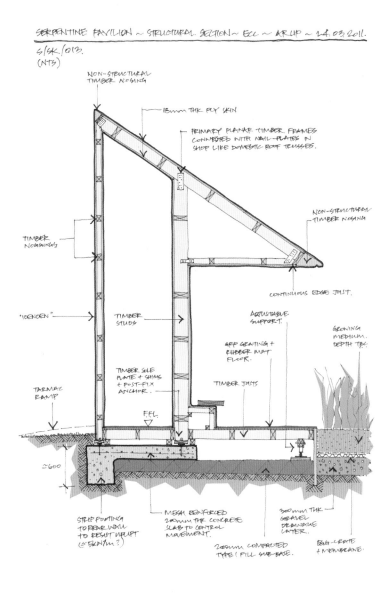

SERPENTINE PAVILION ~ STRUCTURAL SECTION ~ ECC ~ ARUP ~ 24.03.2011.

S/SK/013.
(NTS)

NON-STRUCTURAL
TIMBER NOGGING

18mm THK PLY SKIN

PRIMARY PLANAR TIMBER FRAMES
CONNECTED WITH NAIL-PLATES IN
SHOP LIKE DOMESTIC ROOF TRUSSES.

NON-STRUCTURAL
TIMBER NOGGING

TIMBER
NOGGINGS

CONTINUOUS EDGE JOIST.

"IDENDEN"

TIMBER
STUDS

ADJUSTABLE
SUPPORT.

GROWING
MEDIUM.
DEPTH TBC.

GRP GRATING +
RUBBER MAT
FLOOR.

TIMBER SOLE
PLATE + SHIMS
+ POST-FIX
ANCHOR.

TARMAC
RAMP

TIMBER JOISTS

FFL.

~600

STRIP FOOTING
TO REAR WALL
TO RESIST UPLIFT
(@ 5KN/m?)

MESH REINFORCED
200mm THK CONCRETE
SLAB TO CONTROL
MOVEMENT.

300mm THK
GRAVEL
DRAINAGE
LAYER.

200mm COMPACTED
TYPE 1 FILL SUB-BASE.

EGG-CRATE
+ MEMBRANE.

△▷ Arup structural engineer Ed Clark's section detail of the pavilion illustrates the construction logic and spatial layering from outside to inside. The prefabricated trusses and timber structure were clad with spruce plywood and finished with a coating of black fire-resistant Idenden.

joint and a stable base. All the frames along the two sides of the building also work together and the inclined roof are frame plywood panels screwed and glued along the top to act as a diaphragm to stiffen the entire structure."[39]

The pavilion was constructed of prefabricated pine timber frames with spruce plywood cladding and a scrim impregnated with a black coating of Idenden (a polymer emulsion with a matte-black finish and fire resistance). Prefabricated trusses cantilevered over the seating and circulation areas were clad in black. Black rubber floor mats buffered internal sounds while creating unified floor, wall, and ceiling surfaces. The pavilion absorbs light, with all matte-black surfaces. The only exception is a simple blue pine bench that floated from the wall in contrast to the black surrounds. Changing views and moods of the sky were accentuated against the dark surfaces of the pavilion, while the shaded perimeter walls provided a visually quiet backdrop to the life of the garden. During a rainstorm, the steep roof overhang captured rainwater for the garden, while a "water cut" or small channel at the outer edge of the ceiling gathered rain into a transient vertical screen of water between visitors and the garden.

Clark discussed the attention given to all details of the project, and that even rainwater runoff was an experiential opportunity: "During the early stage of project we impressed that this is London and it rains a lot. Peter saw how that could be beautiful. Development was intentional to make sure that when weather was inclement, that the experience was as delightful as sitting in the summer, sunny, calm, blue-sky morning. The idea of the water cut is that rain lands perfectly within centimeters of the edge of the floor."[40]

Clark underscored the importance of construction mock-ups used by Zumthor and his design team: "Precision was absolutely present in every step of the way. To achieve that, Peter [Zumthor]

△ The black surfaces created a subdued atmosphere, absorbed daylight, and enhanced the sense of mystery and contrast between the building and the garden.

was constantly making prototypes and physical models to study the height of the bench; depth of the bench; height of the ceiling above you; width of the corridor; feeling of tightness or spacious; roof line relative to floor, etc." [41]

LIGHT INSPIRATIONS

In the search for atmosphere and presence in architecture, darkness is as important as light. Despite the hundreds of thousands of people who visit the Serpentine Pavilion installations each year, the 2011 pavilion created an intimate and quiet atmospheric quality through contrast of light and shadow, spatial layering, choice of light-absorbing materials, and the integration of nature. The pavilion was designed as a frame for the garden and, in many ways, it was a "non-building" wrapped in matte-black surfaces to absorb—rather than reflect— light and to create a quiet presence on the site. Zumthor reveals that rich, luminous, and spatial experiences can be realized in a modestly sized building with only a few simple architectural and daylighting strategies. Inverting the balance between architecture and landscape, Zumthor "invites nature to take center stage," as he explains: "I like to be part of this whole creation of plants, and animals etc. And I think it's beautiful to make a piece of architecture where the garden is in the center. It is not me looking at the landscape, but maybe the opposite—the landscape looking at me. [42]

The 2011 Serpentine Pavilion encouraged designers to reconsider a more humble relationship between architecture and nature and to celebrate impermanence, change, and the dynamics of both light and darkness.

DESIGN PROFILE

1. Building Profile
Project: 2011 Serpentine Pavilion
Location: Kensington Gardens, London, England, UK
Architect: Atelier Peter Zumthor
Garden Designer: Piet Oudolf
Client: Serpentine Gallery
Building Type: Pavilion
Square Footage: 396 sq m (4,263 sq ft)
Estimated Cost: Not available
Completion: 2011

2. Professional Team
Architect: Peter Zumthor
Garden Designer: Piet Oudolf
Project Architects: Anna Page, Petra Stiermayr, and Klemens Grund
Structural Engineer: Arup
Main Contractor: Stage One
Project and Construction Manager: Mace
Landscape: The Landscape Group
Town Planning Consultant: DP9

3. Climate Profile
Climate (Köppen-Geiger Climate Classification System): Cfb: oceanic climate
Latitude: 51.28° north latitude
Solar Angles: Noon
June 21: 62.2°
March/September 21: 38.7°
December 21: 15.2°
Length of Day: Approximate Hours of Daylight from Sunrise to Sunset
June 21: 16h 38m
March/September 21: 12h 15m
December 21: 7h 50m
Heating Degree Days: 2303 heating degree days °C (4343 heating degree days °F) (18°C and 65°F base temperature) [43]
Cooling Degree Days: 129 cooling degree days °C (208 cooling degree days °F) (18°C and 65°F base temperature) [44]

4. Design Strategies
Daylighting Strategies: 1) Sidelighting: six alternating entries to corridor and four entries to garden, and 2) Toplighting: open roof aperture above garden.
Sustainable Design and High-Performance Strategies: Daylighting throughout with supplemental electric lighting; no heating or cooling systems required.
Renewable Energy Strategies: None.

Zumthor: Structure and Materials

The exploded diagram illustrates the structural logic and spatial organization of the pavilion. The timber-frame structure and roof trusses are clad in plywood panels and scrim with a fireproof black Idenden coating. Nested spaces progress from darkness in the circulation corridor to the light-filled interior seating area and toplit garden.

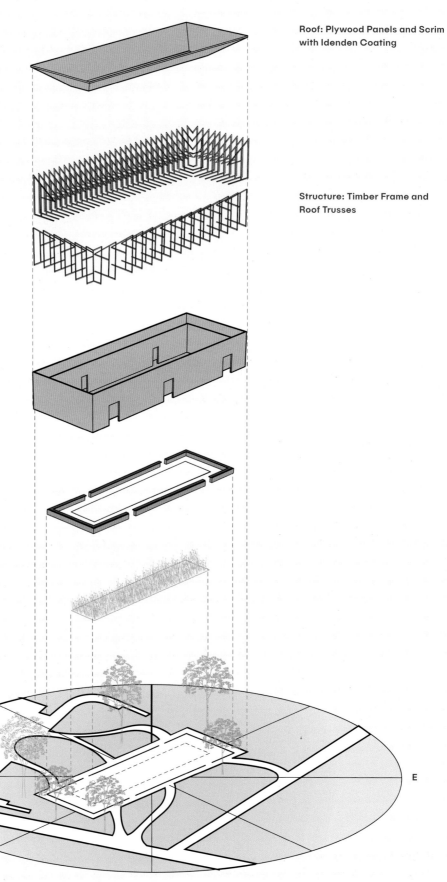

Roof: Plywood Panels and Scrim with Idenden Coating

Structure: Timber Frame and Roof Trusses

Envelope: Plywood Panels and Scrim with Idenden Coating

Seating: Wood Bench

Floor: Black Rubber Floor Mats

Garden: Seasonal Plantings

W

E

S

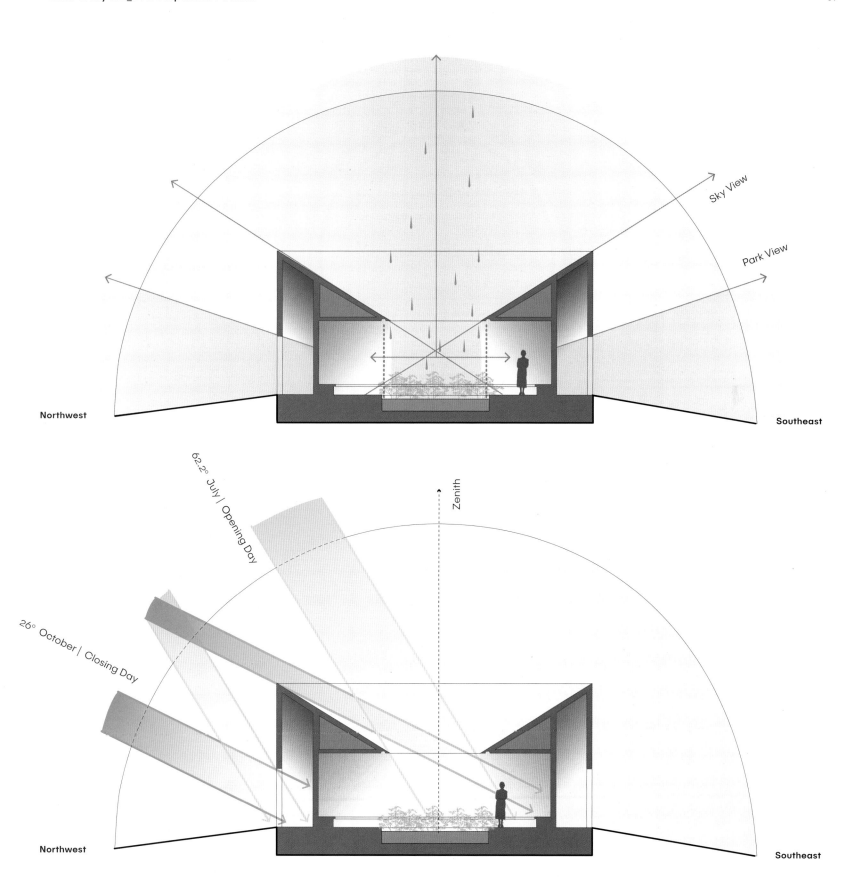

The upper northwest–southeast section illustrates the direct views to Kensington Garden from the circulation corridor and the framed view of the sky from the interior seating area and garden. The lower section illustrates the changing sun angles during the months the pavilion was open in July to the closing in October given the latitude (51.28° north latitude). As sun angles decreased from summer to fall, direct sunlight shifted from the garden to the adjacent seating areas.

Daylight Analysis:
Plans_July Through October_Illuminance

Illuminance studies (in lux) illustrate the procession through the dark circulation corridor into the brightly illuminated garden during the four-month period that the pavilion was open (July to October). Dramatic pools of daylight mark the thresholds into the building entries in contrast to the dark corridor, while toplighting is relatively uniform within the garden and seating area. Light levels decrease as the seasons shift from summer to fall.

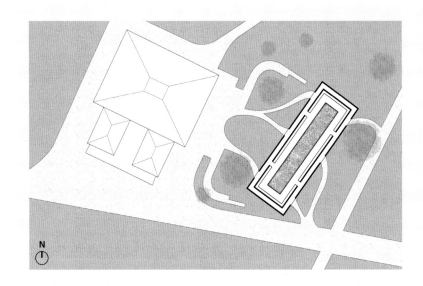

Sunny Skies
Illuminance (Lux)

——————	5,000
——————	4,375
——————	3,750
——————	3,125
——————	2,500
——————	1,876
——————	1,251
——————	626

9:00 am   12:00 pm   3:00 pm

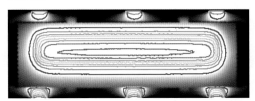 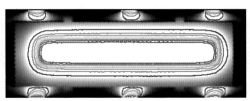 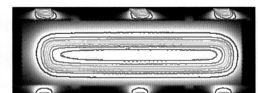

July 21

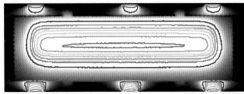 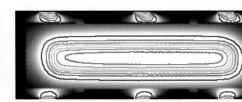

August 21

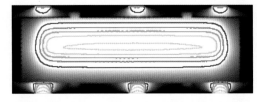 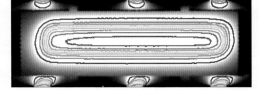 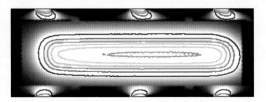

September 21

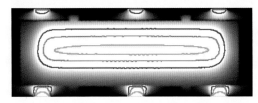 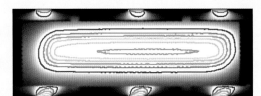 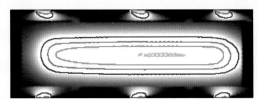

October 21

Daylight Analysis:
Walk-Through_Equinox

Perspective renderings and luminance studies (in candela/square meter; cd/m2) illustrate the visual quality of daylight and contrast ratios from four view locations within the building during the fall equinox (September 21 at noon). There is an increase in light levels and a decrease in contrast moving from the entries through the circulation corridor into the seating areas and garden. The highest contrast ratios occur at the entry thresholds and at the juncture between the sheltering roof of the seating and the roof skylight. Contrast effectively enhances the transition between the outer and the inner gardens.

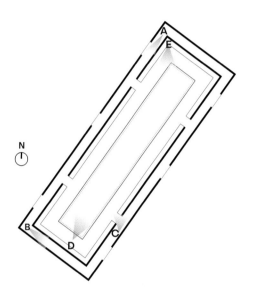

Sunny Skies
Luminance (Cd/m²)

	300
	263
	225
	188
	150
	113
	76
	38

View A: September 21 at 12:00 pm

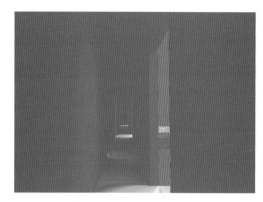

View A: September 21 at 12:00 pm

View B: September 21 at 12:00 pm

View B: September 21 at 12:00 pm

View C: September 21 at 12:00 pm

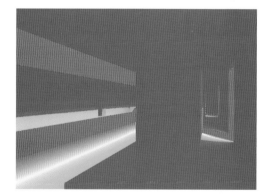

View C: September 21 at 12:00 pm

View D: September 21 at 12:00 pm

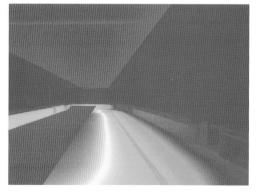

View D: September 21 at 12:00 pm

Daylight Analysis: Plans_July Through October_Illuminance

Time-lapse renderings of the seating area and garden
illustrate the mid-day procession of sunlight during the
months when the pavilion was open in July to October.

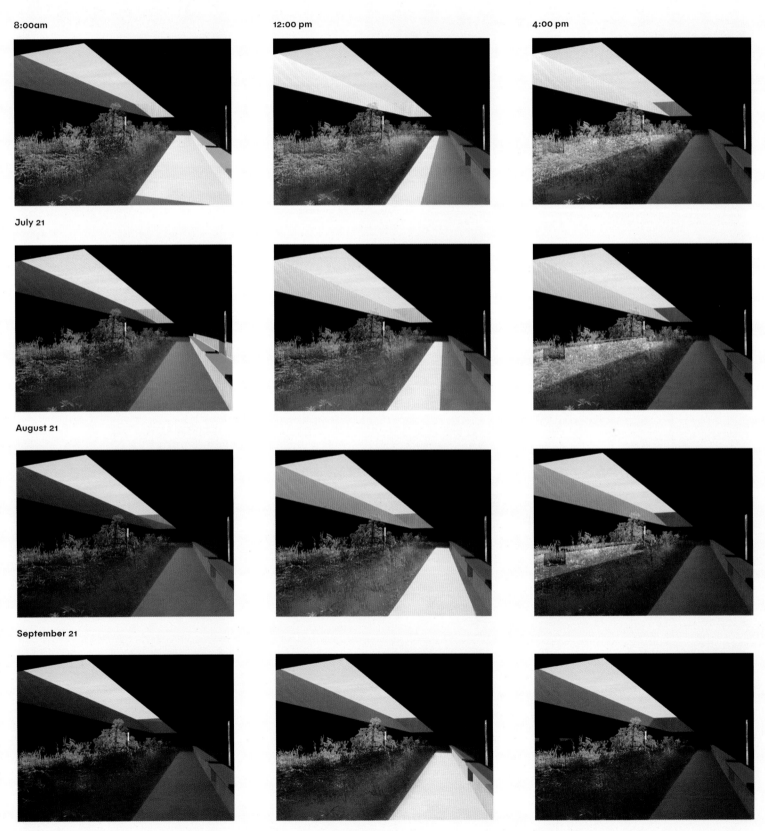

8:00am   12:00 pm   4:00 pm

July 21

August 21

September 21

October 21

Chapter 2: endnotes

Introduction

1 "Atmospheres by Peter Zumthor," Arcspace.com: Danish Architecture Centre, July 19, 2006, http://www.arcspace.com/bookcase/atmosphere-/

2 Peter Zumthor, *Peter Zumthor Atmospheres: Architectural Environments—Surrounding Objects*, Basel: Birkhäuser, 2012, 10–12.

3 Juhani Pallasmaa, *The Eyes of the Skin: Architecture and Polemics*, New York: John Wiley & Sons, 2012, 13.

4 Gernot Böhme, "Encountering Atmospheres: A Reflection on the Concept of Atmosphere in the Work of Juhani Pallasmaa and Peter Zumthor," *OASE*, no. 91 (2013), 100.

5 Juhani Pallasmaa, *The Eyes of Skin: Architecture and Polemics*, 10–11.

6 "Serpentine Gallery Park Nights 2011: Peter Zumthor and Piet Oudolf with Fritz Hauser and Peter Conradin Zumthor," YouTube video, 21:23, posted by "Serpentine Galleries," 2011, https://vimeo.com/92263112.

7 Peter Zumthor, *Peter Zumthor Atmospheres: Architectural Environments—Surrounding Objects*, 22–28.

8 Ibid.

Chapter 2.1

9 Philip Jodidio, *Tadao Ando at Naoshima: Art Architecture Nature*, New York: Rizzoli, 2006, 8.

10 "Climate: Naoshima," Climate-Data.org, http://en.climate-data.org/location/52351/.

11 Jesper Wachtmeister, *Kochuu: Japanese Architecture/Influence & Origin*, (2003; Sweden: Solaris Filmproduktion, 21:47), DVD.

12 "Art Museum Naoshima Project Profile," Tadao Ando Architect & Associates, 1.

13 Werner Blaser, *Tadao Ando: Sunken Courts*, Zürich: Verlag Niggli AG, 2007, 7.

14 "Art Museum Naoshima Project Profile," 1.

15 Werner Blaser, *Tadao Ando: Sunken Courts*, 7–9.

16 Michael Blackwood, *Tadao Ando* (1989; Michael Blackwood Production INC.), YouTube video, 48:20, published on June 28, 2015, https://www.youtube.com/watch?v=61g14g6hF7c.

17 Michael Auping, *Seven Interviews with Tadao Ando*, Fort Worth, Texas: Modern Art Museum of Fort Worth, 2002, http://x-polis.blogspot.com/2010/09/on-light-holl-pallasmaa-zumthor-ando.html.

18 Michael Blackwood, *Tadao Ando*, 44:00.

19 Ibid., 13:58.

20 "Art Museum Naoshima Project Profile," 1.

21 Edan Corkill, "Icon and Iconoclast Tadao Ando's Architectural Vision Goes Way Beyond Buildings: interview with Japan Times," *Japan Times*, December 28, 2008, accessed November 8, 2015, http://www.japantimes.co.jp/life/2008/12/07/style/icon-and-iconoclast/#.VkD_RVWrS1t.

22 Michael Blackwood, *Tadao Ando*, 33:10.

23 "Degree Days: Energy Data for Professionals," Degreedays.net: Weather Underground, http://www.degreedays.net/#generate.

24 Ibid.

Chapter 2.2

25 Peter Zumthor, *Peter Zumthor Atmospheres: Architectural Environments—Surrounding Objects*, Basel: Birkhäuser, 2012, 61.

26 "Serpentine Gallery Park Nights 2011: Peter Zumthor and Piet Oudolf with Fritz Hauser and Peter Conradin Zumthor," YouTube video, 18:14, posted by "Serpentine Galleries," 2011, https://vimeo.com/92263112.

27 Ibid., 20:30.

28 "Average Conditions for London, England," WeatherSpark.com, https://weatherspark.com/averages/28729/London-England-United-Kingdom.

29 "Serpentine Gallery Park Nights 2011," 14:06.

30 Ibid., 10:57.

31 "Peter Zumthor's Serpentine Gallery Pavilion," *The Telegraph*, YouTube video, 1:05, posted by "The Telegraph," June 27, 2011, http://www.telegraph.co.uk/culture/art/architecture/8601393/Peter-Zumthors-Serpentine-Gallery-Pavilion.html.

32 Peter Zumthor, *Peter Zumthor Atmospheres: Architectural Environments—Surrounding Objects*, 10–19.

33 Ed Clark, Engineer, Arup London, telephone interview with author, recorded March 31, 2016.

34 Christine Murray, "AJ editor Christine Murray talks to Peter Zumthor," *Architects' Journal*, June 2, 2011, http://www.architectsjournal.co.uk/news/daily-news/peter-zumthor-my-work-is-not-about-design/8615593.article.

35 "Serpentine Gallery Park Nights 2011," 34:00.

36 Ibid., 21:23.

37 Ed Clark.

38 Amanda Birch, "Serpentine Gallery Pavilion by Peter Zumthor," bdonline.co.uk, June 27, 2011, http://www.bdonline.co.uk/serpentine-gallery-pavilion-by-peter-zumthor/5020460.article.

39 Ed Clark.

40 Ibid.

41 Ibid.

42 Kathern Bullock, "Serpentine Pavilion 2011 by Peter Zumthor," YouTube video, 0:43, posted by "Kathern Bullock," April 20, 2015, http://www.dailymotion.com/video/x2oludh.

43 "Degree Days: Energy Data for Professionals," Degreedays.net: Weather Underground, http://www.degreedays.net/#generate.

44 Ibid.

Chapter 3

Sculpted Light

"Light is not perceptible without form ... to reflect it. Conversely, form is not perceptible without light to reveal it. ... The forms that we see in a building, and the way that we see them, are due to the way in which light is admitted by the form as well as the way in which the form then models the light that has been admitted."[1]

Marietta Millet, Architect and Professor

Early modern architect Louis Sullivan is renowned for his 1896 essay on the "tall office building," in which he penned the famous phrase "form [ever] follows function": "It is the pervading law of all things organic and inorganic, of all things physical and metaphysical, of all things human, and all things super-human, of all true manifestations of the head, of the heart, of the soul, that the life is recognizable in its expression, that form ever follows function. This is the law."[2] Inspired by the Roman architect Marcus Vitruvius Pollio, who wrote in *De Architectura* (*Ten Books on Architecture*) about the architectural qualities of *firmitas*, *utilitas*, *venustas* or "firmness, commodity, and delight," Sullivan inspired architects to explore the richness, value, inherent beauty, and form-giving potential of fundamental elements of architecture such as structure, materials, construction methods, technology, and program.[3] In a similar spirit, Alvar Aalto, the renowned Finnish modern architect, cautioned against the exploration of form independent of context: "Only where form arises at the same time as content or in faithful combination with it, as it were, can we speak of a step forward, but then form as a separate element no longer interests us."[4] Similarly, Louis Kahn, a contemporary of Aalto, characterized the inseparable relationship between form, design, and program: "Form is 'what.' Design is 'how.' Form is impersonal; Design belongs to the designer. Design gives the elements their shape, taking them from their existence in the mind to their tangible presence. Design is a circumstantial act. In architecture, it characterizes a harmony of spaces good for a certain activity."[5]

An ecological variation on this theme can be found early in the development of regenerative design theory, when landscape architect John Tillman Lyle included the concept "Shape Form to Guide Flow," as one of eleven regenerative design strategies. Lyle explained: "This principle could also be stated 'flow follows form follows flow.' Energy and material flows occur within the physical medium of the environment, and the medium largely determines the pace and direction of flow. By shaping the medium (the environment), we can guide the flow."[6]

△ Large skylight monitors with diffusing filters provide
even illumination in the top-floor gallery and control
the abundant sunlight and solar-heat gains. Jumex
Museum, Mexico City, Mexico; David Chipperfield,
David Chipperfield Architects.

△ Passive strategies for seasonal daylighting, natural ventilation, cooling, and heating are integrated with skylight monitors and south-facing glazing. ARPAE Headquarters, Ferrara, Italy; Mario Cucinella Architects.

"Architecture is the learned game, correct and magnificent, of forms assembled in the light."[7]

Le Corbusier, Architect

This principle extends to daylighting design in the ways that form influences the flow of light in its movement, quantity, and quality. The flow of light also shapes form, while the luminous characteristics of natural light inform our perceptions of architectural form and space. The building massing, section, size and placement of windows, detailing of the windows inside and out, and other form-related factors determine how deeply light can penetrate into a space, how light is distributed, and the amount and atmosphere of light.

More recently, Swiss architect Peter Zumthor reflected on the notion that "form follows anything," as Zumthor explained: "In a way I think it's true, form can follow content, it can follow profit, it can follow the truth, it can be used to create presence. ... Architecture is not about form, it is about many other things. ... The light and the use, and the structure, and the shadow, the smell and so on. I think form is the easiest to control, it can be done at the end."[8] Zumthor's variation on Sullivan's famous quote suggests that form can arise out of diverse factors such as place, climate, culture, users, activities, and construction. Although form may not always be the starting point, it is nonetheless of fundamental importance, as Zumthor clarifies: "But if, at the end of the day, the thing does not look beautiful—and I'm deliberately just saying beautiful here ... if the form doesn't move me, then I'll go back to the beginning and start again. So you could say ... my final aim, probably is: The Beautiful Form."[9]

Form and light are inseparable from the activities and purposes of architecture. Whether poetic or pragmatic in nature, an inherent beauty and aesthetic comes from finding the appropriate form for the architectural context and aspirations.

In the following studies of works by David Chipperfield Architects and Mario Cucinella Architects, daylight shapes architectural form, and form shapes the resulting qualities and characteristics of daylight. First is the Museo Jumex in Mexico City, by David Chipperfield Architects (DCA), where the architecture is shaped to address a panoply of issues relevant to creating a public art forum, such as identity, site, climate, program, and luminous goals. David Chipperfield describes the design challenge: "We attempted to create a civic condition. To make a civic building. ... It's a question of, how do you translate those intentions into physical form? ... How do you make a building public?"[10]

Restrictions such as a constrained site, limited solar access, busy roadways, an adjacent railroad, and tall neighboring buildings gave rise to the architectural form. The massing, plan, sections, and envelope are shaped in each orientation to provide a distinct response to site, climate, and programmatic needs. The simple vertical mass, in which all windows are pulled back from the envelope to be shaded and sheltered by exterior terraces, mediates direct sunlight and heat while providing views and connections to the city. Vertical zoning creates two distinct luminous environments. Public spaces on the lower levels are sidelit by the sheltering terraces that open to the city, while the introspective upper level gallery is toplit with diffuse filtered skylights. Architectural solutions, rather than technological responses, gave rise to the building massing, plan, and section.

The next case study is the ARPAE (Regional Agency for Environmental Protection and Energy) Headquarters in Ferrara, Italy, by Mario Cucinella Architects (MCA). Here, the intersection of form and performance was the design priority, as Mario Cucinella explains: "Form and performance is a relationship. Expressing well the idea of architectural form [as] fundamental to the performance of building and [considered] before technology."[11] As a new ecological model for office buildings, all scales of design were considered through the lens of performance, including measurable issues such as illuminance levels, air flow, annual energy consumption, and carbon emissions, along with intangible qualities of health and well-being, beauty, and aesthetics. For Cucinella, the first level of response is to site and climate, with the architecture arising from context. For MCA, testing and assessment are key to the integration of form and performance, with a variety of design methods and qualitative and quantitative metrics employed, ranging from simple daylight models to sophisticated computational analyses and large-scale mock-ups.

David Chipperfield Architects and Mario Cucinella Architects ask designers to consider: How is natural light architectural? How might light shape form? And how might form shape light? Architectural form is found through the meeting of design aspirations, site and programmatic forces, desired qualities, performance goals, and other project-specific design considerations. Just as a sculptor shapes a piece of marble to express a desired intention, so too an architect sculpts the building massing, plan, section, envelope, windows, and interior forms to create a desired luminous environment.

Case study 3.1

Jumex Museum
(Museo Jumex)

Mexico City, Mexico

David Chipperfield, David Chipperfield Architects

"With these types of [museum] spaces I'm very interested in using natural light as much as possible. In this case it was quite a difficult site because it's dwarfed by much taller buildings around it, so we knew that it had to have character, a strong personality – the roof of the Jumex Museum provides light and character." [12]

David Chipperfield, David Chipperfield Architects

◁ △ An aerial view reveals the solar constraints of the small triangular urban site. Adjacent tall commercial buildings necessitated a west orientation for the skylight monitors. Large openings in the façades shelter deeply recessed balconies and terraces to block direct sunlight and solar gains in the lower levels.

LIGHT AND THE QUALITY OF PLACE

Jumex Museum

The Jumex Museum is located within the recently developed New Polanco district of Mexico City. It houses the contemporary art collection of Eugenio López Alonso, founder of the Jumex Foundation and owner of the fruit-juice corporation Jumex Group, which also supports the Jumex Gallery, Jumex Foundation, and a library on the factory grounds in the suburban city of Ecatepec. Designed by David Chipperfield, of David Chipperfield Architects (DCA), the museum's mission is to inspire and support Mexican and international contemporary art and artists, and to explore the role of art in today's world. The new urban location for Jumex Museum enables the Foundation to reach out and engage with a broad public audience.

Mexican Light

Jumex Museum is sited on a triangular wedge of land surrounded by newly constructed office buildings to the east, the aluminum-clad Museo Soumaya by architect Fernando Romero to the west, an active railroad to the north, and a busy street to the south. Given the mildness of the climate, Chipperfield explained that the museum is uniquely open to the site and city: "The question was always: How does a foundation like this present itself to the public? What type of space works best for the art? How does it relate to the city? Then you also have to consider how to do a project in Mexico, how to optimize the light, make it suited to the climate and so on. It's a case of putting all those things together. From the beginning I was very interested in the fact that Mexico City has a climate that allows you to explore the possibilities of opening and closing a building in a much more radical way than you could in northern Europe, for instance." [13]

Mexico City has a subtropical highland climate with temperate weather throughout the year. Located at an elevation of 2,240 meters (7,350 feet), the city is surrounded by mountains in the high plateau of south-central Mexico. Seasonal temperatures vary

The building section and plans reveal
a vertical layering of spaces and light.
Community spaces such as the café and
meeting areas occupy the ground and first
floors, while art galleries are located on
the upper levels.

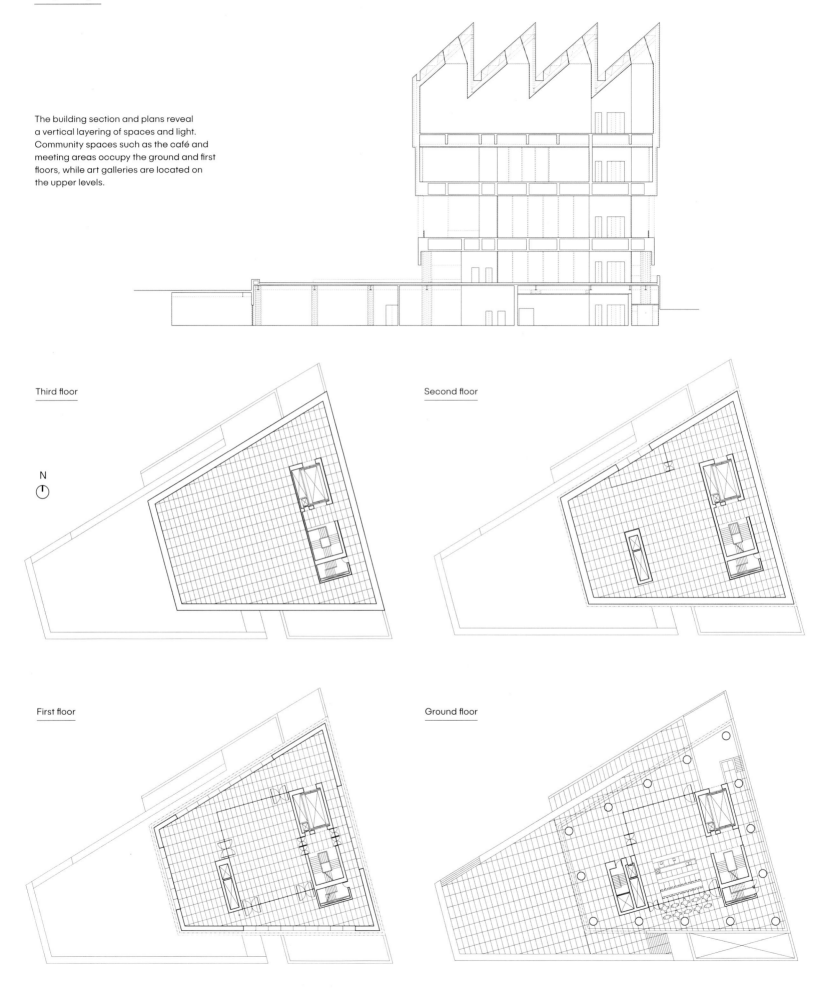

Third floor

N

Second floor

First floor

Ground floor

from an average low in January of 6.1°C (43°F) to an average high in April of 27.2°C (81°F). [14] The rainy season occurs from June to September, while the driest period is during the winter months. There is abundant sunshine throughout the year, even during the rainy season in summer. Located at 19.4° north latitude, the length of day and apparent movement of the sun are relatively consistent throughout the year. The hours of daylight vary from approximately 11 to 12 hours of daylight on the winter and summer solstices. Given the proximity to the equator, the sun appears to move from the south to the north side of the zenith on the summer solstice. High sun angles dominate throughout the year, with the noon solar altitude at 47.1° in December, 70.6° in March/September, and 94.1° in June (when the sun flips to the north side of the building). Seasons are experienced as dry or wet periods of the year.

LIGHT AND THE DESIGN INTENTIONS

Museum Program
The museum program includes spaces for the Jumex Collection, traveling shows, and special exhibitions; areas for public outreach and educational events; and a café, bookstore, and administrative spaces. Chipperfield explained that public engagement was a design priority: "How do you make a balance between the buildings being at the one time protected and internal and at the other time open to the public? ... The idea was to try to expand the boundaries of the building beyond the front door by defining the plaza. ... You arrive at the museum as soon as you've walked up the steps and you're on that platform ... trying to find a way to indicate from outside what is happening inside and vice versa. We are fortunate that the climate is so benign that we can. We could really reduce the barrier between outside and inside." [15]

Climate response and natural light were important programmatic issues, as Peter Jurschitzka, Project Architect at DCA explained: "First, how can you utilize daylight for a museum? We really wanted to make a daylight museum. Secondly, this is Mexico City, a temperate climate with the high elevation, so it doesn't get excessively hot, but it is still a place where you have to provide shade, so you have to protect from the light." [16]

The building is programmatically and luminously separated into two vertically stacked zones, with the outwardly focused public event spaces and café on the two lower levels, and the inwardly focused galleries on the two upper levels.

Sculpted by Site and Light
Peter Jurschitzka emphasized that the strong Mexican sunlight was first and foremost an architectural issue, rather than a technological concern: "To accept the very strong sun in Mexico, we couldn't have direct sun on any windows, so we recessed the windows and then [considered] how to use daylight for the exhibition. It's a question of climate and place, not layers and shading and technology. The firm brought an aesthetic of simplicity, place, culture, and elegance." [17]

The footprint of the museum, which mirrors the form of the site, is pushed to the east boundary, with circulation routes on the north and south, and a generous terrace on the west. Positioned on an elevated plinth and surrounding colonnade, the telescoping mass of the building, large terrace openings, and bold sawtooth profile of the skylight monitors fully optimize daylight despite site constraints. The seemingly solid vertical form of the architecture is punctured by large openings that introduce views and sunlight to the generous terraces and balconies, while recessed glazing and large rooftop monitors capture indirect light from the site and sky.

◁ An outdoor café and exterior exhibition space are located at the ground level to foster connections to the community and public engagement. The sheltering façades create spaces of shadow and relief from the abundant sunlight of Mexico City. Punctured voids in the façades create deep overhangs and exterior rooms to shelter floor-to-ceiling glass walls.

◁ △ The restrained palette of building materials includes travertine, polished white concrete, glass, stainless steel, and wood. Floor-to-ceiling glass walls provide ambient sidelighting while deep balconies shelter the interior from direct sunlight.

LIGHT AND THE DESIGN STRATEGIES

Layered Light

Chipperfield's design fosters a direct relationship between the inside and outside at the ground-level terraces, outside exhibition spaces, and first two floors of the museum. The terrazzo exterior of the building features large openings to admit sidelighting to the balconies and terraces, which is then borrowed indirectly by the glazed interior spaces. Floor-to-ceiling glass walls and pivoting doors are recessed from the outer envelope so that no glazing is exposed to direct sunlight, as Jurschitzka explains: "We wanted to move glazing away from direct light and avoid secondary means of shading on all floors. When you look at the project you will notice it doesn't really have any windows. All the openings are cut into [the] façade, but there is no glass on the surface of [the] façade. As a result of that, all glazing is shaded."[18]

Outdoor terraces are animated by direct sunlight and changing patterns of light and shadow throughout the day, while admitting borrowed indirect sidelighting to the interior. Public spaces, with direct physical and visual connections to the city, transition into quiet, inwardly focused galleries on the top floors. The lower gallery was designed as a flexible space that can be configured as a black box gallery with electric lighting, combined with indirect daylight from a northern terrace when desired. A spacious open-plan gallery is located on the top floor, which culminates the vertical progression. With four large west-facing skylight monitors illuminating the art and space, the gallery was designed for flexibility and to employ daylight as the primary means of illumination.

Given site constraints and limited solar access, west-facing asymmetrical sawtooth monitors on the roof are each sculpted in section to eliminate shading from the adjacent monitor, as Andy

Sedgwick, Director of Lighting at Arup London, explains: "The site in Mexico City generated this geometry where we faced west. And to make matters more complicated, a tall building is immediately to the west, so the third skylight would have received a lot less light because it would be shaded from the afternoon sun. ... What we did in the end was switch the glass from the vertical face of the sawtooth onto the inclined face, and to just have a narrow strip on the top of each of the inclined faces of the sawtooth. That meant they all had the same solar access and get light at the same time. The second breakthrough was to add a second [interior] layer that redistributes the light evenly in the space."[19]

Sedgwick further explained that the design resulted in a slightly more efficient system with less glazing and good levels of daylight uniformity within the gallery. The lowest interior level of the skylight is fitted with fixed louvers to redistribute the light evenly on the gallery walls. Above the louvers is a polycarbonate diffusing layer that scatters daylight (or electric lighting) to the gallery walls and space. Low-iron laminated glass with ultraviolet filters ensures optimal color rendering and conservation of artwork. Daylight and electric lighting are integrated to provide curators and exhibit designers with the ability to stage different lighting conditions based on exhibition needs.

Atmospheric Light

The quiet, elegant atmosphere of the museum results from the refined building form, material quality and detailing, and filtered daylighting. The monumentality and containment of the travertine-clad structure, reminiscent of pre-Columbian architecture, is juxtaposed with open, spacious, light-filled interiors. Simplicity is a poetic and pragmatic response, as Peter Jurschitzka explained: "To achieve a simplicity is also a design quality and a design issue. ... To keep the glass really simple without any issues of overheating and so on. And to avoid the aesthetic issue of dark shaded glass, of blinds,

◁ The second-floor black box gallery is a flexible space with access to a north-facing balcony for daylight and views.

 Vierendeel beams support the skylight monitors and create a large open gallery on the third floor. The deep sections of the monitors help diffuse direct sunlight, while white surfaces, interior louvers, polycarbonate filters, and blackout blinds further filter and redistribute daylight within the gallery.

and complicated mechanisms. To achieve a simplicity is an aesthetic issue."[20] The telescoping building mass, huge terrace openings, and culminating sawtooth monitors not only resolve programmatic and climatic issues, but they also define the quiet, confident character of the architecture.

On the journey from the ground floor to the upper galleries, visitors move through the entry, café, and event spaces that embody an open and welcoming atmosphere connected to the city. The elegantly minimal glass room of the event space draws precedence from the exhibition hall in the National Gallery in Berlin by Mies van der Rohe. While restoring Mies's National Gallery, Chipperfield was inspired to create a similarly flexible space at the Jumex Museum: "In many ways [the National Gallery] is one of the most useless museum space[s]. ... and was highly criticized when it was completed as being a place nearly impossible to hang art ... but what's interesting about the space is that it has become loved over the last fifty years. Its uselessness has become its power. In Mexico I tried to make another 'useless space.' This space [at the Jumex] imitates—in a much smaller way—the hall of Mies's National Gallery."[21]

As visitors move vertically through the museum, the atmosphere transitions from dynamic and active lower levels to inwardly focused and contemplative upper galleries. Warm travertine floors, delicate glass-and-stainless-steel-framed walls, the white concrete structure, and pivoting wood doors lead to a sculptural stair constructed of polished white concrete and wrapped with matte-black steel-clad panels. At the threshold between the

staircase and galleries, a solemn matte-black wall marks the transition into the serene and introspective gallery, filled with filtered sunlight.

LIGHT AND THE ART OF MAKING

Structured and Material Light

A restrained material palette of travertine, white concrete, glass, steel, and wood is brought to life through daylight. No detail is left unresolved, from the asymmetrically pivoting timber doors and refined glass and stainless steel walls to the careful detailing of the handrail. Light and shadow and their changing atmospheric effects accentuate the quiet and elegant spaces and refined detailing for which Chipperfield is renowned. Architectural critic Raymund Ryan praises the craft and design resolution of the museum: "Chipperfield's Jumex never attempts the sculptural or theoretical daring of museum buildings by some of his famous contemporaries. He is drawn to beautiful volumes and elegant details rather than to some universal concept of flexible space."[22]

The structural system is equally well considered, with two systems employed to support distinct programmatic zones. To foster an open connection to the site, the basement and ground-level floors are structurally supported by concrete-wrapped steel columns and the stair cores, while the upper floors are supported by the exterior walls and stair cores. Vierendeel beams are used to create the expansive volume and flexible open plan of the toplit gallery. All of these features create a balance between the artwork in the foreground and the beauty and exquisite craft of the building design and construction.

Daylight Design Process

The design evolved through collaboration between DCA and Arup, with testing and analysis throughout all stages of the process, as Arup's Andy Sedgwick explained: "It's an attitude that the design of the project continues right to the end. It doesn't finish when you send drawings to the contractor. You come back later; in fact it's the process of having it built and watching it built that informs design decisions that still need to be made. You really are designing right through the day the building opens ... and many years afterwards as well."[23]

Peter Jurschitzka explained that DCA intentionally chose a simple approach to solar control, stressing a first preference for architectural solutions to control and mediate daylight, including the building form, section, and skylight design. Interior louvers, polycarbonate diffusing filters, and blackout blinds provide secondary technological means to adjust lighting conditions.

Sedgwick emphasized that rigorous testing and computer analyses were done to optimize the skylights and louver systems during the design phases, but that final material and detail decisions were made on-site during construction: "We were looking for a material that gave adequate diffusion of both the electric lights (in the skylight) and the natural light. ... We wanted to sense the depth of the skylight, so we didn't want a completely diffusing material. That is almost impossible to assess computationally. We found the right materials through trial and error using polycarbonate on-site. We had different panels of louvers made for one bay of the skylight and sequentially went through them. ... Each time we subjectively appraised the light on the wall and also measured it to see how uniform we would get. We [also] were able to choose the most optimal angle for the louvers, and then to have them all fabricated."[24]

LIGHT INSPIRATIONS

A dynamic relationship between inside and outside is fostered through the building form, section, envelope, and program zoning. The Jumex Museum balances the desired openness of the building and welcoming exterior spaces on the lower levels with protective upper-level art galleries. Form thoughtfully responds to the particular forces of place and program. In so doing, Chipperfield has been able to achieve a degree of openness and connection to the site uncommon with most museums, as he explained: "These bottom two floors are all about stimulating and provoking a more dynamic performance from the building ... but I wasn't sure whether this would work and this wasn't in the brief. What's interesting is that this has become the real heart of the building, and it's ensured a dynamic relationship between the city and an otherwise closed treasure box. By creating these two floors we have created a kind of public realm ... adopted by the city."[25] The Jumex Museum uses form, brought to life by daylight, to connect to the site, protect the art, and celebrate the brilliant Mexican sunlight.

DESIGN PROFILE

1. Building Profile
Project: Jumex Museum (Museo Jumex)
Location: Mexico City, Mexico
Architect: David Chipperfield Architects
Client: Jumex Foundation (Fundación Jumex Arte Contemporáneo)
Building Type: Museum
Square Footage: 3,995 sq m (43,000 sq ft)
Estimated Cost: Not available
Completion: 2013

2. Professional Team
Architect: David Chipperfield
Director: Andrew Phillips
Project Architect: Peter Jurschitzka
Project Team: Matt Ball, Jonathan Cohen, Robert Trent Davies, Johannes Feder, Peter Jurschitzka, Christian Felgendreher, Sara Hengsbach, Alessandro Milani, Diana Su
Collaborators: TAAU/Oscar Rodríguez: Cocoy Arenas, Alejandro Castañeda, Rubén Ocampo, Alejandro Rojas, Rafael Sevilla
Structural Engineer: Arup/Alonso y Asociados
Services Engineer: Arup/Iacsa
Electrical Engineer: Asociados A
Façade Consultant: Soluciones en Piedra Franco
Lighting Consultant: Arup
Fire Protection Consultant: BMS i
Building Management System: BMS i
Project Management: Inpros
Quantity Surveyor: Intercost
General Contractor: PC Constructores
Graphics: John Morgan Studio

3. Climate Profile
Climate (Köppen-Geiger Climate Classification System): Cwb: subtropical highland climate
Latitude: 19.4° north latitude
Solar Angles: Noon
June 21: 94.1° (4.1° north of zenith)
March/September 21: 70.6°
December 21: 47.1°
Length of Day: Approximate Hours of Daylight from Sunrise to Sunset
June 21: 13h 18m
March/September 21: 12h 08m
December 21: 10h 57m

Heating Degree Days: 775 heating degree days °C (1533 heating degree days °F) (18°C and 65°F base temperature)[26]
Cooling Degree Days: 533 cooling degree days °C (873 cooling degree days °F) (18°C and 65°F base temperature)[27]

4. Design Strategies
Daylighting Strategies:
1) Sidelighting: floor-to-ceiling glazing shaded by exterior terraces, and 2) Toplighting: west-facing skylight monitors with polycarbonate diffusing layer and interior louvers, and low-iron laminated glass with ultraviolet filters.
Sustainable Design and High-Performance Strategies: High-performance envelope and systems, daylight throughout with supplemental electric lighting in galleries.
Renewable Energy Strategies: None.

Chipperfield: Structure and Materials

The exploded diagram illustrates the structural and material organization of the museum as well as the vertical layering of public meeting spaces and art galleries. The massing, travertine cladding, and minimal openings of the exterior envelope create shaded balconies and outdoor rooms to protect the inner glass façades from direct sunlight and solar gains.

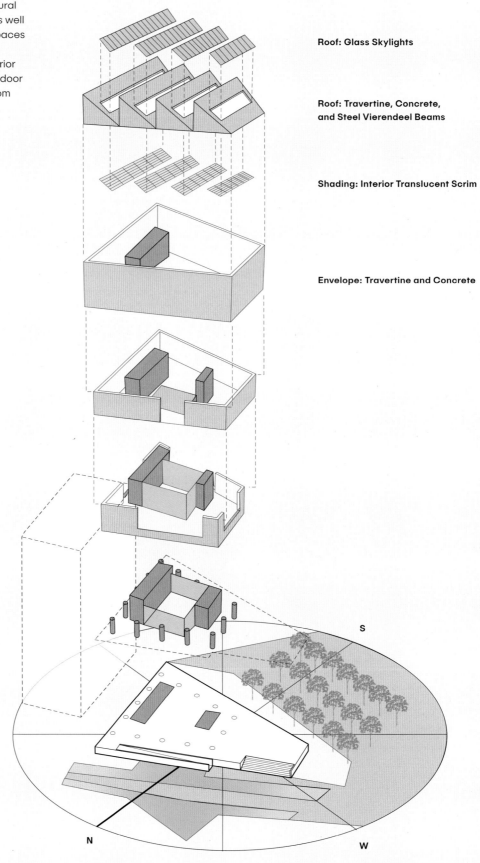

Roof: Glass Skylights

Roof: Travertine, Concrete, and Steel Vierendeel Beams

Shading: Interior Translucent Scrim

Envelope: Travertine and Concrete

Stairs: Black Steel Cladding

Envelope: Travertine, Concrete, and Glass Walls

Structure: Concrete and Steel

S

N

W

The upper southwest–northeast section illustrates the layering of building envelope and the interior views to the site through glazing, balconies, and openings in the exterior façade. The skylights in the top-floor gallery filter direct sunlight while allowing sufficient translucency to view the sky. The lower section illustrates the diffusion of sunlight in the west-facing rooftop monitors as light passes through a translucent polycarbonate layer, louvers, and low-iron laminated glass with ultraviolet filters.

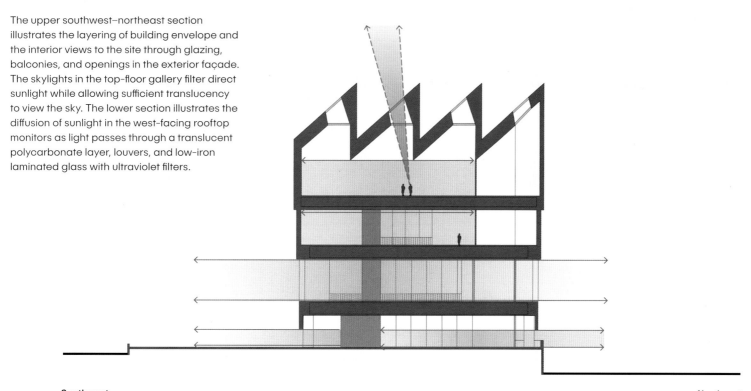

Southwest

Northeast

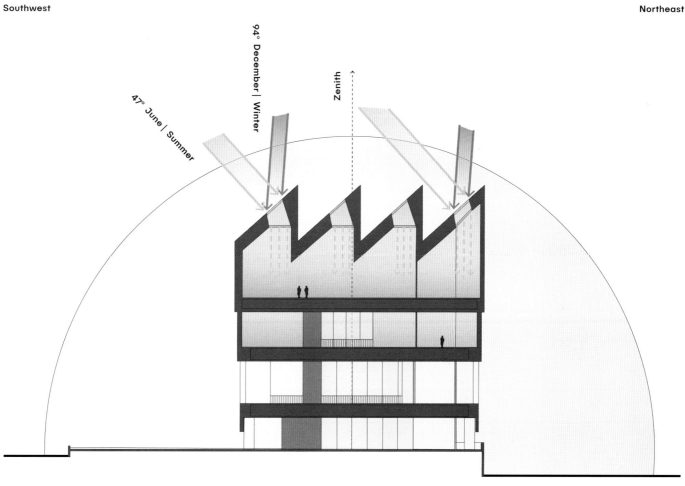

94° December | Winter

Zenith

47° June | Summer

Southwest

Northeast

Arup Daylight Analysis: Section Studies_Four Options

Lighting consultants at Arup worked with architects to develop design concepts, evaluate strategies, and to optimize the skylights and louver systems for the climate and geographic location (19.4° north latitude). Radiance software assesses the sectional effect of the skylight tilt on the light levels and daylight distribution in the top-floor gallery.

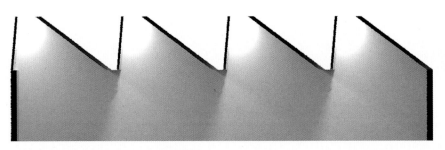

Skylight tilt 0 degrees

Skylight tilt 10 degrees

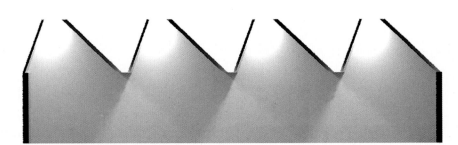

Skylight tilt 20 degrees

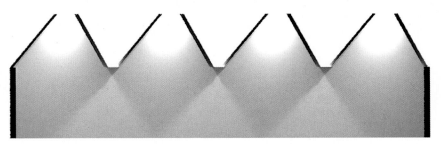

Skylight tilt 40 degrees

Arup Daylight Analysis:
Section Studies_Final Option

In the upper perspective, Arup assessed the quality and distribution of daylight in the west-facing skylight monitors. The lower sections illustrate the effect of louvers on the west glazing and the resulting distribution of the light as a daylight factor. (The DF% is the ratio of daylight inside the structure compared to the daylight outside at the same time and under overcast sky conditions.) Iterative studies assessed a variety of design strategies and details such as the effect of glazing size and orientation, diffusing layers, louvers, and glazing types.

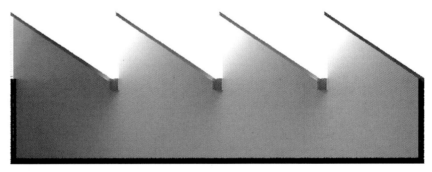

Daylight faotor

Daylight Factor (DF%)

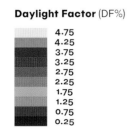

4.75
4.25
3.75
3.25
2.75
2.25
1.75
1.25
0.75
0.25

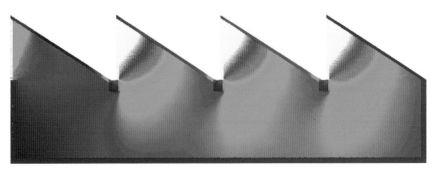

Radiance studies

△ The lower portion of the façade contains floor-to-ceiling glazing, which admits seasonal daylight, natural ventilation, and passive heating. Large rooftop monitors in the upper façade extend beyond the glass façades. Photographed during construction.

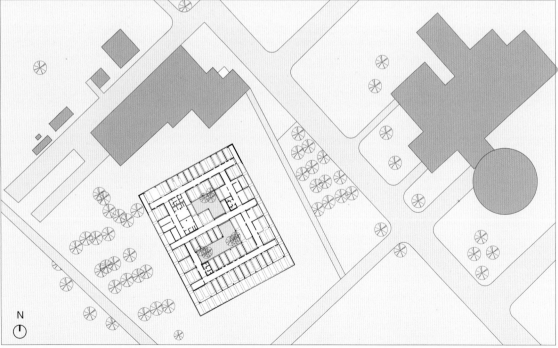

△ A combination of sidelighting, toplighting, and interior courtyards provide daylight, natural ventilation, and views throughout the deep floor plan.

Case study 3.2

ARPAE Headquarters

Ferrara, Italy

Mario Cucinella Architects

"The architecture of form is part of the fundamental performance of the building. ... We look to the future and not the past. We look for ideas of innovation. For thousands of years, architects found this [innovation] with nature, with empathy for the environment. The climatic issue was fundamental. At ARPAE, we try to bridge that. We are working with nature first and then technology." [28]

Mario Cucinella, Mario Cucinella Architects

△ Detail of a rooftop monitor, used to integrate daylighting, natural ventilation, passive cooling, and solar control.

LIGHT AND THE QUALITY OF PLACE

Ferrara and the Po River Delta

Located in the Emilia-Romagna region of northeastern Italy, the new headquarters for the Regional Agency for Environmental Protection and Energy (ARPAE) is a model of ecological innovation. Designed by Mario Cucinella, of Mario Cucinella Architects (MCA), the office building demonstrates the ways in which architectural form can integrate with climate-responsive passive strategies, innovative systems, and new construction methods to create beautiful architecture while meeting the highest standards of performance. Sited west of the Renaissance city of Ferrara in the Po River Delta, the headquarters are just 50 kilometers (31 miles) east of the Adriatic Sea. Flowing eastward from the Alps, the river delta is renowned for its scenic beauty and fertile agricultural lands. Ferrara was a cultural center of the Italian Renaissance and designated a UNESCO World Heritage Site in 1995 for the historic integrity of the architecture and cultural landscape of the river delta. Given its rich biodiversity and wetlands, the Po Delta Regional Park was added to Ferrara's UNESCO designation in 1999. The region remains a significant ecological district and cultural center for planning, architecture, music, and the arts.

Bioclimate and Italian Light

Located on the outskirts of Ferrara, the open suburban site affords excellent access to sunlight, wind, and views. As a humid temperate climate, precipitation and high humidity are common, with relative humidity averaging 60 to 70 percent in the summer months, and 80 to 90 percent in the winter. Precipitation varies throughout the year, with light to moderate rainfall greatest in May and least likely in October. The location experiences only occasional winter snow. The average precipitation ranges from a minimum of 11.6 millimeters (0.45 inches) in March to a maximum of 39 millimeters (1.58 inches) in October.[29] Temperatures are cool in the winter and hot in the summer, with an average low of 2.5°C (36.5°F) in January and an average high of 31°C (87.8°F) in July. [30]

△ View of an interior courtyard that provides daylight, natural ventilation, and views to the garden. Floor-to-ceiling glazing complements the toplighting and stack ventilation from the skylights. Direct sunlight and heat gain can be mediated by interior shades.

Skies are clearest during the summer months and most overcast in the winter. [31] Wind direction is variable throughout the year.

Cucinella describes the soft atmospheric quality of daylight in this region of Italy: "Ferrara is not far from seaside. It's on the plain in a flat area. Here light is diffuse. It's an ethereal light. ... Ferrara [light] is very smooth and soft. It's not aggressive. It's not sharp. You see the different intensities and feelings, how the environment around you makes a difference in the reflection of light." [32]

Located at 44.5° north latitude, mid-way between the Equator and the North Pole, the seasonal position of the sun changes dramatically, with sunrise and sunset moving from the southeast to southwest in winter, to the northeast to northwest in summer. The solar altitude at noon varies from 22° to 69° at the winter and summer solstices. Sky conditions are predominantly overcast in the winter months, and clear in the summer and early fall.

LIGHT AND THE DESIGN INTENTIONS

Sustainable Office Program

Designed to meet the expanding office and laboratory needs of ARPAE, an environmental protection agency, the program brief emphasized sustainable design, technological innovation, ecological performance, and health and well-being. Cucinella designed the headquarters as a model ecological office building to celebrate dynamic luminous and thermal conditions, and challenged the status quo uniform approach to comfort: "ARPAE is about change. ... [In the past,] the future of technology and innovation was a closed building with air conditioning and always the same temperature and the same light. In another office building we surveyed 160 people with a questionnaire. The results were impressive. They cared most about daylighting and the natural variation of [light] intensity. Artificial light has no variation. Daylight is part of the psychology, an emotional part of the story; a bright light and a cloud, it can change completely in intensity." [33] Rather than viewing changing light and thermal conditions as problems, Cucinella designed an office building that fosters varied conditions to improve occupant satisfaction and performance.

◁△ Construction photographs reveal the logic of the nested façade systems. The upper façade and roof act as a "solar visor," protecting the lower recessed glazing while admitting abundant indirect daylight.

Cucinella describes "form and performance" as an interrelationship that is the driving design concept at ARPAE: "Architectural form creates natural performance. ... Combining the idea of daylight and natural ventilation gives extraordinary performance. The only way to improve comfort in summer is with cooling to increase air change and to move air and transport humidity." [34] The summer goal was to mediate the high relative humidity and temperatures with natural ventilation and to provide daylighting without solar gains. The winter goal was to harvest solar gains for passive heating, while providing luminous and thermal control in office and laboratory spaces.

Creative Empathy

To respond to today's ecological challenges, Cucinella argues that architects need a more empathetic understanding of the site and other living things, as he explains: "To be empathic is to have a relationship with someone else or a site ... I call it 'creative empathy.' Showing empathy is an attitude. Using your mind and body to try to understand what is outside [of you]. Empathy is the capacity to listen, to create a relation. The first idea of the climate condition is to make an interpretation of the shape and angles of

the building. I try to find in this information clarity ... to influence and make the building from empathy with the site." [35]

While always looking toward the future, Cucinella also seeks inspiration from bioclimatic design innovations that have been honed over thousands of years in vernacular architecture, which are often inherently empathic to place, culture, and nature. ARPAE provides a fresh interpretation of the traditional wind chimney by coupling light and air to improve performance and enhance awareness of seasonal change.

LIGHT AND THE DESIGN STRATEGIES

Light and Air

Sited south of the existing office building, the rectilinear mass of the new headquarters is oriented to the southeast. A new garden entry creates a transparent connection between the old and new buildings to house the lobby and reception area. The single-story plan comprises a series of offices and labs organized around two L-shaped and interconnected garden courtyards at the heart of the building. In contrast to an open-plan office, Cucinella organized the building as a series of autonomous rooms linked by circulation routes and gardens. Each office and laboratory space has visual connections to either the outside landscape or the interior gardens, and contains one or more roof monitors, or "chimneys," to provide stack ventilation and daylighting. A seemingly "thick" building plan is transformed by the courtyards into a series of thinner spaces with both toplighting and sidelighting in each space. Borrowed light, views, and air are provided through interior and exterior operable glazing.

The building envelope uses two nested-façade systems, with recessed glazing at the ground level and an overhanging wood-clad envelope on the upper portion of the façades and roof monitors. The upper façade acts as a "solar visor" to shade the recessed glass during the warm seasons and to create a sheltered circulation space on the exterior of the building. Less shading is provided on the south to capture low winter sunlight for passive heating and daylight. Roof monitors extend beyond the glass envelope to admit light and air to the exterior circulation paths.

Cucinella calls the roof "a climatic moderator," and explains the essential ecological role of the chimney monitors: "The roof of the building, the so-called fifth façade, is the strongest design feature of the project. A series of chimneys give to the building a strong architectural identity while satisfying the technological requirements of the brief. The chimneys are skylights that filter natural light, promote natural ventilation and reduce the need for mechanical cooling."[36] The undulating rooftop monitors vary in height to avoid shading adjacent monitors and to respond to the east-to-west solar movement.

Sculpted Light

The shape of the plan, massing, and section are integral to the thermal and luminous comfort and energy performance of the building, as Cucinella clarifies: "Shape is part of performance; that's why I like ARPAE. We are really building a bridge with our past when buildings dealt with nature with no energy. That was the job in the past and now."[37] During the summer months, the combined wind chimney and daylight monitor, sidelighting, and self-shading building form are architectural strategies to reduce cooling loads. Winter strategies include direct solar gains, daylighting to reduce electric lighting loads, and high-performance envelope and glazing systems. A geothermal heat pump is connected to a radiant distribution and heat-recovery system to optimize thermal comfort throughout the year.

Additional water savings are realized through a rainwater system that collects runoff from the roof to reuse for heating, irrigation, and graywater. Renewable energy systems include solar hot water heating and a 201 sq m (2,164 sq ft) photovoltaic system. MCA estimates that bioclimatic, passive design, and renewable energy strategies, along with high-performance systems, reduce summer and winter energy consumption by 30 percent and 40 percent respectively when compared to a similar-sized conventional building.[38] The estimated energy profile for winter is 35kWh/sq m (11.1kBtu/sq ft), while summer is 50kWh/sq m (15.9kBtu/sq ft).[39] High-performance mechanical systems are estimated to provide a carbon reduction of 85 percent at 3kg CO_2/year (compared to a standard building).[40]

▽ View of the south glass façade shaded by the overhanging roof monitors. Direct sunlight is blocked during the summer months while direct sunlight and heat are admitted in winter.

◁ Interior courtyards effectively reduce the apparent depth of the floor plan to provide daylighting from the heart of the building massing. Perimeter sidelighting and toplight monitors ensure that all spaces have daylight, natural ventilation, and views to the surrounding landscape or interior gardens. Photographed during construction.

Summer

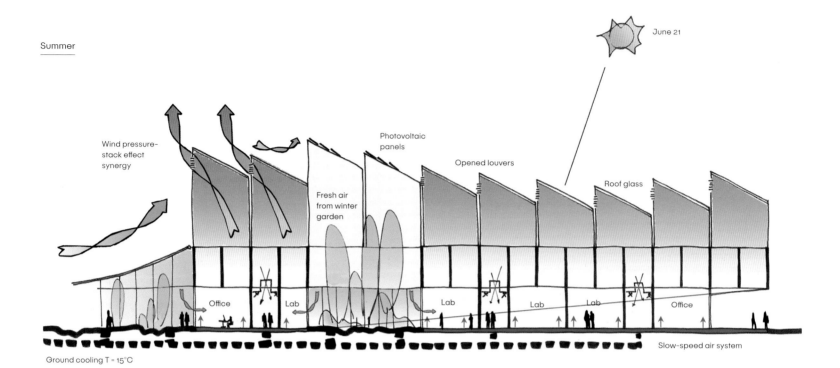

Wind pressure-stack effect synergy

Photovoltaic panels

Opened louvers

Roof glass

June 21

Fresh air from winter garden

Office

Lab

Lab

Lab

Lab

Office

Ground cooling T = 15°C

Slow-speed air system

Winter

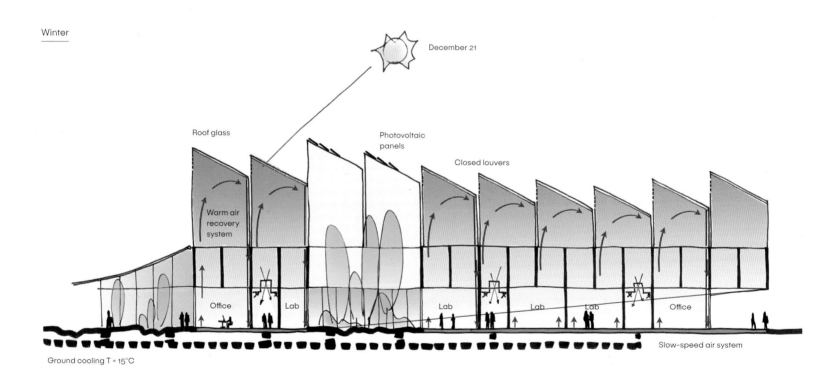

Roof glass

December 21

Photovoltaic panels

Closed louvers

Warm air recovery system

Office

Lab

Lab

Lab

Lab

Office

Ground cooling T = 15°C

Slow-speed air system

△ Seasonal sections illustrate the integration of the building form and section with energy performance, visual and thermal comfort, and building systems for lighting, heating, ventilation, and cooling.
A geothermal heat pump with a radiant distribution and heat recovery system optimizes heating and cooling on a seasonal basis.

LIGHT AND THE ART OF MAKING

Atmosphere and Beauty

ARPAE reconsiders the role of beauty, aesthetics, health, and well-being in office design, as Cucinella explains: "In the last 20 years architects have tried to make office space more efficient. They are so efficient that people are unhappy. If you look at the history of architecture, it was about quality. People are at work eight to ten hours [per day]. We need to take into account that they pass more time in the office than at home. We need to improve the office quality." [41]

Daylight, natural ventilation, and passive strategies invite occupants to experience the changing moods of the day and seasons. Interior and exterior views provide visual relief

△ A detail of the roof under construction shows the distribution of monitors, location of interior courtyards, and construction logic. The timber-frame structure is clad in plywood with an exterior wood rainscreen.

and connections to the landscape, while operable windows and adjustable shading enable occupants to individually tune their environment. The exposed wood structure and the healthy materials, finishes, and furnishings create a friendly and relaxed atmosphere that invites occupants to touch and interact with the envelope, space, and gardens.

Human experience and emotional response to architecture have been design priorities throughout history, as Cucinella explains: "I think of the Gothic architects; we see how much these people made an effort to make the wall so thin, to make colored glass to bring light

inside, to create this emotion. ... ARPAE's new idea of beauty and sustainable design is not an illusion. It's something very real. A connection, a relation to daylight and ventilation and shape. My concept of beauty is something invisible; but there is a part that is visible, that is aesthetic, like the character of a person." [42]

Iterative Design Methods
MCA employ a variety of design methods and tools to support the decision-making process, including diagramming, rendering, physical models, daylight models, and sophisticated analysis tools. The design process and performance testing were interrelated, and set the early trajectory of the project, as Cucinella explains: "In the office we have two people dedicated to this issue of daylight, ventilation, and simulations. They are architects, not engineers. This is very important. When we start the process they present climate condition and the [design] opportunity from climate." [43]

Additional analog and digital tools were used to evaluate bioclimatic issues such as solar access, illuminance levels, glare, natural ventilation, carbon emissions, and energy consumption. Cucinella stresses the importance of physical models to gain

△ Interior construction photograph reveals the construction logic, which includes timber framing, plywood cladding of monitors, steel cross bracing, and expansive floor-to-ceiling glazing on the perimeter of all façades

a tangible experience of natural light in the space: "We always start working with real models to understand and learn by experiencing the quality of light. You can learn so much from a box with a hole. You can see and transform the quality of light inside by changing color, changing surface, changing reflection. You can see the light and 3-D architectural elements. Always make physical models, especially daylight models." [44]

Performance testing is particularly essential in the concept and schematic design phases. Early in-house testing provides essential insights into the architectural form and response to bioclimatic forces, while supporting an informed discussion with engineers and other consultants who can help refine and assess the performance in later design phases. Cucinella encourages architects to reclaim more authority over the early integration of design and performance: "Every step is a learning process to arrive at an architectural

▷ (Right and below right) Abundant daylight from the roof monitors and perimeter sidelighting provide illumination throughout the interior. All spaces have visual access to the site or interior gardens. Light-reflecting surfaces and floors help redistribute daylighting throughout. Photographed during construction.

▽ Roof monitors vary in height to optimize solar access from the south to the north and east to west.

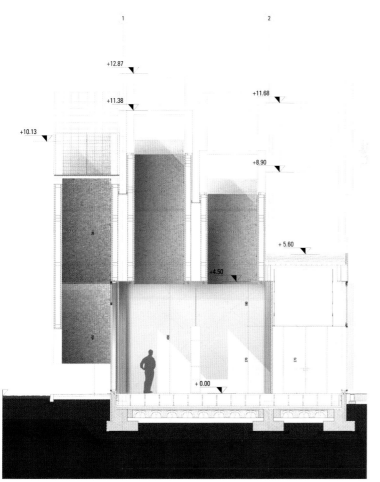

◁▷ Physical daylight models evaluated the quality of light in relation to the building massing and section, height and scale of roof monitors, and size and placement of interior courtyards. Quantitative analyses and computer simulations evaluated the integration of daylight, thermal, and energy performance.

solution. ... [Early analysis is] very preliminary, but immediately there is some feeling of what we're doing, of performance and shape and how shape is working. It's time to come back to the idea that an architect also has engineering competence. I don't want to be an engineer; this is not my work, but I need to know something. Maybe I'm not about to make a precise calculation, but I can simulate something at a preliminary stage ... [to] really work with daylighting and suggest to the engineer how we can integrate natural and artificial light." [45]

LIGHT INSPIRATIONS

Architectural form, performance, and aesthetic experience are at the heart of sustainable design. Architecture is not a static object, but rather a dynamic relationship with site, climate, and users. Cucinella uses architectural form, rooftop chimneys, courtyards, and a layered envelope to celebrate seasonal changes in luminous and thermal conditions, and to invite interactions between the users, architecture, and nature. The ARPAE headquarters elevate the promise of the ecological office, inspire a new definition of sustainable design excellence, and raise the bar for all building types, as Cucinella suggests: "Each building has the potential to redesign the surrounding natural, cultural, and socio-economic systems. Buildings can recreate an intimate relationship—a 'creative empathy'—to link places and their inhabitants ... that are enriching and enabling environments for life and work." [46]

DESIGN PROFILE

1. Building Profile
Project: ARPAE Headquarters: Regional Agency for Environmental Protection and Energy (Agenzia Regionale per la Prevenzione, Ambiente Energia)
Location: Ferrara, Italy
Client: ARPAE Ferrara
Building Type: Office
Square Footage: 5,000 sq m (53,820 sq ft)
Estimated Cost: €4m
Completion: 2016

2. Professional Team
Architect: Mario Cucinella
Project Team: Mario Cucinella, Michele Olivieri (architect in charge), Francesco Barone, Caterina Maciocco, Antonella Maggiore, Giulio Pisciotti, Luca Stramigioli, Debora Venturi, Yuri Costantini (modelmaker)
Structural Engineering: Tecnopolis SpA.
Wood Structures: SWS Engineering
Bioclimatic Study: Manens Tifs SpA. (Roberto Zecchin, Adileno Boeche, Andrea Fornasiero)
Electrical Engineering: Tecnopolis SpA
Construction Business: Montelaghi SpA
Suppliers: Novello Ambiente SpA. (wood); Base SpA. (fixtures)
3D Rendering: Engram Studio
Photography: Moreno Maggi

3. Climate Profile
Climate (Köppen-Geiger Climate Classification System): Cfa: humid temperate climate
Latitude: 44.5° north latitude
Solar Angles: Noon
June 21: 69°
March/September 21: 45.5°
December 21: 22°
Length of Day: Approximate Hours of Daylight from Sunrise to Sunset
June 21: 15h 33m
March/September 21: 12h 10m
December 21: 8h 49m

Heating Degree Days: 2033 heating degree days °C (3794 heating degree days °F) (18°C and 65°F base temperature) [47]
Cooling Degree Days: 1093 cooling degree days °C (1885 cooling degree days °F) (18°C and 65°F base temperature) [48]

4. Design Strategies
Daylighting Strategies: 1) Sidelighting: direct site views and sidelighting in all orientations and borrowed interior daylight throughout, and 2) Toplighting: integrated daylight and natural ventilation roof monitors in all spaces.
Sustainable Design and High-Performance Strategies: Daylight and natural ventilation throughout; solar control and shading; high-performance envelope, glazing, electric lighting, and mechanical systems; rainwater system that collects runoff from the roof to reuse for heating, irrigation, and graywater.
Renewable Energy Strategies: 201 sq m (2,164 sq ft) photovoltaic system mounted to the roof surrounding the courtyards.
Energy: Estimated energy profile for winter is 35KWh/sq m (11.1kBtu/sq ft) and for summer is 50kWh/sq m (15.9kBtu/sq ft).
Carbon: Carbon reduction for the mechanical systems is estimated at a reduction of 85 percent from a standard building at 3kg CO_2/y.

Cucinella: Structure and Materials

The exploded diagram illustrates the structural and spatial organization of the building. The wood and steel structure is clad with floor-to-ceiling glazing on the lower portion that is shaded by the wood-clad upper façade composed of skylight monitors. Sidelighting from the exterior of the building and the courtyards provide bilateral daylight, while the roof monitors provide toplighting and natural ventilation throughout.

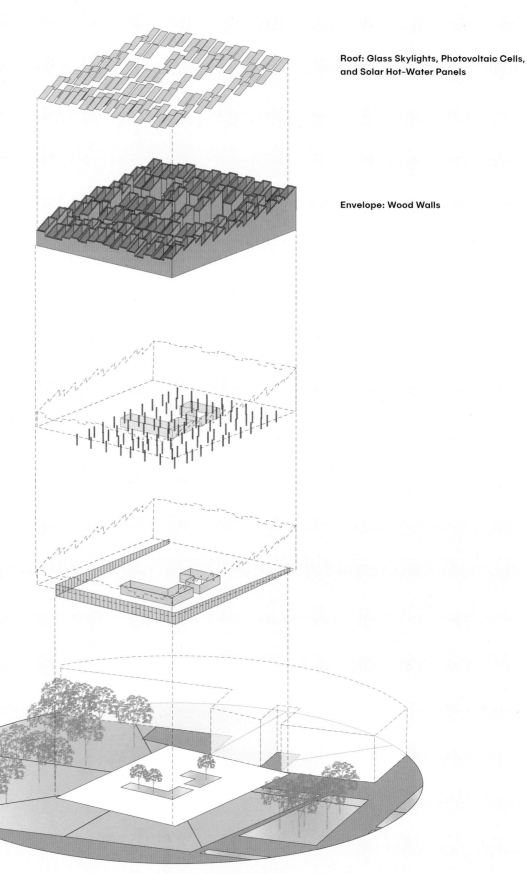

Roof: Glass Skylights, Photovoltaic Cells, and Solar Hot-Water Panels

Envelope: Wood Walls

Envelope: Wood Columns and Steel Cross Bracing

Envelope: Glass Walls

S

E

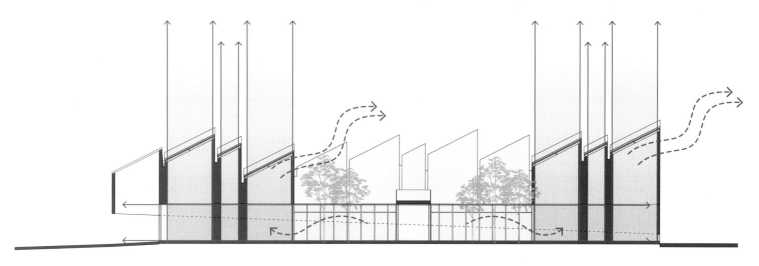

Southeast

Northwest

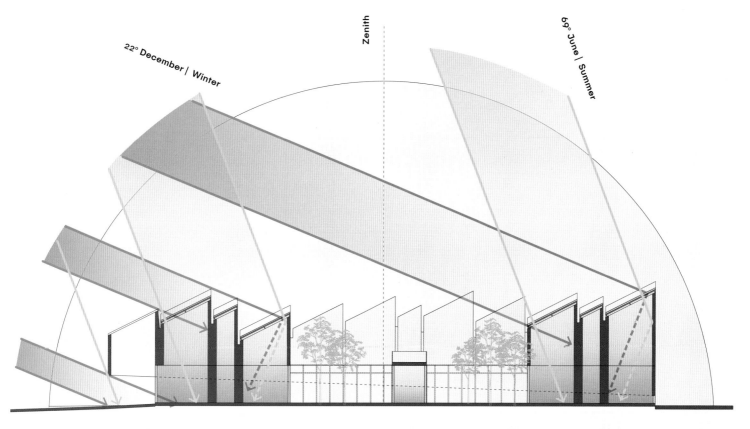

22° December / Winter

Zenith

69° June / Summer

Southeast

Northwest

The upper southeast–northwest section illustrates the integration of daylight and natural ventilation in the roof monitors. Warm air vents through louvers in the vertical façades of the roof monitors, while natural light enters skylights and reflects from walls of the light well. The lower section illustrates the seasonal and diurnal sun angles given the geographic location (44.5° north latitude) and varying length of day (15h 33m on June 21 and 8h 49m on December 21). Roof overhangs, shading, and high-performance glazing are used to seasonally control solar gains and visual and thermal comfort.

Cucinella Daylight Analysis: Solar Access and Ventilation

Daylighting and bioclimatic studies were conducted in-house and with consultants from Manens Tifs SpA. Example studies include a solar site analysis to evaluate the form and distribution of roof monitors. The effectiveness of natural ventilation was analyzed using Fluent 5.5 computation fluid dynamic software to assess the sectional contours of temperature in kelvin (k) and thermal comfort. Quantitative daylighting analyses were developed using Radiance software to evaluate the daylight factor (DF%) and illuminance levels (in lux) to meet program and energy goals.

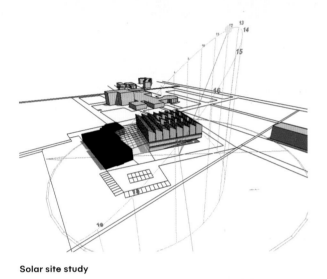

Solar site study

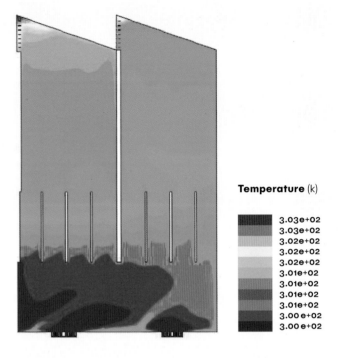

Temperature (k)

3.03e+02
3.03e+02
3.02e+02
3.02e+02
3.02e+02
3.01e+02
3.01e+02
3.01e+02
3.01e+02
3.00e+02
3.00e+02

Contours of temperature

Cucinella Daylight Analysis: Daylight Factor and Illuminance

Daylight factor

Radiance study

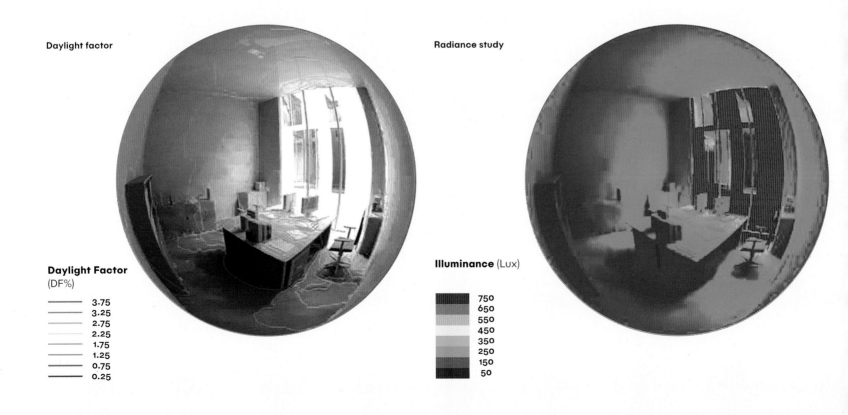

Daylight Factor
(DF%)

3.75
3.25
2.75
2.25
1.75
1.25
0.75
0.25

Illuminance (Lux)

750
650
550
450
350
250
150
50

Chapter 3: endnotes

Introduction

1 Marietta S. Millet, *Light Revealing Architecture*, New York: Van Nostrand Reinhold, 1996, 47–48.

2 Louis Sullivan, "The Tall Office Building Artistically Considered," *Lippincott's Monthly Magazine*, March 1896, 403–409.

3 Louis Sullivan, *Autobiography of an Idea*, New York: American Institute of Architects, 1924, 108.

4 Aarno Ruusuvuori, Göran Schildt, and J.M. Richards, *Alvar Aalto: 1898–1976*, Helsinki: The Museum of Finnish Architecture, 1978, 155.

5 John Lobell, *Between Silence and Light: Spirit in the Architecture of Louis I. Kahn*, Boston: Shambhala, 1985, 28.

6 John Tillman Lyle, *Regenerative Design for Sustainable Development*, New York: John Wiley & Sons, 1994, 43.

7 Le Corbusier, "Design Quotes," *Life of an Architect*, http://www.lifeofanarchitect.com/design-quotes/.

8 "Royal Gold Metal Lecture 2013 – Peter Zumthor," Royal Institute of British Architects, YouTube video, posted by "Royal Institute of British Architects," February 2013, 22:00, https://vimeo.com/60017470.

9 Peter Zumthor, *Atmospheres: Architectural Environments— Surrounding Objects*, Basel: Birkhäuser, 2012, 71–73.

10 "Nobel Center, David Chipperfield," Stockholm Association of Architects, YouTube video, posted by the Stockholm Association of Architects, April 4, 2014, 2:33, https://www.youtube.com/watch?v=ceSKkeLD7Dg.

11 Mario Cucinella, Mario Cucinella Architects, telephone interview with author, recorded December 9, 2015.

Chapter 3.1

12 "Museo Jumex Complete – David Chipperfield Interview," *Designboom*, November 18, 2013, http://www.designboom.com/art/museo-jumex-complete-david-chipperfield-interview-11-18-2013/.

13 Ibid.

14 "Average Weather for Mexico City," WeatherSpark.org, https://weatherspark.com/averages/32574/Mexico-City-Distrito-Federal.

15 "Nobel Center, David Chipperfield," Stockholm Association of Architects, YouTube video, posted by the Stockholm Association of Architects, April 4, 2014, 1:02, https://www.youtube.com/watch?v=ceSKkeLD7Dg.

16 Peter Jurschitzka, Project Architect, David Chipperfield Architects, telephone interview with author, recorded September 25, 2015.

17 Ibid.

18 Ibid.

19 Andy Sedgwick, Director of Lighting, Arup, telephone interview with author, recorded September 25, 2015.

20 Peter Jurschitzka.

21 "Nobel Center, David Chipperfield," Stockholm Association of Architects, 6:53.

22 Raymund Ryan, "Museo Jumex in Mexico City by David Chipperfield Architects," *The Architectural Review*, February 11, 2014, http://www.architectural-review.com/today/museo-jumex-in-mexico-city-by-david-chipperfield-architects/8658048.fullarticle.

23 Andy Sedgwick.

24 Ibid.

25 "Nobel Center, David Chipperfield," Stockholm Association of Architects, 0:50.

26 "Degree Days: Energy Data for Professionals," Degreedays.net: Weather Underground, http://www.degreedays.net/#generate.

27 Ibid.

Chapter 3.2

28 Mario Cucinella, Mario Cucinella Architects, telephone interview with author, recorded December 9, 2015.

29 "Ferrara Monthly Climate Average, Italy," World Weather Online, http://us.worldweatheronline.com/ferrara-weather-averages/emilia-romagna/it.aspx.

30 Ibid.

31 "Average Weather for Ferrara, Italy," WeatherSpark.com, https://weatherspark.com/averages/32276/Ferrara-Emilia-Romagna-Italy.

32 Mario Cucinella.

33 Ibid.

34 Ibid.

35 Ibid.

36 "ARPAE Project Profile," Mario Cucinella Architects, 2015, 1.

37 Mario Cucinella.

38 "ARPAE Project Profile," 1.

39 Ibid.

40 Ibid.

41 Mario Cucinella.

42 Ibid.

43 Ibid.

44 Ibid.

45 Ibid.

46 Mario Cucinella, "Beyond Zero Housing," University of Nottingham, SlideShare, PowerPoint Presentation, posted by Creative Energy Homes, October 24, 2012, http://www.slideshare.net/CreativeEnergyHomes/bzch-mario-cucinella.

47 "Degree Days: Energy Data for Professionals," Degreedays.net: Weather Underground, http://www.degreedays.net/#generate.

48 Ibid.

Chapter 4

Structured Light

"Anytime you write a poem, you need to find the balance between your thoughts and your language. Nothing should disturb the essence of the idea. It is the same with architecture. Whoever cannot put his poetic ideas into a built structure has no architecture basics. Structure is the core of architecture, and it cannot be expressed in numbers. It is the original part of the story an architect can tell about life and people." [1]

Sverre Fehn, Architect

Louis Kahn, the master of daylight in American modern architecture, proclaimed that "structure is the giver of light," and that to select structure is to select the quality of natural light. [2] The column and beam, the dome, and the vault each define a particular character and rhythm of light. Following on the modernist ethic of an honest expression of structure and materials, Kahn concludes that the choice of material is also a choice of structure, as he explains in his famous conversation with a brick: "You realize that something has a certain nature ... you consider the nature of brick. You say to brick, 'What do you want, brick?' Brick says to you, 'I like an arch.' If you say to a brick, 'Arches are expensive, and I can use a concrete lintel over an opening. What do you think of that, brick?' Brick says, 'I like an arch.'" [3] From this perspective, the choice of materials is a choice of both structure and quality of light. The form, size, depth, detailing, and character of the window and resulting daylight is, in part, determined by the choice of structure and materials.

In *Light Revealing Architecture*, Marietta Millet discusses two different concepts regarding the relationships between structure and light: "The structure defines the place where light enters. ... Where the structure is, there is no light. Between the structural elements, there is light. It seems unlikely that light could conceal structure, since light reveals what is there, and structure is always present in a building. However, sometimes structure is hidden purposefully or thoughtlessly. Sometimes the pattern and rhythm of the light contradicts the pattern and rhythm of the structure. ... Structure orders and releases light eloquently only when it has been designed to do so." [4]

A structure that carries the load to the perimeter of the building suggests window and enclosure characteristics that are consistent with the construction system and materials. In contrast, if loads are carried internally, then the building envelope has great flexibility and freedom in the choice of window form, size, and placement. The resulting pattern and quality of light may or may not reinforce the structural expression.

In the past, the necessity for load-bearing structural systems such as brick, stone, rammed earth, and adobe necessitated a limited and strategic use of windows to maintain the structural integrity of the wall. Today, many materials such as brick and stone are used as veneers with no structural role, providing an opportunity to intentionally express an ambiguity or creative expression between structure and materials. More delicate, yet structurally strong, frame systems such as wood, steel, and aluminum provide the freedom to open much larger expanses of glazing between load-bearing frames. Additionally, the proliferation of innovative curtain walls and structural glass systems allows even the primary structural systems to be transparent. Whether revealed or hidden, the choice of structures and materials expresses the pragmatic and expressive potential of structured light.

The following studies of works by Sverre Fehn and Undurraga Devés Architects explore decidedly different approaches to structural expression, building envelope, and the resulting qualities of daylight. First is Sverre Fehn's Ulltveit-Moe Pavilion at the National Museum - Architecture in Oslo, Norway, where the structural logic is clearly revealed on both the interior and exterior of the building. For Fehn, "structure is the core of architecture," and it is inextricably linked to design intentions and human experiences

△ Structure, space, and light create distinct zones in the Ulltveit-Moe Pavilion. The exterior concrete wall, glazed façade, and perimeter space shelter the inner zone from direct sunlight and solar gains. National Museum - Architecture, Oslo, Norway; Sverre Fehn.

of space, light, and place. [5] A clear structural logic is revealed in the pavilion, with the loads of the concrete roof carried by interior concrete columns, while the perimeter is structurally independent and enclosed by a delicate glass curtain wall. Outside the pavilion, a freestanding concrete wall acts as a quiet visual backdrop for the exhibitions, while mediating direct sunlight and views. Mechanical and electrical systems, as well as rainwater drainage, are skillfully integrated within the interior concrete columns. This layered structural system supports Fehn's poetic, spatial, and luminous design intentions. From the exterior, the pavilion appears as a delicate and ephemeral structure, with the glazed envelope wrapping up and over the edge of the roof to create a minimal exterior enclosure that contrasts with the robust concrete columns and sheltering roof on the interior.

Next is the Chapel of Retreat in Valparaíso, Chile, by Undurraga Devés Architects, which is a series of nested boxes recessed into a

"Structure is the giver of light. When I choose an order of structure that calls for column alongside of column, it presents a rhythm of no light, light, no light, light, no light, light. A vault, a dome, is also a choice of a character of light."[6]

Louis Kahn, Architect

subterranean landscape. The structural concrete box is expressed on the exterior as a series of mass planes spanning the landscape void. The interior is a dark wooden box, seeming to float in space, suspended above the glazing that wraps the lower perimeter of the chapel. While the structure is hidden from the interior, it is fully expressed on the exterior. The integration of structure and daylight creates the illusion of a hovering box of shadow suspended within a light-filled subterranean landscape. In an interview with Douglas Murphy for *ICON*, Cristián Undurraga explained the role of structure in the chapel: "The expression of the structures and the materials have to be clear and transparent."[7] In critiquing the structural expression, Murphy concludes: "But here form still follows function: it's just that the function is to symbolise the ineffable."[8]

Both projects illustrate that structural logic is, in part, a conceptual choice and an attitude regarding the expressive interaction of structure, materials, and light. Fehn juxtaposes the interior concrete structure with a delicate structural glass wall to minimize the sense of enclosure, while Undurraga conceals the load-bearing concrete structure from the interior view and creates the illusion of a heavy box of shadow that appears to be mysteriously supported by ground-reflected light within the landscape void.

The integration of the structure and daylight is tied to essential design intentions and goals: What are the desired spatial, atmospheric, and luminous qualities? Should the structure be hidden or revealed? What choices of structure and materials support the program and activities? Fehn and Undurraga demonstrate that, regardless of the choice of structural system, the use of daylight as an essential building material is inextricably tied to structural logic and poetic expression.

◁ With structural loads carried to the perimeter of the subterranean landscape void, the wood cladding and structural glass walls of the chapel appear to float within a volume of light. The hidden structure enhances a sense of mystery and timelessness. Chapel of Retreat, Sanctuary of Auco, Calle Larga, Los Andes Valley, Valpariaíso, Chile; Christián Undurraga, Undurraga Devés Architects.

△ Exterior view of the exhibition pavilion reveals the structural layers, which include the exterior freestanding concrete wall and ambulatory space, structural glass envelope, and interior concrete columns and roof.

Case study 4.1

Ulltveit-Moe Pavilion, National Museum - Architecture
(Nasjonalmuseet Arkitektur)

Oslo, Norway

Sverre Fehn

"You're … always trying to find the simplest solution. There are a lot of factors you have to take into account, but a simple solution often provides answers to several different questions. But you can't just begin building, you have to reach an architectonic expression before you start. To be a good architect actually requires great humility. You have to make the most of the very small amount of knowledge you possess."[9]

Sverre Fehn, Architect

△ The juxtaposition of the contemporary exhibition pavilion and historic Norge Bank building fosters an architectural conversation on form, structure, materials, and light across space and time.

LIGHT AND THE QUALITY OF PLACE

National Museum
The National Museum in Oslo, Norway, includes the National Museum - Architecture, which, in 2008, moved into a newly renovated and expanded museum complex designed by Norwegian architect Sverre Fehn. The National Museum - Architecture comprises a new glass and concrete exhibition pavilion and Fehn's renovation of both the 1830 Norges Bank building, originally designed by architect Christian Heinrich Grosch, and an addition to the bank building completed in 1910. Sited in the heart of the city, the museum is designed to house permanent and temporary exhibitions, archives, a library, bookstore, café, and a variety of architecture- and design-related events and performances. Surrounded by historic buildings and located adjacent to the 13th-century medieval Akershus Castle, the museum is several blocks from the scenic waterway, islands, and distant hills of the Oslo Fjord.

Oslo Climate and Light
Dr. Nina Berre, Director of Architecture at the National Museum of Art, Architecture, and Design, explains Fehn's sensitivity to place: "Fehn's contribution is a very site- and target-specific approach. He never copied his own solution. [Architecture] is a local effort related to site and conditions. He was always inventing new architecture. He was very concerned with topographical solution, to site and nature."[10] In this urban context, Fehn established a subtle relationship with the forces of nature by siting the pavilion to the south and within the sheltering form of the historic buildings, ensuring solar access and select views to the urban streetscape and sky.

At 59.9° north latitude, Oslo is characterized by seasonal extremes of light and darkness, which provides challenges for daylighting design. Located just south of the Arctic Circle, daylight on the summer solstice extends for over 18 hours, with twilight persisting through the remaining evening hours. During the winter solstice, there are only 6 hours of daylight, with a maximum noon sun altitude of 6.6° above the horizon, compared to 53.6° on the summer solstice.

△▽ The building section and plan clarify the layering of structure and light to mediate direct sunlight and solar gains. Defined by four concrete columns and the roof, the inner zone is sheltered from direct sunlight by a perimeter space wrapped in a structural glass curtain wall. The exterior ambulatory space and freestanding concrete wall shelter the glass façades from direct seasonal solar gains while providing a backdrop for interior exhibitions.

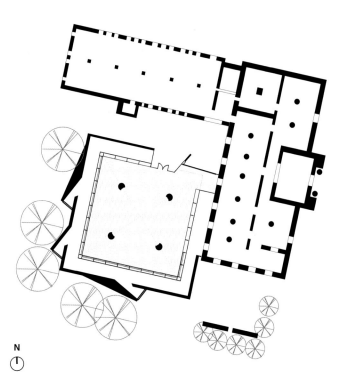

N

Despite the high latitude, Oslo has a surprisingly mild climate, as it is tempered by the Oslo Fjord and proximity to the Gulf Stream in the Baltic Sea. It has a warm–humid continental climate, with the average low temperature of –10°C (14°F) occurring in February and the average high of 10.5°C (69°F) in July. [11] With 50 percent overcast skies, the chance of precipitation throughout the year ranges from a low of 52 percent in May to a high of 72 percent in December. Winds are variable throughout the year, with prevailing winds shifting from south in the summer to north and northeast in the winter.

LIGHT AND THE DESIGN INTENTIONS

Museum Program

The renovated 1830 Norges Bank building includes the museum entry, reception area, café, bookstore, and main hall, while the permanent collection, archives, library, and supporting spaces are in the 1910 addition. The least sensitive temporary installations are housed in Fehn's new glass exhibition pavilion, in which the experience of light and time are at the heart of the design concept and program response. Martin Dietrichson, project architect at KIMA Architecture, explains: "[Fehn's] main idea was to make a pavilion for different kinds of exhibitions in contrast to the old building, but also that had some familiarity with each other. He wanted to make an open space, and he wanted it to be filled with daylight, but in some way we had to control it. His intention was to enter the building and in the morning [feel] that it was in the morning, and the same in the middle of [the] day and evening." [12]

Museum Director Nina Berre explains that the pavilion is most suitable for three-dimensional and non-sensitive materials that can accommodate changing levels of illumination and potential exposure to sunlight. Berre underscores the fact that these apparent restrictions have actually afforded creative approaches to exhibition

◁ △ Views through the northern façades of the exhibition pavilion provide a visual and physical connection to the renovated historic Norge Bank building, which houses additional exhibition galleries, archives, and support spaces. During the daytime, the masonry façades of the bank reflect indirect daylight to the perimeter of the exhibition pavilion. Given the northern latitude and short winter days, daylighting and electric lighting integration provide quality lighting throughout the year.

△ View to the west reveals the layering of the exterior and interior space. Seasonal sidelighting is mediated by supplemental shading and drapes hung from ceiling recesses along the perimeter glass wall. Flexible track lighting illuminates exhibitions, while electric uplighting emphasizes the vertical columns and structure.

designs while honoring Fehn's desire to celebrate the beauty and changing qualities of light: "Working with temporary exhibitions, we often asked what Fehn wanted. … The pavilion is a very perfect beautiful space to exhibit architecture models. The most challenging is exhibiting drawings that have strict limits regarding light conditions. We've had many good experiences in the pavilion. It is possible to really use the exhibition in different ways. There is always a balance between the vision and intention of doing an interesting exhibition and to be sensitive to Fehn's architecture, to be very conscious but not afraid of trying to do other things. … Experimentation was an intention, to experiment and test; to do something speculative."[13] The pavilion itself becomes part of the museum exhibition, with changing moods, atmosphere, and movement of light and shadow.

Pavilion of Light

The pavilion is located on the open southern portion of the site, protected on the north by the historic buildings. With the street grid offset from the cardinal directions, the pavilion opens to the southwest and northwest. The simple square mass of the pavilion is tucked within the sheltering L-shaped form of the existing buildings and linked on the north by a common entry. Designed as a "pavilion" rather than a "building," the intention was to provide a simple sheltering roof animated by the changing moods of the light, seasons, and weather, as Dietrichson explains: "Fehn wouldn't have had a façade at all, just a roof. He would have had just the light entering and just the roof. Of course we needed to have a

climate edge [façade], so we started on this idea of glass. Fehn was interested in working with glass as minimal construction."[14]

The concrete roof and structural columns define a flexible and open exhibition space that is subtly enclosed by a structural glass façade. Layered space, structure, and surfaces create two nested zones, with four columns defining an inner exhibition space beneath the vaulted concrete roof, and a second zone along the glass perimeter. The pavilion is wrapped on the outside with an ambulatory space and a freestanding battered concrete wall, reminiscent of the neighboring medieval castle. This exterior space creates a quiet visual backdrop for the exhibitions, shields the pavilion from views to the site, and is also used for exhibitions and performances. Strategic gaps in the exterior concrete wall provide select views to the sky, trees, street, and neighboring historic buildings.

LIGHT AND THE DESIGN STRATEGIES

Museum Atmosphere

Fehn's colleague Per Olaf Fjeld explained that Fehn would start a project with inspiration from the site and an atmospheric intention: "We developed a word for it, for the atmosphere or the feeling of a project that you have in your head before anything is put down on paper: *Room Picture*. For Sverre, this 'room picture' was clear before he sat down to discuss anything with the people in the office."[15]

Martin Dietrichson confirmed that the atmospheric quality of daylight was a design focus for the pavilion: "There are very extreme daylight differences in winter to summer that's really nice in this pavilion. You get the feeling of that [seasonal change] when inside the building."[16] He further clarified that the exhibition pavilion creates "an intentional conflict" between the dynamic qualities of daylight in the pavilion and the controlled light in the museum

△ ▷ Reminiscent of the historic 13th-century Akershus Castle, the exterior battered concrete wall is strategically broken to provide select views to the urban site and to admit daylight. In this northern latitude, the mood and quantity of light as well as seasonal sun angles dramatically vary on a seasonal basis.

◁ An exterior detail of the structural glass façade reveals the construction logic and attention to detail. The structural glass wall is slightly elevated from the surrounding ambulatory space and sheltering concrete perimeter wall. With roof loads carried by the interior concrete columns, the structural glass façade carries only the load of the envelope. Vertical fins provide structural support, while translucent horizontal solar louvers control solar gains and diffuse direct sunlight.

galleries in the historic building, emphasizing the distinction between the two architectural eras. [17]

The pavilion floor, walls, and ceiling act as a canvas for the seasonal qualities of light and weather in this northern locale. Architectural critic Ada Louise Huxtable shared Fehn's atmospheric description of "northern light": "Norway's 'horizontal' light and 'long shadows—a flickering, sensitive light' ... 'offer an infinite number of variations ... architecture is frequently invisible, enveloped in mist.'" [18] Low light levels and environmental moods are affected by the phase change of precipitation from rain into snow, sleet, and fog during the winter months. The dark days and nights of winter give way to the absence of true "night" in the summer, when the space is bathed in the soft warmth of twilight throughout the evening. While direct sunlight enters the pavilion throughout the year, it is filtered through solar louvers on the glass façade.

Inside and Outside

The section of the pavilion is designed to admit and control sunlight on a seasonal basis, including the carefully defined floor-to-ceiling heights, room depths, form of the vaulted ceiling, length of the roof overhang, and height and placement of the exterior concrete wall. The layering of the glass façade, ambulatory space, and exterior concrete wall resolve Fehn's desire to create both an internally focused pavilion while maintaining direct experience of the dynamic forces of nature within an urban context. Dietrichson explains how the design responds to Fehn's seemingly contradictory goals of creating an introverted, yet open and spacious daylit space: "To get the light atmosphere in the pavilion we worked with the glass and also with the concrete construction. ... For the outside concrete wall, the main idea is to make the space larger and that the wall should be a kind of back wall to the exhibition. ... [It's an] introverted space inside a building that is full of light. And in contact with the sun and trees, but you don't have direct views straight out to the city. It's a special atmosphere and very introverted in a way ... we do that with all the direct sunlight that is allowed in." [19]

The low winter sun enters the glass façade over the exterior concrete wall and is reflected from the sloped ceiling to the perimeter zone, which effectively shelters the inner space within the concrete columns. Higher summer-sun angles are mediated by

◁ △ The exterior concrete wall and outdoor ambulatory space provide a backdrop for exhibitions and periodic art installations and performances.

the length of the overhang of the sloped roof above the perimeter zone. Exterior horizontal glass sunshades reflect direct solar gains and diffuse the summer sunlight. Although direct views to the urban site are restricted, a consistent presence of nature is experienced through a horizontal slice of the sky and treetops that is framed above the exterior concrete wall.

LIGHT AND THE ART OF MAKING

Structured and Material Light

Structure and poetic intention are inseparable, as Fehn explained: "For me, there is no architecture without construction. We work with our alphabet [of] materials such as wood, concrete, bricks [and] with them, we write a story which is inseparable from the structure. And the structure is supported by the poetic idea."[20] Per Olaf Fjeld elaborated on Fehn's perspective: "The structure was the most important thing to [Fehn]. He saw structure in most things. But not in a technological way, he didn't necessarily strive to maximise structural efficiency. … What concerned him was finding the right relationship between space, light and shadow."[21]

To achieve the desired degree of openness, transparency, and minimal sense of enclosure, Fehn pushed the limits of construction and technology in glass size and structural performance. The

◁ Curators have designed a great variety of exhibition display systems including various moveable walls, display surfaces, and pedestals to accommodate diverse types of work and lighting needs.

exhibition pavilion was one of Fehn's final works, and collaboration with experts in a variety of areas was essential. Rigorous iterative studies and testing of structure, construction details, and building systems were conducted over a four-year period, using physical models and architectural drawings at a variety of scales, including 1:1, 1:2, 1:10, 1:15, and 1:20. Dietrichson described the collaborative process: "Regarding the design process, we spent a lot of time with [the] concept and defining what was important. But we also needed to get the right people on the team for the glass, concrete works, and wooden structure in the floor as well as the technical [systems] for air and electric. We worked with the contractor, Kåre Hagen AS, from the beginning." [22]

The load-bearing concrete structure, comprised of four columns and the roof, is thoughtfully integrated with mechanical, electrical, and drainage systems. The concrete roof and columns carry the structural loads as well as the air supply and return, rainwater from the roof, and electrical systems. Concrete columns define two distinct zones, with an internally focused and protected zone beneath the curved ceiling and between the columns, and a more open and light-filled zone along the perimeter of the structural glass wall. As structural loads are carried by the concrete columns, the glass curtain wall and structural glass fins are self-supporting and float free of the roof structure. Outside the columns, the sloped ceiling cantilevers out 6 meters (19.6 feet) and is enclosed by the layered structural glass façade that wraps up and over the roof to create the illusion of a glass box from the exterior. Beneath the pavilion is a space for the heating and mechanical systems. Fehn's approach to structure was integral to his architectural vision and inspiration for the project, its use, and the users. His intention was to create the most minimal of structures: essentially an open pavilion with a roof overhead. The structural logic and choice of materials, while seemingly simple, skillfully integrate practical considerations such as gravity, water, and comfort with atmospheric and experiential qualities to create an open, spacious, and light-filled space.

Envelope Details

The envelope details, energy, and lighting studies were developed in collaboration with Skandinaviska Glassystem (SGS). Stefan Abrahamsson of SGS explained that the double-pane structural glass façades, which span 5.8 meters (19 feet) in height and are supported by external structural glass fins, combined different glazing technologies to meet luminous and thermal goals. The façade glass employs AGC Glass Company's Stopray Safir, a neutral solar-absorbing glass with an approximate visible light transmittance of 60 percent and G-value of 32 percent. Vertical glass fins are constructed of low-iron Optiwhite glass to provide high visible-light transmission and to optimize view. Horizontal glass sun shades are mounted on the upper portion of the façade and between the vertical glass fins. The sun shades include a pyrolytic coating, using AGC's Stopsol Supersilver, which is designed to reflect solar energy while maintaining a high level of visible light transmission and aesthetic quality. Two-millimeter (0.08-inch) wide translucent white stripes are screen-printed on the sun shades to diffuse light. The roof glass, which wraps over the upper edge of the building, is electrically heated, and the outer pane has both screen-printing and a Stopray Safir coating. [23] Track lighting along the outer and inner ceiling zones of the pavilion provides supplemental electric lighting, and a recess along the perimeter of the ceiling and glass façade accommodates drapes or blinds. Moveable exhibition walls and interior shading allow exhibition designers additional strategies for exhibition display and lighting control, including flexible and sliding walls, black boxes, black and white curtains, and a range of interior screens and shading elements.

LIGHT INSPIRATIONS

The Ulltveit-Moe Pavilion is an expression of Fehn's rigorous attention to structure, materials, and detailing, and his quest to celebrate the relationship between architecture and nature, as referred to in his general views on site design: "I hope that seeing the building in its setting will give rise to a new consciousness of the beauty of the place." [24]

Dietrichson reflected on working with Fehn and his response to the luminous experience in the pavilion: "It was fantastic to work together with him. At his age he [still had] a very young mind; he was always searching for something. When almost finished, I entered the building with Fehn. He was extremely happy. ... I'm also happy every time I enter into the pavilion. I have a feeling of something new. And that's also an intention with the concepts and the light." [25]

Seemingly simple in massing and section, the pavilion reveals a meticulous integration of structure, form, materials, systems, and daylight with an economy of means. Practical requirements such as structural loads, thermal performance, and illuminance levels are met while also creating a quiet and contemplative exhibition space brought to life by northern light. The delicate crystalline pavilion rises above the sheltering concrete wall to stand in quiet conversation with Grosch's steadfast masonry architecture and the massive stone ramparts of the medieval Akershus Castle.

▽ Interior view of the temporary installation "Ode to Osaka" by Manthey Kula Architects, which was located within the four concrete columns of the pavilion during the summer of 2015. As a reinterpretation of Sverre Fehn's competition proposal for the Scandinavian pavilion for the 1970 World Fair in Osaka Japan, the inflatable fabric structure with a wood-framed entry airlock elevated the contrasting luminous, structural, and spatial qualities of the pavilion and temporary installation.

DESIGN PROFILE

1. Building Profile
Project: Ulltveit-Moe Pavilion, National Museum – Architecture (Nasjonalmuseet Arkitektur)
Location: Oslo, Norway
Architect: Sverre Fehn
Client: Statsbygg & the National Museum
Building Type: Museum
Square Footage: 3,800 sq m (40,903 sq ft)
Estimated Cost: Not available
Completion: 2008

2. Professional Team
Architect: Sverre Fehn
Project Architect: Martin Dietrichson
Project Team: Marius Mowe, Kristoffer Moe Bøksle, Henrik Hille
General Contractor: Kåre Hagen AS

3. Climate Profile
Climate (Köppen-Geiger Climate Classification System): Dfb: warm–humid continental climate
Latitude: 59.9° north latitude
Solar Angles: Noon
June 21: 53.6°
March/September 21: 30.1°
December 21: 6.6°
Length of Day: Approximate Hours of Daylight from Sunrise to Sunset
June 21: 18h 49m
March/September 21: 12h 20m
December 21: 5h 53m
Heating Degree Days: 4367 heating degree days °C (8072 heating degree days °F) (18°C and 65°F base temperature) [26]
Cooling Degree Days: 43 cooling degree days °C (69 cooling degree days °F) (18°C and 65°F base temperature) [27]

4. Design Strategies
Daylighting Strategies: Sidelighting: floor-to-ceiling glazing in all orientations diffusing glass at north entry; structural glass façades with exterior horizontal solar glass shading with translucent white stripes screen-printed on glazing; vertical structural glass fins; adjustable interior drapes and varied temporary solar-control strategies with moveable walls, partitions, and exhibitions.
Sustainable Design and High-Performance Strategies: High-performance glazing systems, mechanical systems, and electric track lighting.
Renewable Energy Strategies: None.

Fehn: Structure and Materials

The exploded diagram illustrates the structural layering and spatial organization of the pavilion. On the exterior is located a freestanding concrete wall that provides a neutral backdrop for exhibitions and creates a sense of privacy. The pavilion is clad with a delicate glass curtain wall that is structurally autonomous from the roof loads carried by the interior concrete columns.

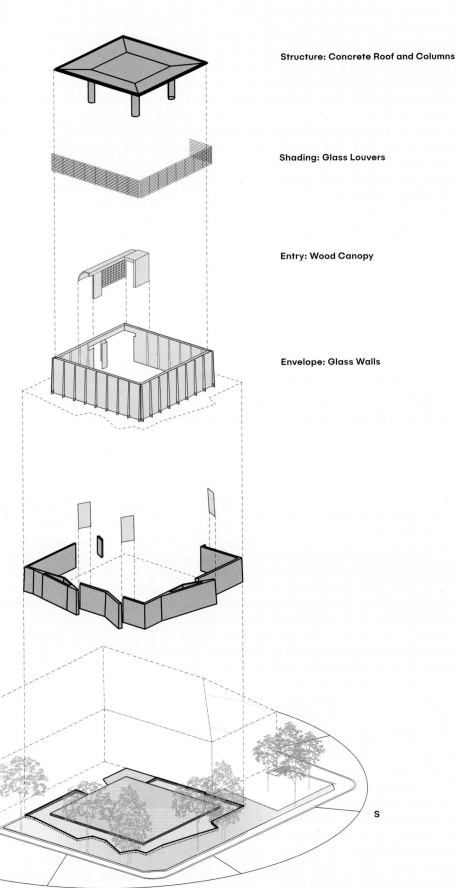

Structure: Concrete Roof and Columns

Shading: Glass Louvers

Entry: Wood Canopy

Envelope: Glass Walls

Envelope: Freestanding Concrete and Glass Walls

Floor: Concrete and Wood

N

S

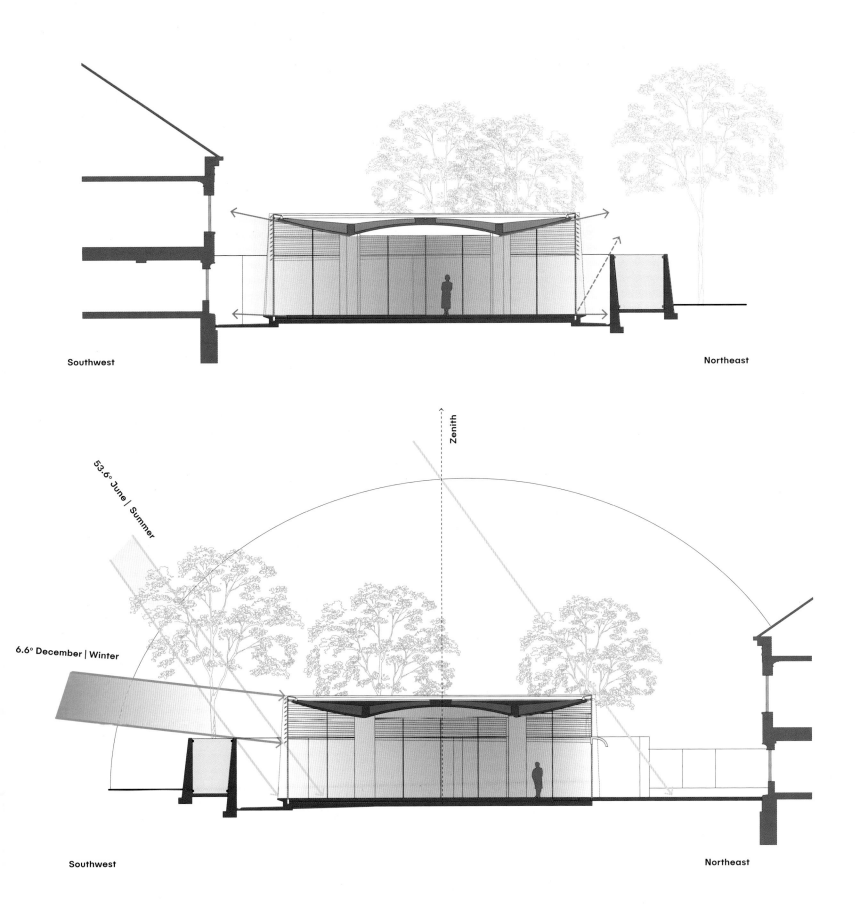

Southwest

Northeast

Zenith

53.6° June | Summer

6.6° December | Winter

Southwest

Northeast

The upper southwest–northeast section illustrates the layering of structure, materials, and daylight. A freestanding concrete wall and ambulatory space defines the outside boundary. A structural glass façade with horizontal solar glass louvers and translucent glazing mediates sunlight and solar gains. Four concrete columns define perimeter and interior exhibition spaces.

Daylight Analysis: Seasonal Plans

Illuminance studies (in lux) illustrate the seasonal and diurnal light levels and distribution. Given the high latitude and dramatically changing length of day from winter to summer, the analysis studied the "midway-point" between sunrise, noon, and sunset for each season. The analysis reveals the different light levels and quality of daylight along the perimeter zone of the glass façade and the interior zone defined by the four concrete columns.

Sunny Sky Illuminance (Lux)

——— 500
——— 438
········· 375
——— 313
——— 250
——— 188
——— 126
——— 63

N

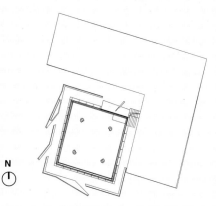

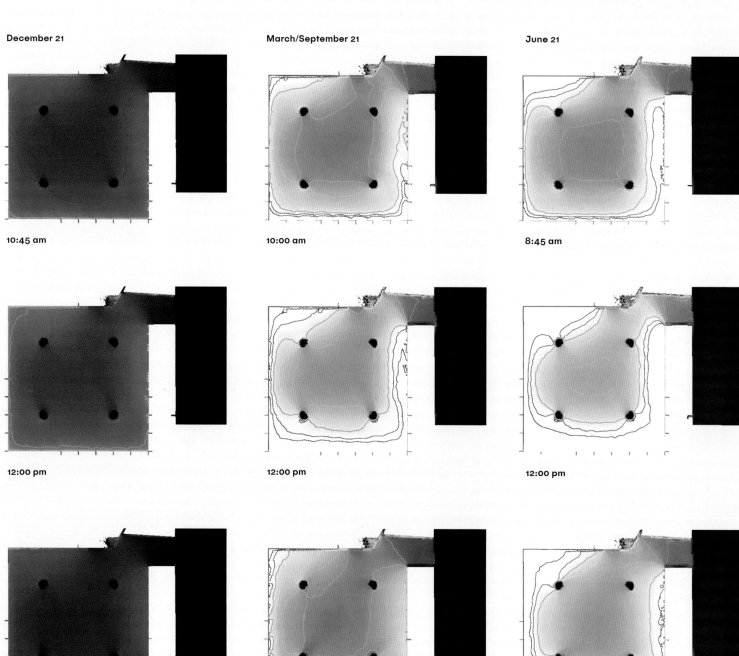

December 21

10:45 am

12:00 pm

1:45 pm

March/September 21

10:00 am

12:00 pm

12:00 pm

June 21

8:45 am

12:00 pm

12:00 pm

Equinox Walk-Through

Perspective renderings and luminance studies (in candela/square meter;cd/m2) illustrate the visual quality of daylight and contrast ratios from four view locations within the exhibition space during the fall equinox (September 21 at noon). The highest contrast occurs in areas of direct sunlight adjacent to the window wall. Temporary drapes and shading at the glass façade can mediate direct sunlight, illuminance levels, and visual and thermal comfort based on program needs.

**Sunny Sky
Luminance** (Cd/m²)

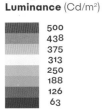

500
438
375
313
250
188
126
63

View A: March/September 21 at 12:00 pm

View A: March/September 21 at 12:00 pm

View B: March/September 21 at 12:00 pm

View B: March/September 21 at 12:00 pm

View C: March/September 21 at 12:00 pm

View C: March/September 21 at 12:00 pm

View D: March/September 21 at 12:00 pm

View D: March/September 21 at 12:00 pm

Seasonal Timelapse_Looking Southwest

Time-lapse renderings of the pavilion illustrate the dramatic seasonal and diurnal changes in the quality and distribution of daylight throughout the year given the high geographic latitude (59.9° north latitude) and varying length of day (18h 49m on June 21 and 5h 53m on December 21).

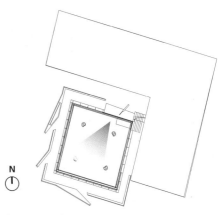

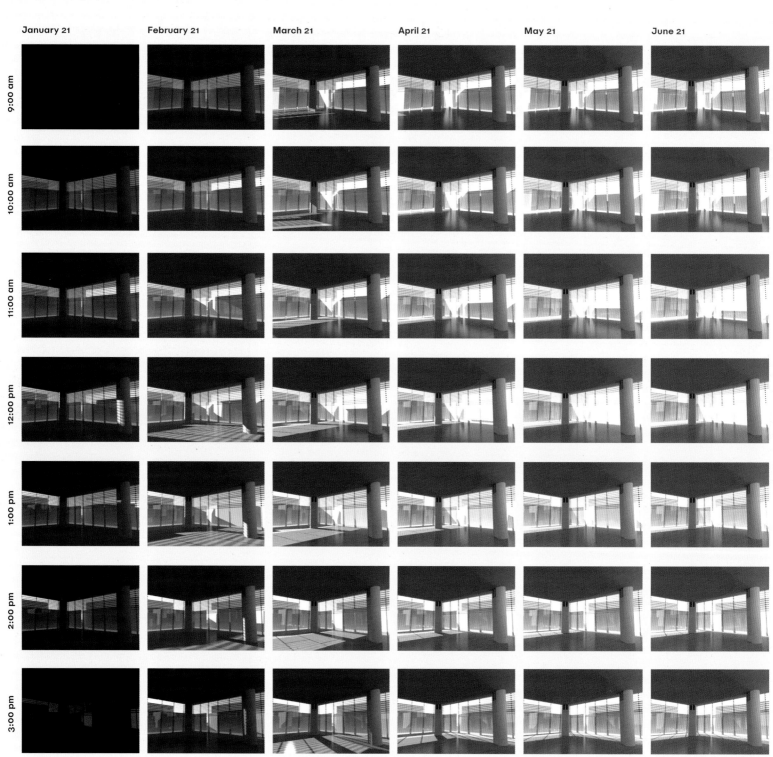

July 21   August 21   September 21   October 21   November 21   December 21

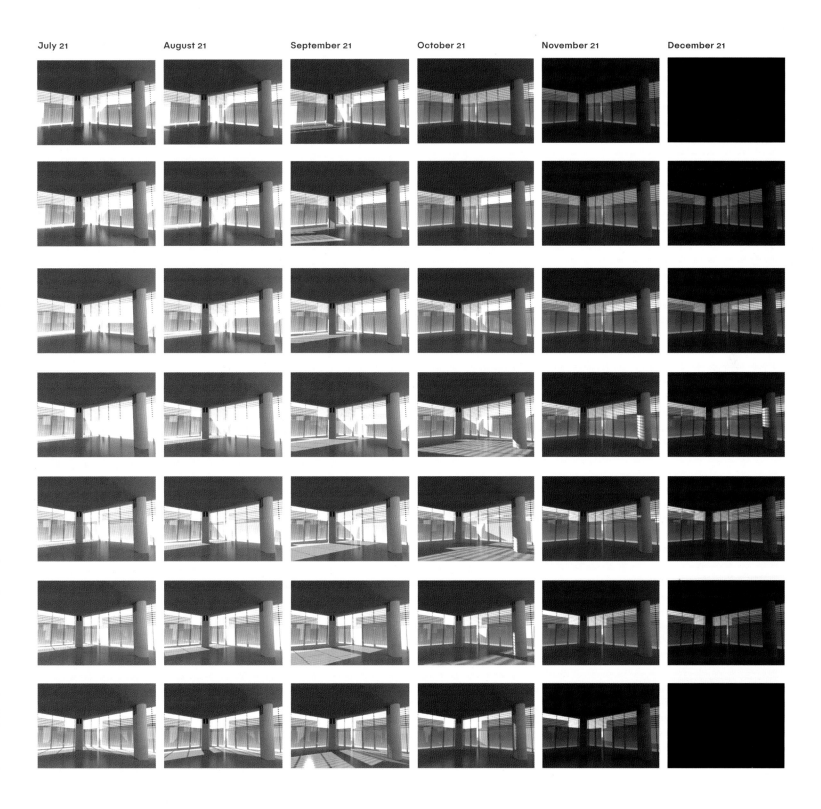

Case study 4.2

Chapel of Retreat
(Capilla del Retiro)

Sanctuary of Auco, Calle Larga,
Los Andes Valley, Valparaíso, Chile

Cristián Undurraga, Undurraga Devés Architects

"Daylight is the first material. Light is what gives the atmosphere that we are always seeking, [like] calm, beauty, a trusting experience. ... Light runs through spaces like water. It moves through spaces in a particular way. Every material has a different quality to interact with light. The material that reveals light has specific conditions, [such as] the reflection of materials to keep the darkness." [28]

Cristián Undurraga and Pablo López, Undurraga Devés Architects

◁ △ The entry descends through the site into the subterranean landscape void surrounding the chapel. Nested layers of the façade are revealed as the exterior concrete mass of the upper portion of the chapel hovers above the structural glass façade and suspended wood-box interior. Photograph is prior to the installation of native landscaping.

LIGHT AND THE QUALITY OF PLACE

A Place of Pilgrimage

The Chapel of Retreat, designed by Cristián Undurraga, Undurraga Devés Architects (UDA), is adjacent to the Carmelite Monastery of Auco and the Sanctuary of Teresa of the Andes in Calle Larga, Chile. The site is surrounded to the east by the spectacular Andes Mountains and to the west by the coastal mountain range and the Pacific Ocean. Santiago lies some 70 kilometers (43 miles) to the south. The natural beauty of the Andes and the rich agricultural lands and vineyards of the Andes Valley form a serene and contemplative context. Architect Cristián Undurraga emphasizes the importance of place in Chilean culture: "Geography is very close to you, even in the city. The mountains are outside every day. So we don't have a strong history, we have a strong geography. We are always relating to the geography." [29]

The chapel, in which pilgrims experience a cave-like subterranean space surrounded by stone walls and gardens, is a counterpoint to the mountainous landscape, as Undurraga explains: "You're surrounded with mountains all the time. [At the chapel] you go through a primitive experience to the cave. It is so simple, from the interior we keep intimacy and at the same time connect with the mountains and geography. This is achieved through the stone walls and geometry. You feel that spiritually in the geography. People go outside the chapel as part of the spiritual retreat; they also walk and climb to the mountains. It is all connected." [30]

Calle Larga and Chilean Light

Undurraga describes daylight as an abundant natural resource and a building material in its own right: "We are very lucky to have light in the central part of the country and in the valley. Natural light is beautiful all year. For us, natural light is just another material. It is the most archaic material we have. We work with it intuitively." [31]

Located at 32.8° south latitude in the Valparaíso region, Calle Larga is considered a local steppe climate with dry-mild weather

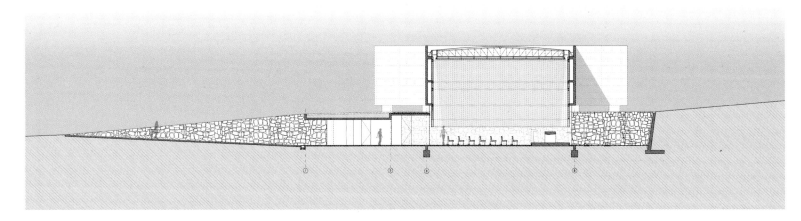

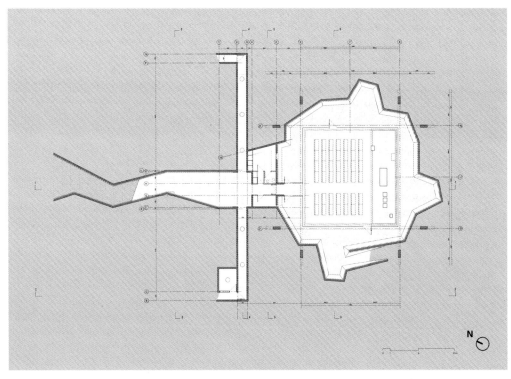

◁ △ Building section and plan illustrate
the contrasting geometries of the
square chapel within the organic form
of the subterranean landscape void.

throughout the year. The average low temperature of 3°C (37.4°F) occurs in June, and the average high of 31°C (87.8°F) in January. [32] With mild and fairly consistent seasonal conditions, sunlight is plentiful throughout the year, ranging from approximately 14 hours on the summer solstice to 10 hours on the winter solstice. The sun reaches the highest noon altitude of 90.7° in December (when the sun flips to the south side of the chapel) and the lowest noon altitude of 33.7° in June (when the sun is on the north). With little or no rainfall during the months of December through March, and only modest rainfall the remainder of the year, the qualities of daylight are characterized by high contrast, brilliant sunlight, deep shadows, and high levels of illumination. At the chapel, direct sunlight and solar gains are mediated by the self-shading

building form and subterranean section. Due to the mild climate, no mechanical heating or cooling is required. Cross-ventilation is accomplished by operable doors at the lower level of the chapel, and electric lighting is provided to supplement daylight.

LIGHT AND THE DESIGN INTENTIONS

A Contemplative Program

As a pilgrimage site for Saint Teresa of the Andes, the first Chilean to be canonized by the Roman Catholic Church, hundreds of thousands of pilgrims visit the region each year to honor the saint, explore the numerous pilgrimage destinations, and retreat for prayer and meditation. As a patron saint for the young and sick,

Saint Teresa is revered for her teachings on peace, simplicity, and humility. Undurraga translates these seemingly intangible teachings into architectural design. In this spirit, the chapel provides a peaceful, simple, and humble space of contemplation. The Chapel of Retreat supports the specific contemplative practices of the pilgrims, but is also designed to provide a place of spiritual respite for all visitors, as Undurraga explained: "Not all people who visit are religious. People go there for a peace[ful] moment; a transcendent moment. They are not only Catholic; the atmosphere is something everyone can understand." [33] The activities in the chapel may include informal contemplation and meditation as well as ritual ceremonies and retreat events. The exterior terrace and stone-walled gardens can be accessed by visitors for walking and contemplation. Support spaces are discreetly located at the subterranean entry.

Light, Form, and Space

The chapel is sited a respectful distance south of the monastery and other pilgrimage destinations, which include the Sanctuary of Auco church, a library, crypt, guest house, and visitor services. Visual, acoustic, and spatial separations create a quiet and contemplative transition for visitors and people on retreat. From the exterior, the chapel is a simple, seemingly solid, concrete mass— yet on approach, a subterranean landscape space is revealed within the earth. The platonic form of the chapel is juxtaposed against an irregular landscape void, which creates the illusion of the chapel floating mysteriously in space. At the subterranean level, the lower portion of the building envelope is fully glazed to further the illusion of levitation, while the contrasting concrete mass hovers over the stone walls of the recessed landscape.

Pablo López, project architect at CUA, emphasized that daylighting is integrally related to the tectonic nature of the chapel. The massing can be described as a "box within a box," in which an interior wooden box is nested with a concrete box suspended over a glazed and daylit subterranean garden, as Undurraga explains: "There are two different geometries. The geometry and materials drastically change from outside to inside; with different layers from bottom to top and outside to inside. … Light comes through the space that is generated by two different geometries. This is very important; light comes through those two different orders." [34]

The walls and ceiling of the wooden box are constructed of reused railroad ties, with a rough texture and dark value to contrast with the clean lines of the concrete floors, glass walls, and refined interior surfaces of stone, steel, and wood. The lower perimeter is wrapped in a glass envelope to create a visual gap and horizontal band of light between the dark overhead volume and the illuminated subterranean ground plane. The transparent boundary of the glass wall dissolves the visual distinction between inside and outside to form a contrasting yet intimate relationship between the shadowed interior of the chapel and the dynamic play of sunlight on the garden walls.

▷ A detail of the contrasting rustic stone walls of the landscape and the precise geometry and smooth surfaces of the concrete and glass façades. Photograph is prior to the installation of native landscaping.

LIGHT AND THE DESIGN STRATEGIES

Sacred Light Redefined

While drawing on traditions of Gothic architecture, the chapel takes a decidedly different approach to sacred space, by revealing to pilgrims an earthly expression of the sacred. Undurraga expresses this connection to the sacredness of everyday experience through the elegantly restrained architectural form, materials, and exquisite detailing revealed by the movement of light and time. In an interview with *ArchDaily*, Undurraga discussed the relationship to the Gothic tradition and his reinterpretation: "The whole of this piece, which appears to levitate over the ground, refers us to the spiritual dimension inside. This space is illuminated from the lower part, leaving a space to view a weightless body in the interior that hides the rationality of its supports, whilst the exterior affords us a view of the stone wall that surrounds the patio. The upper light has been restricted so as to maintain a certain half-light in the box, which is heightened by the dark color of the wood. Here, the duality of the rational exterior / metaphysical interior, so typical of Gothic architecture, assumes a new expression of a commitment to modernity." [35]

Undurraga clarifies his design intention for using reflected light from the floor and stone walls of the subterranean garden: "In traditional churches daylight comes from above. [In the chapel] light comes from the ground, not from above. I think that God is here. God is sitting next to me in a chair." [36]

Strategies of Light and Darkness

Daylight is admitted into the chapel as ground- and wall-reflected sidelight from the landscape void and also through a small skylight that runs along the top and perimeter of the walls of the interior wooden box. Toplighting gently grazes the dark, distressed surfaces of the railroad ties to reveal irregular textures, varied colors, and a subtle play of shadows. Ground-reflected light provides illumination from below to further emphasize the nested volumes and landscape void. The simple form of the chapel and the stone walls and gardens intersect to create a square volume of darkness and shadow floating above and within an irregular and organic volume of sunlight. Darkness is essential in achieving the contemplative atmosphere, sheltering the cave-like space, and creating the desired quality of a floating box, as Undurraga explains: "The heavy massive floating box was possible because the structure was going outside of the square [of the box]. The weightless floating body is supported by the light. The light between the earth and the box. For the idea of the floating box we needed contrast. We needed darkness to see the light. We needed a heavy and dark material to achieve the sense of the floating box." [37]

LIGHT AND THE ART OF MAKING

Dynamic Stillness

The inner journey of the pilgrim is reflected in the physical journey through the site as the visitor moves incrementally from arrival at the monastery, through formal gardens, into a gradually descending linear landscape cut into the earth, then passing through a tunnel and glazed lobby, before finally entering the chapel. Once inside, the pilgrim is held within the shadow, darkness, and stillness of the nested boxes of the chapel. The dark, cosmic, and timeless quality of the sanctuary is juxtaposed with the dynamic movement of sunlight and shadow in the garden. The chapel altar is framed

△ A delicate glass passageway marks the threshold between the subterranean entry pathway, the sunlit subterranean garden, and the quiet and cool darkness of the chapel. Visually discreet glass doors provide direct access into the garden.

▷ Structural loads of the chapel are carried to exterior piers in the rock walls of the garden. From the interior, the rustic wood volume appears suspended inside the structural glass curtain wall. Sunlight reflected off the stone walls into the lower portion of the chapel through the glass façades is complemented by a soft band of daylight from a narrow skylight at the top of the chapel.

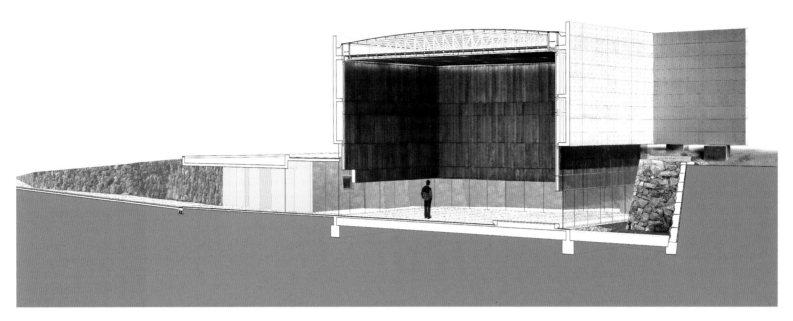

◁△ The building section, concept diagrams, and construction details illustrate the nested layers of structure and materials to create the illusion of a floating box within the volume of light. The dynamic movement of direct sunlight in the landscape contrasts with the quiet and mysterious darkness of the chapel.

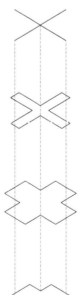

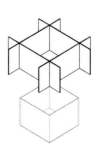

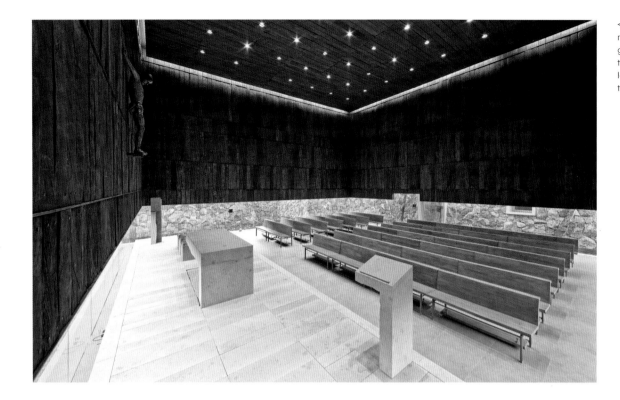

◁ The crisp geometry and restrained materials palette of concrete, stone, glass, and steel contrast with the textured stone walls and native landscape. Photograph taken prior to installation of the gardens.

against the south wall, which captures the nuanced movements of the sun and weather throughout the day and the seasons to reveal infinite variations in light and shadow grazing the three-dimensional terrace walls and native plants. Inner stillness is contrasted with outer movement.

Structured Light

The structure of the chapel is defined by the concrete planes of cruciform beams that carry loads to the boundary of the terrace walls so that the heavy-mass box appears to float delicately within the landscape void. The structure is not hidden, but rather it is removed from the interior view. In his interview with *ArchDaily*, Undurraga explained the relationship between structure, material, and form: "Concrete is the main material of the building's structure.

∇ Sketches of the Church of St. George in Ethiopia from the 13th century. One source of inspiration for the "mystical cave," and a contemporary interpretation of sacred architecture.

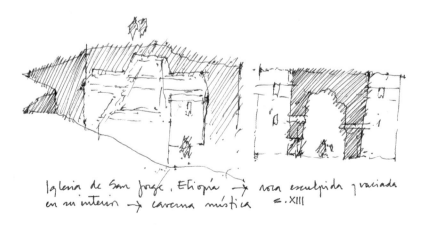

Iglesia de San Jorge, Etiopía → roca esculpida y vaciada en su interior → caverna mística   s. XIII

Its volume, strictly economical, rises up from a crosspiece of four beams in the shape of a cross that is supported with the least possible structural elements so that its relationship with the ground is slight but sufficient. Shape and structure here are an indissoluble synthesis." [38]

The structure and material palette of concrete, glass, steel, wood, and stone are detailed to create a calm and introspective atmosphere. The chancel, altar, and lectern are constructed of local stone. The asymmetric altar is detailed with a hand-hewn stone interior surface and a smooth polished exterior surface. Heavy wooden doors contrast with the minimalist structural glass walls, while wooden pews appear to float on delicate steel frames. Clean lines and refined details are juxtaposed with the rustic textures of the wooden box and the rugged stone walls of the garden.

To achieve this level of refinement, Pablo López explains the importance of on-site testing and modeling: "When developing the chapel, we experimented with large-scale models to balance and verify the results. During construction, things were adjusted and changed, from light luminous wood to a dark and heavy material. ... It was a process of adjustment." [39]

Undurraga emphasized that in Chile, the design process continues into the construction phase: "Here in the south construction is different from the north. When under construction you can make changes and experiment. For example, at the beginning the box was white wood. In the process of developing the project we thought it would be more dramatic if the box was darker. ... And we discovered that the distance between the ground and the box was very big. We added another line of wood to make the distance shorter and the experience of material more dramatic [in the interior]." [40]

△ Wall detail illustrates the structure, material, and spatial layering of the stone wall, concrete structure, structural glass façade, and interior wood box.

LIGHT INSPIRATIONS

The Chapel of Retreat embodies design simplicity. The space and atmosphere that so beautifully support inner reflection, silence, and stillness resulted from rigorous iterative studies and seamless integration of form and structure.

Daylight, including darkness and shadow, is conceived as a material in its own right, fully integrated with design, structure, and material intentions. The resulting clarity of the chapel in form and light is deceptively simple, as Undurraga explained: "It was a long process to arrive at a simple box. From the beginning we didn't want traditional light coming from above. [But] how to represent the precedent in a new way? We started working and searching for a new way. We didn't have the answer. It was then a long process to arrive at this elemental and simple box." [41]

Recipient of the International Prize for Sacred Architecture, the Chapel of Retreat embodies a fresh interpretation of sacred architecture in which light and darkness are integrated with structure and materials to support the mystery of the contemporary pilgrim's often intangible inner journey.

DESIGN PROFILE

1. Building Profile
Project: Chapel of Retreat (Capilla del Retiro)
Location: Sanctuary of Auco, Calle Larga, Los Andes Valley, Valparaíso, Chile
Architect: Undurraga Devés Architects
Client: Roman Catholic Church
Building Type: Chapel
Square Footage: 620 sq m (6,674 sq ft)
Estimated Cost: Not available
Completion: 2009

2. Professional Team
Architect: Cristián Undurraga
Project Team: Cristián Larraín Bontá, Pablo López, Jean Baptiste Bruderer
General Contractor: Terrano SA
Structural Engineer: José Jiménez, Rafael Gatica Engineers
Altar Design: José Vicente Gajardo
Photography: Sergio Pirrone

3. Climate Profile
Climate (Köppen-Geiger Climate Classification System): BSk, dry steppe climate
Latitude: 32.8° south latitude
Solar Angles: Noon
June 21: 33.7°
March/September 21: 57.2°
December 21: 90.7° (0.7° south of zenith)
Length of Day: Approximate Hours of Daylight from Sunrise to Sunset
June 21: 9h 58m
March/September 21: 12h 06m
December 21: 14h 20m
Heating Degree Days: 1202 heating degree days °C (2291 heating degree days °F) (18°C and 65°F base temperature) [42]
Cooling Degree Days: 1224 cooling degree days °C (2104 cooling degree days °F) (18°C and 65°F base temperature) [43]

4. Design Strategies
Daylighting Strategies:
1) Sidelighting: floor-to-ceiling glazing in all orientations; shading provided by recessed landscape void, and 2) Toplighting: thin linear skylight along the perimeter of exterior walls with deep lightwell and interior baffle to control direct sunlight.
Sustainable Design and High-Performance Strategies: Daylight throughout with supplemental electric lighting; cross-ventilation with operable doors; no heating or cooling required.
Renewable Energy Strategies: None.

Undurraga: Structure and Materials

The exploded diagram illustrates the nested structural systems and materials. The structural loads of the chapel are carried to the perimeter of the stone walls in the landscape void, creating the appearance of a floating concrete and wood volume. The lower walls of structural glass provide views into the landscape void, while the dark interior walls and ceilings are clad in recycled railroad ties to create a mysterious and inwardly focused atmosphere.

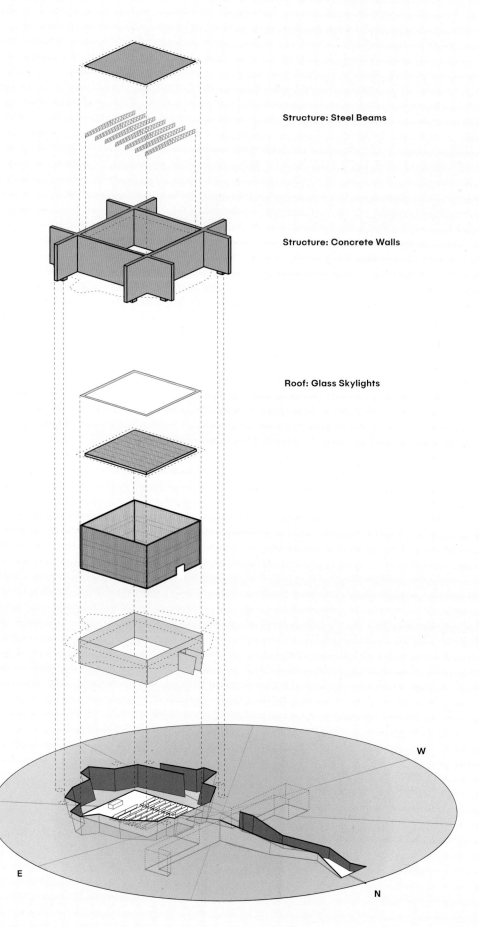

Structure: Steel Beams

Structure: Concrete Walls

Roof: Glass Skylights

Interior: Wood Ceiling and Walls

Envelope: Glass Walls

W

E

N

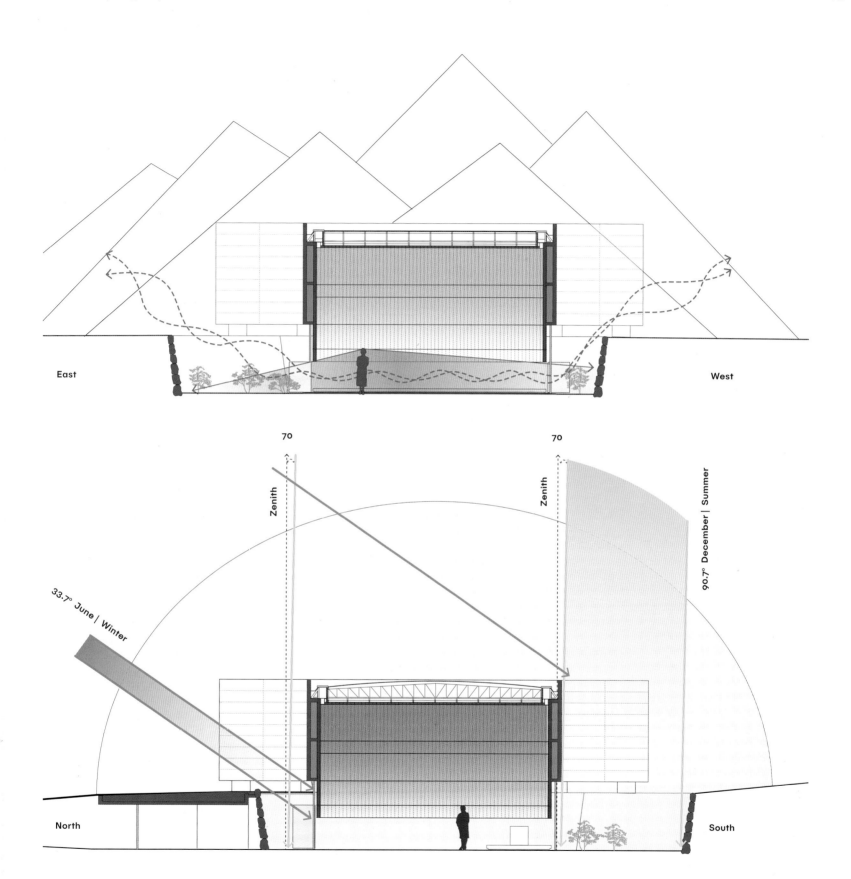

East

West

70

70

Zenith

Zenith

33.7° June | Winter

90.7° December | Summer

North

South

The upper east–west section illustrates the subterranean landscape surrounding the chapel and the visual chand physical access for views, light, and air. Sidelighting enters the lower level of the chapel through the glass façade, while toplight enters through a narrow slot along the perimeter of the ceiling. The lower north–south section reveals the seasonal sun angles. Located in the southern hemisphere and in proximity to the equator, the sun moves from the north façade in June (winter) to the south façade in December (summer).

Daylight Analysis: Seasonal Plans

Illuminance studies (in lux) illustrate the seasonal and diurnal light levels and distribution. Sidelighting is provided at the perimeter of the chapel from reflected sunlight on the stone walls of the landscape void. The inner area of the chapel has low light levels throughout the year.

Sunny Sky Illuminance (Lux)

	150
	131
	113
	94
	76
	57
	38
	20

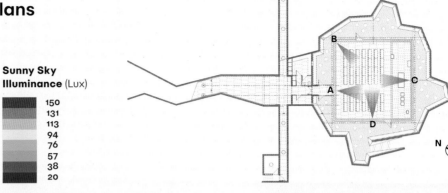

December 21

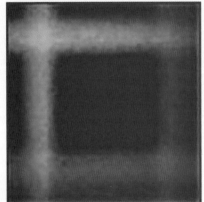

9:00 am

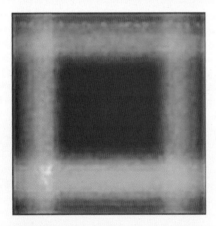

12:00 pm

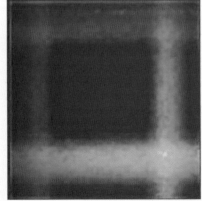

3:00 pm

March/September 21

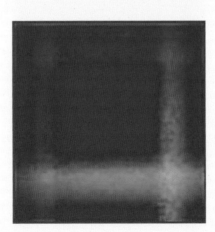

June 21

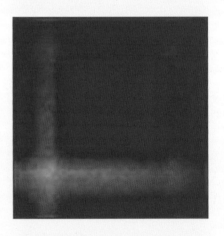

Solstice (December_Summer) Walk-Through

Perspective renderings and luminance studies (in candela/square meter; cd/m2) illustrate the visual quality of daylight and contrast ratios from four view locations within the chapel during the summer solstice (December 21 at noon). The extreme contrast between light levels in the subterranean garden and the dark interior of the chapel enhance the separation from the everyday world to create a quiet and sheltering contemplative atmosphere.

Sunny Sky
Luminance (Cd/m²)

	75
	66
	56
	47
	38
	29
	20
	10

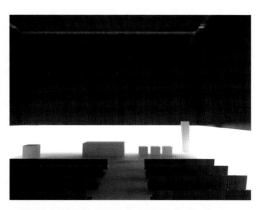

View A: December 21 at 12:00 pm

View A: December 21 at 12:00 pm

View B: December 21 at 12:00 pm

View B: December 21 at 12:00 pm

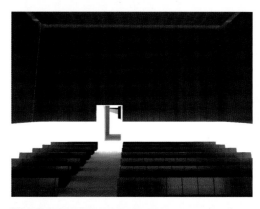

View C: December 21 at 12:00 pm

View C: December 21 at 12:00 pm

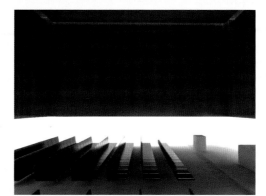

View D: December 21 at 12:00 pm

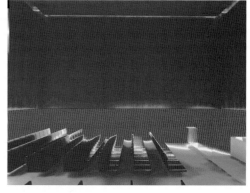

View C: December 21 at 12:00 pm

Seasonal Perspectives_Looking Southeast

Perspective renderings and luminance studies (in candela/square meter; cd/m2) illustrate the changes in the quality and distribution of daylight throughout the year given the proximity to the equator (32.8° south latitude) and length of day (9h 58m on June 21 and 14h 20m on December 21). The perspective renderings reveal the diurnal and seasonal movement of direct sunlight across the stone walls of the landscape. Direct and reflected sunlight enter the perimeter of the chapel, while the innermost space remains in relative darkness. High contrast ratios at the glass façades enhance the distinction between the inner sanctuary and the outer world.

December 21

March/September 21

June 21

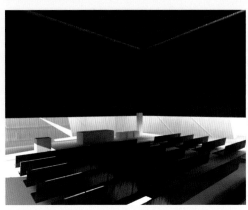
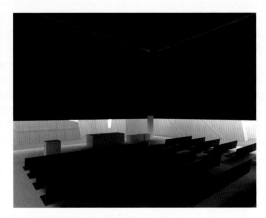

8:00 am

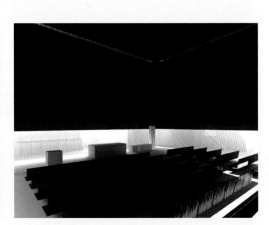

12:00 pm

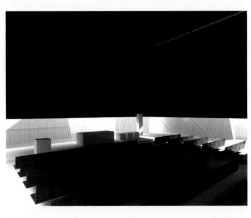
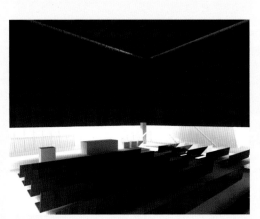
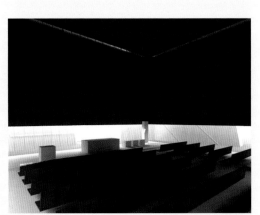

4:00 pm

Sunny Sky
Luminance (Cd/m²)

75
66
56
47
38
29
20
10

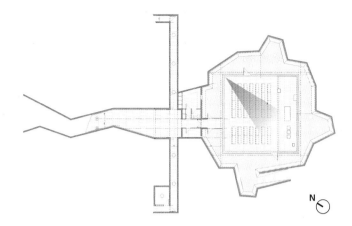

N

December 21

March/September 21

June 21

8:00 am

 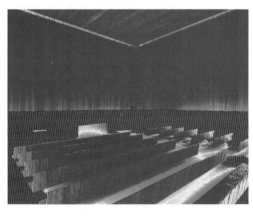 

12:00 pm

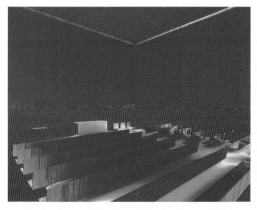  

4:00 pm

Seasonal Sections_Looking East

Seasonal sections illustrate the changing light
levels (in lux) from sidelighting and toplighting as
sun angles change throughout the day and year.

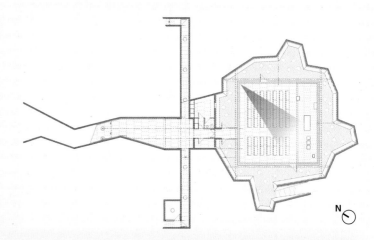

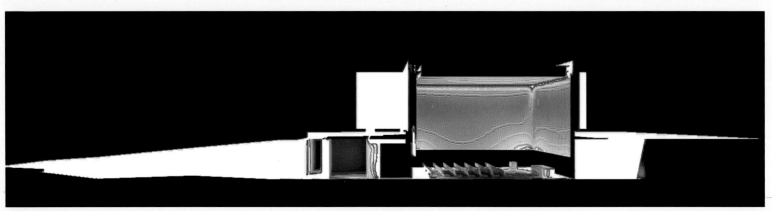

December 21 at 12:00 pm

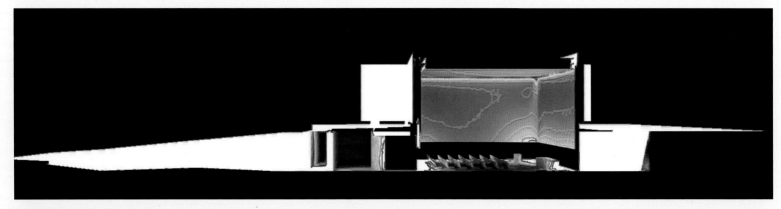

March/September 21 at 12:00 pm

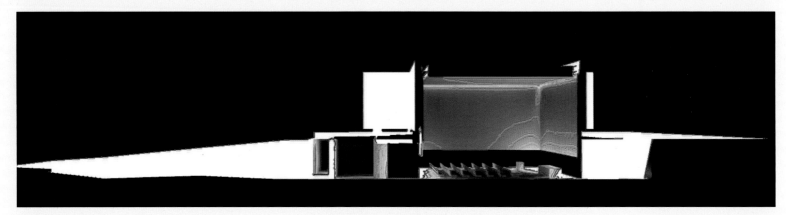

June 21 at 12:00 pm

Seasonal Sections_Looking South

Sunny Sky
Illuminance (Lux)

500
438
375
313
250
188
126
63

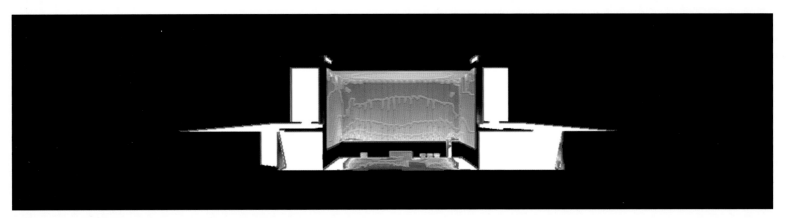

December 21 at 12:00 pm

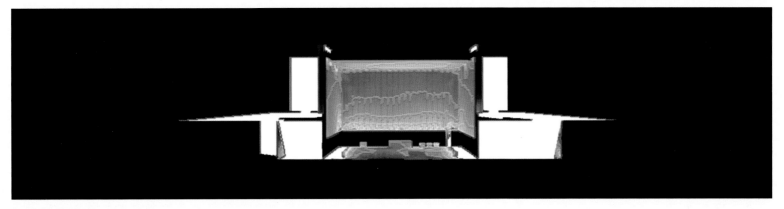

March/September 21 at 12:00 pm

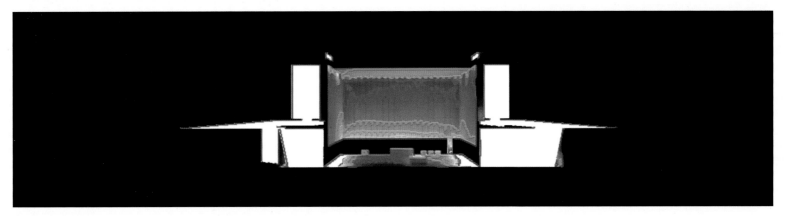

June 21 at 12:00 pm

Seasonal Timelapse_Looking Southeast

Perspective renderings illustrate the movement of
sunlight on the stone walls of the landscape void
throughout the day and seasons, while the inner
chapel remains in relatively uniform darkness.

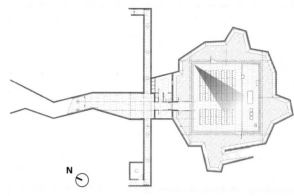

N

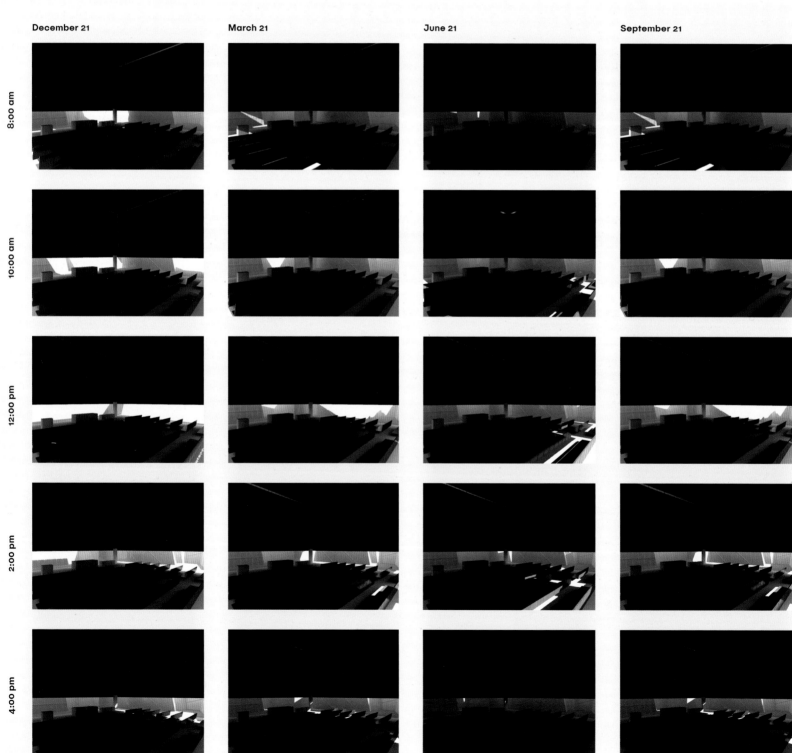

December 21   March 21   June 21   September 21

8:00 am

10:00 am

12:00 pm

2:00 pm

4:00 pm

Chapter 4: endnotes

Introduction

1 "Sverre Fehn, 1997 Laureate: Biography," *The Pritzker Architecture Prize*, Madrid: The Hyatt Foundation, http://www.pritzkerprize.com/1997/bio.

2 John Lobell, *Between Silence and Light: Spirit in the Architecture of Louis I. Kahn*, Boston: Shambhala, 1985, 34.

3 Ibid, 40.

4 Marietta Millet, *Light Revealing Architecture*, New York: Van Nostrand Reinhold, 1996, 65.

5 "Sverre Fehn, 1997 Laureate: Biography," *The Pritzker Architecture Prize*.

6 John Lobell, 34.

7 Douglas Murphy, "The Capilla del Retiro by Undurraga Devés," *ICON*, March 31, 2010, http://www.iconeye.com/architecture/news/item/4346-the-capilla-del-retiro-by-undurraga-deves.

8 Ibid.

Chapter 4.1

9 Ingerid Helsing Almaas, "People Have to Be Strong to Cope With Good Architecture: An interview with Sverre Fehn," *Arkitektur N*, May 10, 2010, http://architecturenorway.no/stories/people-stories/fehn-97/.

10 Nina Berre, Director of Architecture, National Museum of Art, Architecture, and Design, telephone interview with author, recorded September 7, 2015.

11 "Average Weather for Gardermoen, Norway," WeatherSpark.com, https://weatherspark.com/averages/28859/Gardermoen-Akershus-Norway.

12 Martin Dietrichson, KIMA Architecture, telephone interview with author, recorded October 15, 2015.

13 Nina Berre.

14 Martin Dietrichson.

15 Per Olaf Fjeld, *Architect Sverre Fehn: Intuition – Reflection – Construction*, Helsinki: Museum of Finnish Architecture, 2009, http://www.e-architect.co.uk/finland/sverre-fehn-architecture-exhibition.

16 Martin Dietrichson.

17 Ibid.

18 Ada Louise Huxtable, "Essay: The Paradox of Sverre Fehn," *The Pritzker Architecture Prize*, Hyatt Foundation, http://www.pritzkerprize.com/1997/essay.

19 Martin Dietrichson.

20 "Sverre Fehn, 1997 Laureate: Biography," *The Pritzker Architecture Prize*, Hyatt Foundation, http://www.pritzkerprize.com/1997/bio.

21 Tanja Lie, "The Word Thief: An Interview with Per Olaf Fjeld on the Words of Sverre Fehn," *Arkitektur N*, November 5, 2009, http://architecturenorway.no/stories/people-stories/fjeld-on-fehn-09/.

22 Martin Dietrichson.

23 Stefan Abrahamsson, Skandinaviska Glassystem, email message to author, December 11, 2015.

24 Norwegian Ministry of Foreign Affairs, "The Architecture Behind Nordic Modernism," The Royal Norwegian Embassy, Bratislava, Slovakia, http://www.norway.sk/travel/sports/Sverre_Fehn_architect/#.Vnm2wsYrK1s.

25 Martin Dietrichson.

26 "Degree Days: Energy Data for Professionals," Degreedays.net: Weather Underground, http://www.degreedays.net/#generate.

27 Ibid.

Chapter 4.2

28 Cristián Undurraga, Undurraga Devés Architects, telephone interview with author, recorded August 28, 2015.

29 Ibid.

30 Ibid.

31 Ibid.

32 "Climate: Calle Larga," Climate-data.org, http://en.climate-data.org/location/148314/.

33 Cristián Undurraga.

34 Ibid.

35 "Capilla del Retiro: Undurraga Devés Arquitectos," *ArchDaily*, April 2, 2012, http://www.archdaily.com/221334/capilla-del-retiro-undurraga-deves-arquitectos/.

36 Cristián Undurraga.

37 Ibid.

38 "Capilla del Retiro: Undurraga Devés Arquitectos," *ArchDaily*.

39 Pablo López, Undurraga Devés Architects, telephone interview with author, recorded August 28, 2015.

40 Cristián Undurraga.

41 Ibid.

42 "Degree Days: Energy Data for Professionals," Degreedays.net: Weather Underground, http://www.degreedays.net/.

43 Ibid.

Chapter 5

Material Light

"The capacity of light to penetrate matter and temporarily produce an inward glow and intensity of being is a timeless source of human wonder. At such moments, light exerts a mesmerizing, even miraculous, power to transform otherwise mute objects and dull materials and make them shine with an elevated beauty and a sense of being more fully alive. Throughout history, we find examples of buildings being rendered luminous by the manipulation of materials to increase their sensitivity to light. [1]

Henry Plummer, Professor and Photographer

The quality and character of place is an amalgam of geographic setting, latitude, sky conditions, and the living interactions between light, materials, and the physical environment. A place can be defined by the special qualities of its natural light: the shimmering liquid light of Venice; the soft, diffused refracted light of a misty morning in London; the brilliant sunlight and high contrast of light and shadow on a summer day in Lisbon, or the dramatic seasonal transition from light to darkness in Helsinki. Daylight is an ephemeral building material that can be shaped and sculpted like concrete, brick, or wood. Yet it is also dynamic and alive; transforming continuously in its interactions with the material world to create luminous qualities that delight the senses and animate the experience of architecture in unexpected and transient ways. Fundamental questions that can be addressed by considering light as an "architectural material" include: What is the inherent language of light for the locale and climate? What are the diurnal and seasonal attributes and moods of natural light? What atmospheric and expressive qualities of light might be celebrated? What character of light is desired and appropriate?

"Material light" depends on the interactions between the place-based attributes of daylight, and various properties of architectural materials. These physical properties include the material's hue, chroma, and value; texture; reflectance or absorbance; and specularity or diffusion, as Swiss architect Peter Zumthor explains: "Materials react with one another and have their radiance, so that the material composition gives rise to something unique. ... There's a critical proximity between materials, depending on the type of material and its weight. You can combine different materials in a building, and there's a certain point where you'll find they're too far away from each other to react, and there's a point too where they're too close together, and that kills them." [2]

Careful consideration of the architectural materials with which the light will interact is critical in defining the resulting luminous environment: How do the properties of building materials support, enhance, or enrich the desired lighting effects? What palette

▷ A threshold between two toplit galleries illustrating the even, diffuse daylight filtered through the skylight monitors and interior perforated concrete ceiling screen. Clyfford Still Museum, Denver, Colorado, USA; Brad Cloepfil, Allied Works.

◁ Interior courtyards provide sheltered gathering spaces and views to the gardens beyond. A perforated metal "light-catcher" suspended within the courtyard gathers daylight and provides visual interest. Maggie's Centre, Lanarkshire, Airdrie, North Lanarkshire, Scotland, UK; Neil Gillespie, Reiach and Hall Architects.

of building materials reinforces the lighting goals and desired outcomes? How might the chosen materials enhance daylight and thermal comfort? How might visual, tactile, and sensory experiences of light and materials interact?

In the following studies of works by Allied Works Architecture and Reiach and Hall Architects, light is expressed as a material in its own right and as an interactive medium that is transformed and mediated by the physical properties of the building materials and surface characteristics. First are the art galleries of the Clyfford Still Museum in Denver, Colorado, by Brad Cloepfil of Allied Works Architecture, which use daylight to reveal the art and the material qualities of the architecture. Next is Maggie's Centre, Lanarkshire, in Airdrie, Scotland, by Neil Gillespie of Reiach and Hall Architects, in which daylight and materials are coupled to create a healing environment for cancer patients and their family and friends.

The exterior of the Clyfford Still Museum is a heavy concrete mass with few windows, creating an effective connection of the building to the earth, while within the galleries, Cloepfil sought to transform the solidity of concrete into a light-emitting surface suspended beneath deep skylights. A seemingly liquid quality of light results from the interaction between the daylight, depth of the lightwell, and the size and patterning of oblong openings within the perforated concrete ceiling screen. Cloepfil muses that light and concrete "are like alchemy," underscoring the magical transformation of materials by natural light.

At Maggie's Centre, the predominantly overcast high-latitude climate of Scotland means that daylight, and particularly sunlight, is scarce and highly valued. The facility is designed as a sequence of garden and building spaces within a protective wall of perforated white Danish brick. Exterior gardens and the building

interior are animated by the changing qualities of light to create a welcoming and healing environment. The calm and friendly atmosphere is enhanced by strategic garden views, the maximum possible daylight, and a visually quiet and light-reflective material palette. Walls of blond Finnish birch, white-stained pine ceilings, and limed-oak floors create an atmosphere that celebrates the soft, quiet, and diffuse low-angle sunlight. Elements of surprise and discovery are revealed in toplit interior courtyards, which include perforated gold stainless steel light-catchers that capture light to the innermost spaces while framing and reflecting the sky and surrounding treetops.

The projects by Allied Works Architecture and Reiach and Hall Architects had different luminous goals, yet both demonstrate that the interplay between light and materials is essential in meeting the luminous program, addressing the functional roles of light, and creating desired atmospheric qualities. While the projects may appear simple in form, they embody complex interactions between the daylighting and the building sections, spatial organization, envelope detailing, and characteristics of materials and surfaces. In both, light as a material and an interactive medium enlivens the spaces and programs while expressing the unique luminous qualities of each locale and climate. Materials are transformed by their interactions with light, and light is transformed by the materials.

"We must remember that everything depends on how we use a material, not on the material itself. ... New materials are not necessarily superior. Each material is only what we make it."[3]

Mies van der Rohe, Architect

▷ Partial walls, two-story light wells, and wall openings foster visual connections between the top-floor galleries and the lower-level entry and support spaces. Clyfford Still Museum, Denver, Colorado, USA; Brad Cloepfil, Allied Works.

△ (Top) Aerial view of the museum illustrates the proximity of David Libeskind's Denver Art Museum Addition to the west. The Clyfford Still Museum is set back from the north side of the site to provide a public space, recessed landscape entry, and a quiet street presence.

Case study 5.1

Clyfford Still Museum

Denver, Colorado, USA

Brad Cloepfil, Allied Works Architecture

"Still's work, with the power of his color and contrast, the tactility of his surfaces, has never been shown in natural light. The entire body of the museum building is a source of light for his work—the fractured exterior surface dematerializes in light and shadow, the lobby presses darkness to the earth, then above—the liquid, heavy light of the galleries—is light that holds and awakens the work."[4]

Brad Cloepfil, Allied Works Architecture

◁ △ The sheltering façades are composed of vertically striated concrete walls, strategically located windows, and wood screens. Roof gardens on the northwest and southeast corners of the second floor overlook the neighboring city. A deeply-recessed entry provides a transition from the street into the museum.

LIGHT AND THE QUALITY OF PLACE

Clyfford Still

The paintings of artist Clyfford Still are animated by vivid natural light in the Clyfford Still Museum in Denver, Colorado, USA. As one of the most influential abstract expressionist painters of the 20th century, Still's work is known for its textural qualities, thick impasto, rich colors, dynamic forms, and large immersive scale. When Still died in 1980, his will bequeathed the body of his work to an unspecified American city that would create a museum dedicated solely to his roughly 3,125 paintings, drawings, and studies, created between 1920 and 1980. The city of Denver was chosen by Still's widow Patricia as the beneficiary of the estate, which contained 95 percent of his artwork. Brad Cloepfil describes the body of work to be housed in the museum that Allied Works Architecture (AWA) was subsequently hired to design: "His work is so powerful. It's a deeply spiritual work. It's elemental with emotive qualities from the form and color and contrast of light. ... All elements have to do with the power of the landscape where he grew up in South Dakota and eastern Washington. The paintings are beautiful in rooms made especially for that art that is as intimate as possible. It's a chapel to Clyfford."[5] While controversial as an artist during his lifetime, Still's impact has grown over the decades since his death, and his importance has been reinforced with the inauguration of the museum.

Site and Place

Located in Denver's civic center, just south of the Civic Center Park and west of the Colorado State Capital, the Clyfford Still Museum is in the heart of a dynamic arts community. It is in the company of other notable modern and contemporary works of architecture, including the Denver Art Museum's North Building by Gio Ponti, the Frederic C. Hamilton Building (Denver Art Museum addition) and museum residences by Daniel Libeskind, and the Central Library by Michael Graves.

Denver is at an elevation of 1,610 meters (5,280 feet) above sea level and is poised on the western edge of the High Plains of central

Colorado, at the eastern edge of the Rocky Mountains. Considered a cold semi-arid steppe climate, Denver is dry and mild, with four distinct seasons and extensive sunshine throughout the year. Water is a precious resource, with an average of 400 millimeters (15.7 inches) of rain per year in the form of intense thunderstorms and light showers during mid-summer. The winter months experience significant snowfall, with an average of 1,372 millimeters (54 inches) per year. An average low temperature of –7.2°C (19°F) occurs in December, and an average high of 30.5°C (87°F) in July. [6] Prevailing winds are from the south and southwest. The sun is an abundant resource in this predominately clear climate, with an average of 3,100 hours of sunshine per year. Located at 39.7° north latitude, the city experiences significant changes in the hours of daylight throughout the year, ranging from 9.5 to 15 hours on the winter and summer solstices. The solar altitude at noon varies seasonally from a low of 26.8° to a high of 73.8° on the corresponding winter and summer solstices.

Cloepfil clarifies his perspective on Denver and the influence of location: "The concept of building on the site is in response to Denver as a prairie town. It's a surface town, not a mountain town. We wanted this to be about the earth." [7] The 1-acre (0.4-hectare) rectilinear site is bound on the west by Libeskind's Frederic C. Hamilton Building (with its visually dynamic gestural form); to the north by Gio Ponti's original Denver Art Museum; to the south by

a two-story building, and by active streets to the west and north. Cloepfil set the museum back from the north boundary of the site to create a landscaped forecourt at the street entry, as he explains: "The first act prepares the site by creating a dense grove of deciduous trees—a place of shadow and light, a place of refuge from the endless summer sun. The second act of architecture looks to the earth, the weight and stillness of it. The new building derives its presence from the earth, pressing down into it, being held by it. The museum is conceived as a solid, a mass of concrete, crushed granite, and quartz—a single construction that is opened up by natural light. The body of the building becomes the source of light for the art. Light is amplified, diffused and obscured by each surface of the building." [8]

The site and landscape design, developed in collaboration with Reed Hilderbrand Associates, creates an urban refuge, with the building accessed through a series of thresholds created by an elevated landscape plinth, pathways, shaded grove of London plane trees, upper lawn, and benches. The layered site features create a quiet and contemplative transition into the Clyfford Still Museum.

LIGHT AND THE DESIGN INTENTIONS

Programmed Light
Unusual in housing only the work of a single artist, the mission of the Clyfford Still Museum is to "advance the understanding and

◁▷ Building plans and sections illustrate the internal focus and spatial and luminous interconnections. Windows are strategically located to provide sidelighting, while light shafts foster a visual connection between the two floors. Large skylights, partition walls, and openings ensure views and daylighting throughout the galleries.

N

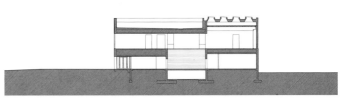

North–south

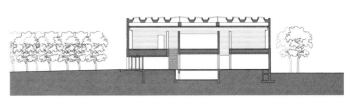

North–south

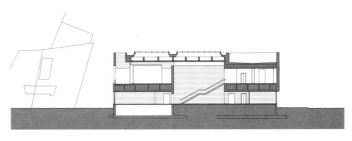

East–west

appreciation of Clyfford Still's art and legacy" through presentation, research, interpretation, preservation, and stewardship. [9] Daylight was an integral aspect of the programming. Christopher Rush, Senior Lighting Designer at Arup New York, explains how the artwork and the daylighting goals shaped the program: "It was decided early on that the character of the space, materials, and daylighting can embrace the mood of Clyfford Still's artwork. Brad [Cloepfil] really liked the idea of a moodiness, a raw emotion in all aspects of the building design and that influenced the daylight. One thing we took away from that was to embrace the variability of daylight on a particular day, or a week, or throughout the year. As clouds come and go. Not to actively manage it. Not to make it a uniform, sterile, consistent, constant condition—to accept this natural variation." [10]

Cloepfil emphasizes that natural light was at the heart of the design: "From the beginning, because Denver has 300 days of sunlight, the body of the building was to be [a] source of light from outside to inside. No one has ever seen the work in natural light. … Our mission was to make the paintings come alive in light." [11] While daylight was carefully considered throughout the museum, the design challenges in the galleries were to celebrate the changing character of natural light, create the desired mood and atmospheric quality, and to obtain an appropriately uniform distribution of light and illuminance levels on the gallery walls.

In response to the program and daylighting goals, the 7,648-square-meter (28,500-square-foot) museum is vertically zoned on two floors. More dynamic and variable daylight is allowed in the lower-level entry and public spaces, while strict conservation and lighting requirements are met within the upper galleries, including regulation of illuminance levels, distribution of light, ultraviolet radiation, color rendering, temperature, and relative humidity. The ground floor contains the entry lobby, reception area, research lab, storage and administration, archives, and circulation corridors, which include an exhibition of the historic timeline for the artist. Visitors are invited to circulate around the ground level to look into the conservation lab, painting storage, and archive areas. An elegant glass and wood staircase leads visitors to the nine upper-level galleries. Six of the painting galleries are illuminated by skylights, while light-sensitive works are exhibited in more intimate, electrically illuminated galleries. The upper level also includes an education gallery, a conference room, and two sheltered terraces on the southwest and northeast corners that provide screened views to the surrounding city.

▽ The entry lobby overlooks the recessed north entry and exterior landscape. A vertical wood screen wraps the threshold to mark a spatial and luminous transition between inside and outside.

Lightscape

A journey of discovery and surprise unfolds as visitors move from the landscaped exterior of the building to the light-filled interiors. On the outside, the sheltering enclosure is animated by a dramatic play of light and shadow as sunlight streams across the vertical striations of the concrete façades and wooden slats of the screened windows and terraces. As an internally focused building, direct visual connections to the site are provided only by recessed glazing at the north entry and select windows on the lower and upper floors. On entry to the museum, visitors are welcomed by expansive light-filled double-story volumes in the main stairway and circulation corridors that bring gentle indirect daylight from the upper floor while providing glimpses to the daylit galleries above. Ascending the stairway, visitors move through a sequence of daylit and electrically illuminated galleries, of varied size and intimacy, corresponding with the media, scale, and program requirements for the artworks.

LIGHT AND THE DESIGN STRATEGIES

Galleries and Liquid Heavy Light

In addition to creating a sublime mood and character of light, the galleries needed to meet practical conservation requirements and lighting goals, which were achieved through a combination of diffuse toplighting, vertically screened and filtered sidelighting, borrowed indirect light from adjacent galleries, and supplemental electric lighting. The intimate scale and relatively low height of the galleries, ranging from 3.6 to 4.9 meters (12 to 16 feet), enable visitors to engage with smaller drawings and to be fully immersed in the larger canvases.

Oriented on an east to west axis, the gallery skylights include translucent triple-glazing with an ultraviolet polyvinyl butyral (PVB) interlayer. Below the exterior glass surface is a deep 2.1-meter (7-foot) lightwell that reflects daylight before it enters the gallery. A shade with 50 percent visible light transmittance is provided within the skylight to mediate seasonal light levels and to darken the galleries. The perforated-concrete ceiling plane on the interior, which is suspended beneath the skylights, contains oval openings that provide 25 percent visible light transmittance into the gallery. Rooftop photo-sensors and dimming switches

▽ The low and sheltering ceiling of the lobby transitions into a variety of spatial experiences as floor plates open to two-story light shafts and the stairway leads to toplit galleries on the upper level.

△ Partial walls, view openings, and light shafts foster an interplay of light and space. Exterior roof terraces and gardens provide a sheltered exterior space to view the surrounding city.

coordinate the diurnal and seasonal integration of daylighting and electric lighting, which includes HIR PAR38 wallwashers for large paintings, and MR16 lamps for smaller works. Small heaters are integrated into the skylights to prevent condensation.

Light Alchemy

Cloepfil explored a variety of toplighting strategies for the galleries before choosing the deep skylight monitor and perforated-concrete interior screen: "I wanted it to be like the concrete was emitting light through the ceiling. I wanted the light to come through and off the concrete. I wanted the ceiling to be perforated in some way. We actually tried it with the structural engineers and it worked. It ended up being a quality of light I've never seen before." [12]

The transformation of concrete, a heavy-mass material, into a seemingly ethereal light-emitting surface distinguishes this design solution from other contemporary daylit museums, as Cloepfil emphasized: "Something magic happened here, that's the way it felt to me. There's design intention and then there's experiential phenomenon and in this case, the experience was so much richer than we hoped. When we work with our structural engineers we talk about concrete being alchemy, but daylight is *really* alchemy." [13] The ceiling structure and its interaction with natural light provide a dramatic visual counterpoint to the bold and textural paintings in the galleries below.

LIGHT AND THE ART OF MAKING

Material Light

Reminiscent of the heavy impasto of Still's paintings, the striated concrete surfaces on the museum's exterior and interior include vertical fins with rough edges that were created using two depths of formwork with beveled edges and varied gaps. Cloepfil

◁ Intimate electrically-illuminated galleries for small light-sensitive works complement the larger daylit galleries for paintings.

describes his fascination with concrete: "Concrete is like alchemy, you add a little of this or a little of that and you can make it into an entirely different entity. I love the mystery of concrete and how much it can do."[14] He characterizes the surfaces as "corduroy concrete," with the textured surfaces fostering a dynamic play of light and shadow, and is delighted that, in the galleries, the appearance of heavy concrete could be transformed in density and weight through form and detail, while at the same time creating a water-like quality of light: "The choices you make to model and shape the light, give the light a particular presence."[15] Cloepfil sought a presence and tactile character of daylight in the galleries, as he explains: "There is awareness of the [ceiling] filter. ... The pattern wasn't a geometric pattern that you recognize. The surface quality is like water. It has that quality; it's not an obvious pattern, but a ripple of light, it has a sense of water."[16] As though immersed in an underwater world with a dappled play of light on the surface, the abundant sunlight is transformed to diffuse light by the depth of the skylight and perforated concrete surface of the light-emitting ceiling. Rough concrete walls, rainscreens of western red cedar, stained white oak-wood casework, polished concrete floors, and an elegant wood and glass staircase bring visual and tactile warmth to the interiors.

◁ An overhead plane of soft diffuse daylight illuminates the second-floor galleries. The abundant sunlight in Denver enters the translucent glazing of the east–west skylights, reflects off the white walls of the deep light well, and is further diffused through the ovoid perforations of the concrete ceiling screen.

▷ Early concept studies exploring the spatial organization and luminous concepts in plan and section.

▽ Construction detail of the concrete ceiling screen.

Performance and Process

Allied Works Architecture used diverse design methods and processes to explore, develop, and refine the project. Early design phases included charcoal and pastel concept studies, freehand sketches, iterative concept diagrams and models, freehand and digital renderings, photo-collages, and conceptual material studies. Physical and digital studies were critical in the early phases, as Cloepfil explains: "The way we work on this kind of project is with physical models, which you can see in front of you and turn around, or to work in a digital 3D space that you can work on quickly. The Clyfford Still Museum was the first project where we explored the interior of the building through a digital 3D model study. We made sure that we could see through the building the way we wanted to, that everything was supporting the experience we were after."[17] As the design scenarios coalesced, more detailed qualitative rendered studies were done using Rhino, SketchUp, and Maxwell Render as well as physical and computer daylight models.

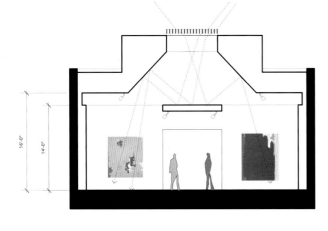

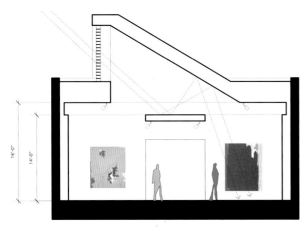

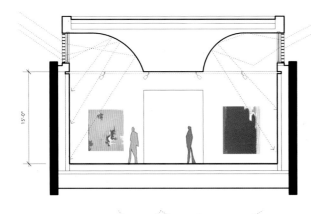

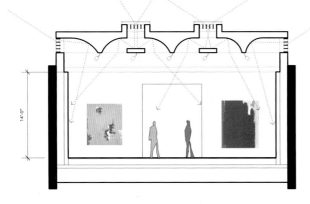

△ Early conceptual section studies explore methods of admitting daylight and mediating heat gains, and solar control.

Collaborations with Brian Stacy and Christopher Rush, engineers at Arup New York, were essential in realizing the desired quality and atmosphere while meeting lighting performance goals. Rush explained the daylight design process: "We used small-scale physical models with accurate geometry and computer simulations throughout the design process to be sure we were on target and that the design allowed some flexibility. ... This caliber of project usually includes a full-scale mock-up to fine-tune the design when the gallery is nearly complete and to do some measurements for exterior conditions so the interior condition tracked with predictions. In the final stages of this design we did a full-scale mock-up for one section of gallery on the ground next to building while it was under construction. This was a last check to confirm everything ... and it was partially a confidence booster to be comfortable with the construction, the skylight details, water proofing, finishes ... and that the daylight levels were correct." [18]

Iterative physical and computer models and on-site construction tests verified that the design was successful at meeting conservation goals of limiting daylight exposure to less than 65,000 footcandle-hours per year (65Kfc-h) while achieving a consistent 20-footcandle (215.2-lux) illuminance on the gallery walls at a 1.5-meter (5-feet) height. Arup described their approach to lighting targets: "[The] approach was based on cumulative exposure on the art for a typical year instead of maximum illuminance at any one time. The Museum agreed with this, enabling the daylight systems to be designed for appropriate annual exposure, rather than the single brightest hour of the year." [19]

The integration of daylighting strategies, daylight photo-sensors, dimming controls, high-performance glazing, and electric lighting systems resulted in an electric lighting power density of 0.062 watt per square meter (0.67 watt per square foot), with exclusions, for a code compliance at 30 percent below ASHRAE 90.1-2004 standards. [20] Mechanical, electrical, and plumbing engineers worked with the design team to optimize other building systems and overall performance. A demand-control ventilation system with CO_2 sensors adjusts fresh air based on occupancy loads and reduces the volume of air that is conditioned, while monitoring humidity and temperature. Arup, which had also provided the engineering services for the Frederic C. Hamilton Building by Libeskind, proposed and developed shared building systems. By absorbing excess chilled water and hot water capacity from the neighboring building, steam-to-hot-water heat exchangers and other accessories were eliminated from the Clyfford Still Museum. [21]

▷ (Top and bottom) A variety of design methods and tools were used to explore and develop the architecture, daylighting, and construction details, including concept studies, iterative massing models, physical daylight models, sketches, rendering, performance analyses, energy assessments, and full-scale on-site physical mock-ups.

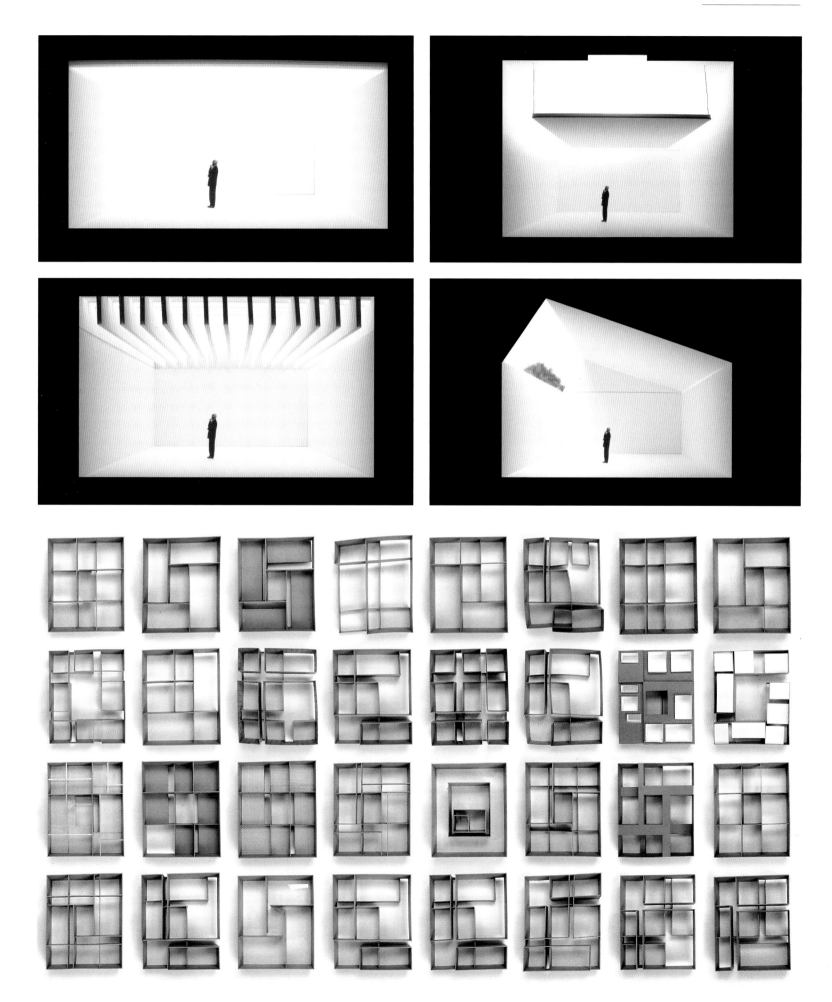

◁ Computer renderings of varied daylight, structure, and material strategies using Maxwell Render. Detailed quantitative daylighting analyses with Arup included large-scale physical daylight models, performance assessment with Radiance, and full-scale mock-ups.

LIGHT INSPIRATIONS

At the Clyfford Still Museum, Cloepfil has achieved a meaningful conversation between the body of art and the body of architecture. Light, materials, structure, and space come together to create a tangible architectural and luminous presence that complements and reveals the power and mystery of Clyfford Still's artwork. Celebrating the natural variations of daylight as it interacts with physical materials and space is an essential design concern. The diverse design processes and methods used by Brad Cloepfil and Allied Works enable direct engagement with the physical and emotional potential of daylight as a dynamic building material. Cloepfil underscores the way in which the experience of light and material influenced the firm's choice of design processes and methods: "We'd want any tool we use to help us realize our vision for what the space is going to be like, in terms of its experience. I'd say that materials are key, light is key, and the order of the space is key." [22]

For Cloepfil, design always returns to creating a meaningful human experience in which light plays an essential role: "The goal is that architecture should move you in a way you haven't been moved before. ... Moments of wonder are what we all want." [23]

▽ Detail of the material juxtaposition of the glass railings, striated concrete partition walls and ceilings, and the seemingly ephemeral perforated-concrete ceiling screen.

DESIGN PROFILE

1. Building Profile
Project: Clyfford Still Museum
Location: Denver, Colorado, USA
Architect: Allied Works Architecture
Client: Clyfford Still Museum
Building Type: Museum
Square Footage: 2,648 sq m; 929 sq m exhibition galleries (28,500 sq ft; 10,000 sq ft)
Estimated Cost: $29m ($15.5m construction)
Completion: 2011

2. Professional Team
Design Principal: Brad Cloepfil
Project Lead: Chris Bixby
Project Team: Brad Cloepfil, Chris Bixby, Dan Koch, Brent Linden, Susan Barnes, Robin Wilcox, Scott Miller, Chelsea Grassinger, Andrew Hamblin, Jonathan Ledesma, Emily Kappes, Matthew Bunza, Elliot Meier
Landscape Design: Reed Hilderbrand Associates
Structural Engineering: KPFF Consulting Engineers
Mechanical Engineering: Arup
Lighting Design: Arup
Project Management: Romani Group Inc.
General Constructor: Saunders Construction Inc.
Photographer: Jeremy Bittermann

3. Climate Profile
Climate (Köppen-Geiger Climate Classification System): BSk: cold semi-arid steppe climate
Latitude: 39.7° north latitude
Solar Angles: Noon
June 21: 73.8°
March/September 21: 50.3°
December 21: 26.8°
Length of Day: Approximate Hours of Daylight from Sunrise to Sunset
June 21: 14h 59m
March/September 21: 12h 12m
December 21: 9h 21m
Heating Degree Days: 3219 heating degree days °C (5955 heating degree days °F) (18°C and 65°F base temperature) [24]
Cooling Degree Days: 906 cooling degree days °C (906 cooling degree days °F) (18°C and 65°F base temperature) [25]

4. Design Strategies
Daylighting Strategies:
1) Sidelighting: Entry sidelighting; select interior sidelighting for views and illumination; and borrowed daylight between interior rooms, and 2) Toplighting: gallery skylights include translucent triple-glazing with an ultraviolet polyvinyl butyral (PVB) interlayer, deep skylight well, and concrete perforated screen at ceiling; daylight photo-sensors; and select interior openings for borrowed daylight between floors.
Sustainable Design and High-Performance Strategies: High-performance envelope, glazing, mechanical systems, electric lighting, and control systems; demand-control ventilation with CO_2 sensors to adjust the fresh air based on occupancy loads and reduce the volume of air that is conditioned; and shared building systems with the Frederic C. Hamilton Building.
Renewable Energy Strategies: None.
Energy: 0.062 watt per square meter (0.67 watt per square foot) with exclusions. [26]
Code Compliance: 30 percent below ASHRAE 90.1-2004. [27]

Allied Works: Structure and Materials

The exploded diagram illustrates the structural and material organization of the museum. Strategically placed windows admit sidelighting through the concrete façades, while skylights provide abundant toplighting on the upper floor. Two-story light shafts bring daylight to the lower level and visually connect the ground and upper floors. Two terrace spaces on the upper floor provide screened views of the surrounding city.

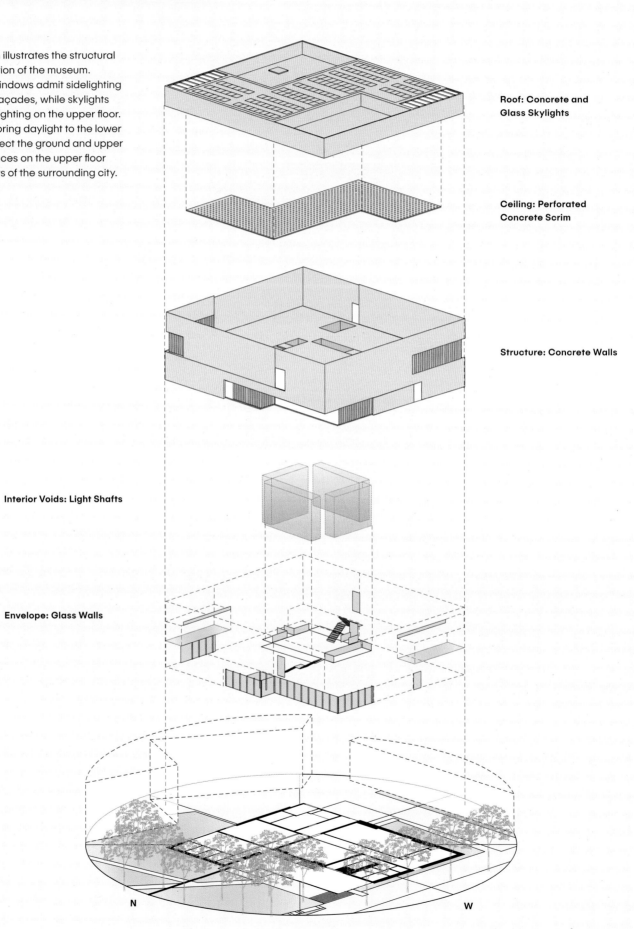

Roof: Concrete and Glass Skylights

Ceiling: Perforated Concrete Scrim

Structure: Concrete Walls

Interior Voids: Light Shafts

Envelope: Glass Walls

N   W

The upper west–east section illustrates views to the site, sky, and interior spaces. The lower north–south section illustrates the inter-connection between the ground-floor and second-floor galleries through the two-story light shafts. The top-floor galleries are illuminated by skylights that include translucent triple-glazing with an ultraviolet interlayer, deep light well, and perforated concrete screen to diffuse and redistribute daylight within the gallery.

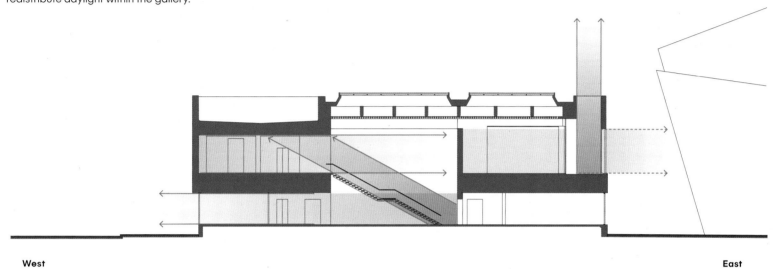

West

East

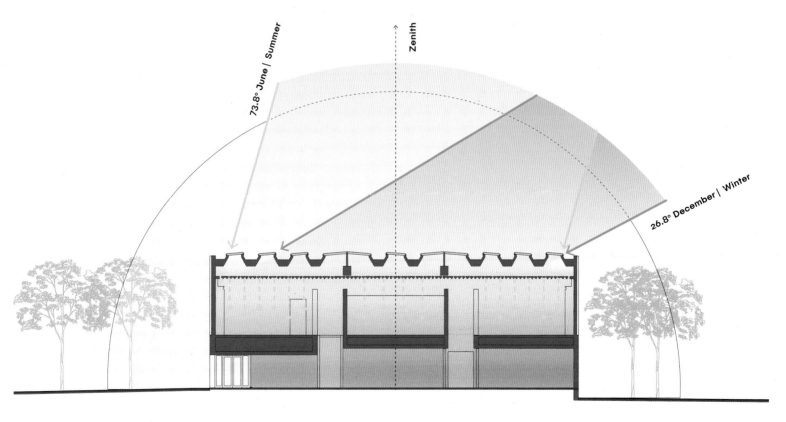

North

South

Arup Daylight Analysis: Solar Exposure, Illuminance, and Luminance

Lighting consultants at Arup worked with architects to develop design concepts, evaluate strategies, and to refine construction details for the climate and geographic location (39.7° north latitude). In the upper image, Radiance software is used to evaluate the integration of daylighting and electric lighting, the center image explores the annual sun exposure on façades and roofs (hours per year), and the lower image illustrates the illuminance levels in daylight factor. (The DF% is the ratio of daylight inside the structure compared to the daylight outside at the same time and under overcast sky conditions.)

Daylight and electric light rendering

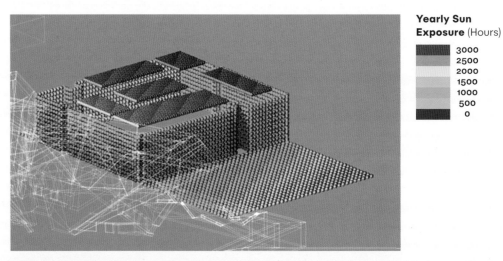

Yearly Sun Exposure (Hours)

	3000
	2500
	2000
	1500
	1000
	500
	0

Yearly sun exposure

Daylight Factor (DF%)

	85.5
	45.7
	24.5
	9.5
	2.7
	0.8
	0.4
	0.2

Illuminance in daylight factor (DF%)

Arup used physical scale models, full-scale room mock-ups, and computer simulations to develop and refine design strategies and details. The upper images illustrate a physical daylight model to test design strategies and daylight performance within a select gallery. The lower images illustrate Radiance computer simulations to evaluate the visual comfort, lighting quality, and luminance (in nits). Luminance, or the light reflected from a surface, is measured in candela/square meter (Standard International Units) or nits (Imperial Units). The analyses illustrate the even distribution of daylight on room surfaces and relatively uniform brightness to ensure visual comfort and lighting performance.

Daylight physical model

Luminance
(nits)

	0.75
	0.65
	0.55
	0.45
	0.35
	0.25
	0.15
	0.05

Luminance study (nits), above, and light rendering (right)

◁ Detail of the sheltering brick wall that wraps the perimeter of the center. Glazed Danish bricks of varying sizes and view openings create a sense of shelter while allowing glimpses of the surrounding community and landscape.

Case study 5.2

Maggie's Centre, Lanarkshire

Airdrie, North Lanarkshire, Scotland, UK

Neil Gillespie, Reiach and Hall Architects

"I was interested in whether we could make a very modest building, a building that made people feel comfortable, a simple goal. We had no real intention to create a masterpiece or an icon. We were interested in creating a very different atmosphere from the hospital. Most of our interest was on materials, light—particularly daylight—and gardens. And how we use the building related to the outside and to living things like grass and trees."[28]

Neil Gillespie, Reiach and Hall

△ View of the south façade and the perforated brick wall that defines the boundaries of the center and interior gardens.

LIGHT AND THE QUALITY OF PLACE

Maggie's Centres

Over the past three decades, leading architects from around the world have designed, or are planning, more than twenty Maggie's Centres at National Health Service (NHS) hospital sites in the United Kingdom and abroad. In 1995, co-founder and landscape architect Maggie Keswick Jencks developed a "blueprint" for a facility that provides personalized support for patients, families, and friends of cancer patients, based on her experience of living with cancer. After Maggie's death in 1995, her husband, architect Charles Jencks, continued to work with her former oncology nurse Laura Lee (now Chief Executive of Maggie's), Marcia Blakenham (Vice-Chairman), and others to launch the first Maggie's Centre at Western General Hospital in Edinburgh in 1996. The recently completed Maggie's Lanarkshire, designed by Neil Gillespie of Reiach and Hall Architects, demonstrates how architecture, daylighting, and landscape design can support health and well-being.

Scottish Light

Maggie's Lanarkshire is located in Airdrie, Scotland, which has a warm temperate climate with mild and wet weather and overcast skies much of the year. Winters tend to be cold and overcast, with mild springs and relatively cool summers. Rainfall and periodic snow occur throughout the fall and winter. Average temperatures range from 3.7°C (38.6°F) in January, to 15.1°C (59.1°F) in July.[29] In describing the quality of light in Scotland, architect Neil Gillespie reflected on diurnal and seasonal transitions: "In the summer, the nights are short, it's still daylight until nine o'clock in the evening. Winter daylight is only until half-past two in the afternoon. In the winter and autumn we have very short days. I'm interested in twilight. We live in a zone where we have long twilights, lights are not switched off suddenly. There are long periods of 'gloaming'; this is an in-between light. I enjoy that as a philosophy. The architecture in a sense is slightly in the shadows … and shaped by light."[30]

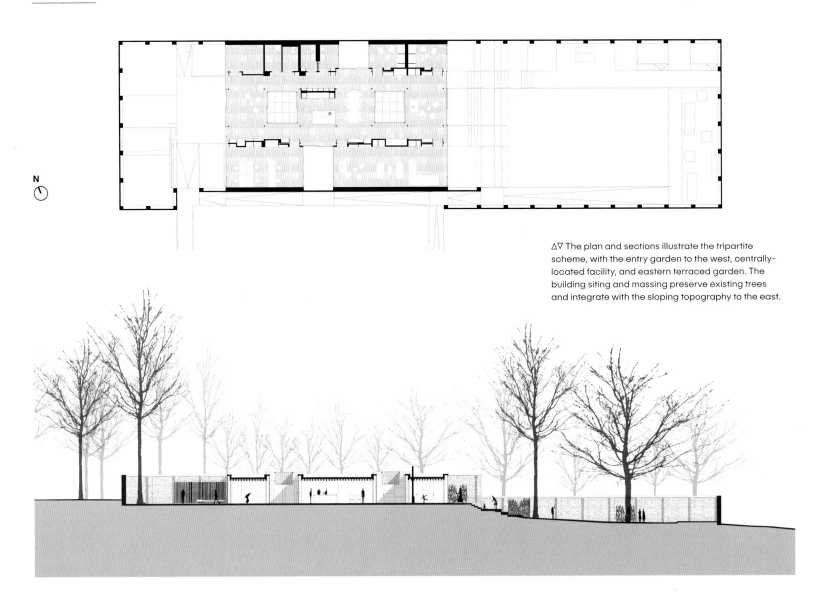

N

△▽ The plan and sections illustrate the tripartite
scheme, with the entry garden to the west, centrally-
located facility, and eastern terraced garden. The
building siting and massing preserve existing trees
and integrate with the sloping topography to the east.

Located at 55.9° north latitude, the seasonal extremes in daylight extend from 7 to 17 hours respectively on the winter and summer solstices, with twilight persisting throughout the summer nights. The maximum noon sun altitudes are 10.6° and 57.6° on the winter and summer solstices.

LIGHT AND THE DESIGN INTENTIONS

Maggie's Program

Maggie's Centres provide free nonmedical services to any person needing care during cancer treatment, including stress management, dietary assistance, exercise and relaxation, work and benefits advice, caregiver support, emotional and psychological counseling, spiritual guidance, and bereavement support. Architect, critic, and co-founder, Charles Jencks, explains that Maggie's Centres have a hybrid program: "It is like a house which is not a home, a collective hospital which is not an institution, a church which is not religious, and an art gallery which is not a museum ... the amalgam makes them more effective in carrying forward their work. Why? ... it creates a sense that everyone is in it together, patients and fundraisers, carers [caregivers] and those who drop in for tea, staff and doctors. This informal continuity, the mixture, overcomes the sense of isolation."[31] Architect Neil Gillespie emphasizes that the center is designed first and foremost to create a supportive environment for the patients and staff, while project architect Laura Kinnaird describes the architecture as part of the "everyday backdrop" of the programs and activities.

Garden Spaces

Located on a former estate bequeathed to the community in 1919 by Sir John Wilson, Maggie's Lanarkshire is on the grounds of the Monkland Hospital, approximately 25 kilometers (15 miles) east of Glasgow. Reiach and Hall Architects (RHA) artfully transformed a parking lot on the northern boundary of the property into a sequence of healing spaces and gardens, as RHA explain: "The design ... is simply a tale of enclosed gardens. ... The literal meaning of paradise is a 'walled enclosure' from *pairi-* 'around' and *-diz* 'to create a wall'. ... The brick walls of the new Maggie's take up these ideas of paradise, enclosure, and fence."[32]

Despite the proximity of the adjacent hospital, parking area, and neighbors, the facility celebrates the beauty and healing qualities of nature through carefully screened gardens, inner courts, nature views, and the changing qualities of light.

The landscape and building comprise a sequence of intimate spaces that move from the hospital grounds into a garden retreat. Oriented along an east–west axis, a perforated brick wall weaves between existing lime trees to define the rectilinear boundary of the gardens and building. Using a tripartite scheme, the center is located between a west and an east garden, which creates a calm and relaxing environment, as explained by Laura Kinnaird: "The entrance garden is a moment of reflection. The sound of the rill [stream] has a calm movement. You're immersed in a garden, which slows everything down. You enter a light-filled space with light punctures down into the center of the plan. You can always look from one end of building and ... meander to arrive in a larger garden. It's a journey between two gardens that metaphor [the] inside and outside."[33]

The west-entry garden is an informal and welcoming space with a small terrace, bench, and water feature. On entering the building, glazed walls and four inner courts provide direct views to both gardens and the sky. On passing through the building, the east garden opens into a series of landscape terraces. Described by RHA as a place for "dignified reflection," the terraces terminate in a still

◁ The main entry at the southwest corner of the center allows visual access into the west garden to create a welcoming first impression.

▽ ▷ A landscaped entry and floor-to ceiling glazing provides visual transparency for visitors and an informal residential quality. The west garden includes seating, native plantings, and a sculptural element with moving water.

pool of water to provide a quiet contemplative space that reflects the moods and qualities of the sky and provides a prospect over the healing gardens.

LIGHT AND THE DESIGN STRATEGIES

Inside-Outside

Gillespie's intention was to draw visitors gently into the garden and through the building by creating soft thresholds and transparency: "We create a wall which goes around a series of trees; but the wall itself is perforated so you can see through it before entering the garden. You haven't entered the building but you have already crossed a threshold. This is one of the biggest problems Maggie's has, particularly with men, which is to get them to come to the center. ... The first garden acts as a threshold. The reason the building is quite glassy is so that you're looking through the building and it's not a huge decision to enter. I'm trying to 'de-risk' the entry; so you can see [what's] ahead." [34]

On approach, visitors catch glimpses of the garden and transparent building through the perforated brick wall. A seating area in the garden provides a place to pause to experience the landscape without having to enter the building. Gillespie explains his intentions behind the building transparency: "[Visitors] can see through the plan. At the entrance there's no reception desk, just tables and chairs. You can pick up a leaflet and leave. The notion of the building is that if you drift through it, you end in another garden at the other end." [35]

Within the rectilinear form, an alternating rhythm of exterior and interior gardens on the east–west axis dissolves the boundaries between building and landscape. On the north–south axis, the building is organized into three zones, with the most intimate private counseling and meeting areas to the north, the most public areas of the kitchen and informal gathering spaces in the middle, and group gathering areas to the south. The kitchen is the heart of the building, as Gillespie explains: "Virtually all Maggie's plans evolve from the kitchen table, around having somewhere to go from the moment you enter the building. Our plan too develops from the kitchen table outwards to the courtyards, the trees and beyond."[36] Long views to the gardens and inner courts are afforded throughout, with diagonal views provided between strategic openings in the interior walls.

The rectilinear mass is relieved by four interior courts that provide intimate internal gardens, enhance transparency and daylight at the heart of the building, and introduce sky views and toplighting. Two centrally located courts are glazed on all sides, with sliding doors allowing access to seating areas that open to the sky. Gold-colored stainless steel light-catchers are suspended in the roof opening to reflect light and frame the changing weather and sky. The highly polished light-catchers have small triangular perforations to admit a dappled play of sunlight on clear days. Gillespie collaborated with architect and lighting designer Jonathan Speirs of Speirs + Major to design the light-catchers: "The eye goes through [the] courtyard; but we wanted to put something in the [space]. … We didn't want to put a tree in it, so we devised a sculptural object. It's different than other objects in the interior. Instead of [being] soft and absorbing, the light-catcher captures

◁ △ Large floor-to-ceiling glass walls on the east and west provide direct views through the center to adjacent gardens. Meeting areas are located to the south, community gathering spaces in the center, and private meeting areas to the north. Two centrally-located courtyards bring toplighting to the heart of the building. Two additional courtyards are located on the perimeter of the north and south walls.

△ A refined palette of materials creates an informal, welcoming, and relaxed atmosphere, including Finnish birch walls, white-stained pine ceilings, and limed-oak floors

▷ View of the sky through the gold stainless steel light-catcher in a central courtyard, providing a protected "inside-outside" space at the center of the facility.

light and reflects it; it sparkles. Eyes are lifted up—rather than horizontally—to the canopy of the big trees and the sky." [37]

In contrast, the two courts on the north and south perimeter walls have sliding glass doors with views into the intimate garden and through the perforated brick wall to the surrounding site. The height, depth, and porosity of the openings in the brick walls are designed to filter seasonal solar gains while allowing a visual connection to the site. Simple interior drapes provide flexibility to adjust views, privacy, lighting levels, and admission of sunlight.

Healing Atmosphere
Maggie's provides an atmosphere of welcoming comfort, safety, and discovery from the moment of arrival. Gillespie explained that the quality of light and shadow were priorities: "Shadow is as important as light. There is active light and shade throughout the building. You can sit in the shadow; there are different opportunities and moods." [38] Views are carefully choreographed to frame nature, changing

△ ▷ A perimeter courtyard admits daylight while providing privacy and screened views of the landscape. Operable windows and interior drapes adjust the quality of space, light, and air. Furnishings and electric lighting are flexible to reconfigure spaces for varied programs and activities

weather, and seasons while ensuring privacy. Spatial, structural, and material order underlies the project to support the calming atmosphere, as Kinnaird discussed: "There is a design rigor and much work behind the scenes with architectural detailing. It's a very considered work, yet there is a casualness and relaxedness to the building. It feels non-intimidating. Everyone says it's bright and friendly. There's no [architectural] moment that doesn't belong. That allows Maggie's [staff] to do what they do well. The architecture is not in conflict with them."[39] The visual arts also foster a sense of beauty and inspiration. Poems by the poet Thomas Clark are engraved into the water elements in both gardens, while contemporary paintings by Alan Johnston and Steven Aalders grace the entry and gathering spaces.

LIGHT AND THE ART OF MAKING

Structured and Material Light
RHA are renowned for their exquisite architectural craft and elegant detailing. Gillespie explains that RHA's founder Alan Reiach admired the work of Alvar Aalto and other early modern Scandinavian architects. Following in this tradition, Maggie's Lanarkshire expresses a clear structural and material order, yet creates a feeling of warmth and friendliness with finishes, detailing, and light. The building is given form by three structural elements: 1) a "perforated brick screen wall" that weaves between existing trees to define the boundaries of the site; 2) a "grove of columns" to define the building interior; and 3) a "tartan grid" that overlies the site and building.

Of particular importance is the design and material quality of the perforated brick wall, which defines a sense of enclosure without isolating the visitor from the hospital community and site, as Gillespie explains: "It's a filter ... the wall was slightly perforated;

but not [with] a mechanical perforation. We use a repetitive pattern [and] introduced a rogue brick. ... It's an active surface, with a number of different goals."[40] Constructed of handmade white Danish bricks, the wall uses nine different sizes, including a longer Kolumba brick, which contributes to the complex pattern. With subtle irregularities from the hand-crafting process, the brick wall conveys a human scale and an informal luminous quality as light is admitted through patterned openings.

Interior materials and finishes were chosen to create a warm, yet flexible, atmospheric quality, as Kinnaird explained: "You can create your own environment and rooms can do different things. One day [a space is] quiet, dark, and inwardly focused or bright and purposefully happy. Our approach is to give Maggie's a light and airy building that is easy to read and dress with curtains and fabric and furnishing to make moods. It's about a series of rooms that can be set up with four or five different levels of subtle detail."[41]

Walls of Finnish birch, white-stained pine ceilings, and limed-oak floors respond to the changing qualities of Scotland's weather and seasons, as Gillespie explains: "We were interested in creating a very mellow set of interiors that are very soft. We know Scottish light and its low [sun] angle. Light is coming through a lot more atmosphere and is softer. We lightened every material. The ceiling is stained white and we took almost all the saturation out of the colors. The weak northern light is received by surfaces that are sensitive. There is no strong color so we create an atmosphere that is very soft and quiet."[42]

◁ View of the east façade, terraces, and native gardens. The transparency of the building allows direct views through the glazed façades to each garden.

Seasonal Lighting

The integration of daylighting and electric lighting was developed in collaboration with Speirs + Major. Physical models were used during the early design phases to study the building form and light courts and to assess seasonal conditions. Gillespie underscores the importance of physical models to assess daylight strategies and to experience the seasonal atmosphere and material qualities: "There is no shortcut to really understanding space from your own experience. What we try to do is make models. You can stick your head in [the physical model] and imagine them as a real place. You have a sense of material you can't get in a drawing." [43] Given the short winter days, the daylighting and electric lighting were considered in response to the dramatic shift from summer to winter.

Kinnaird clarified that the building design "always maximizes daylight in any season," from long daylight hours in summer to the long nights of winter. Electric lighting is integrated quietly into the architectural structure and interior details. Wallwashers provide soft reflected light at the boundaries of the room, while downlights illuminate the volume of space as needed. Task lighting is located strategically to provide higher levels of illumination at desk surfaces, reading areas, and in gathering spaces.

▽ Site and building physical massing models, digital renderings, and detail models were used to study the building and daylighting design.

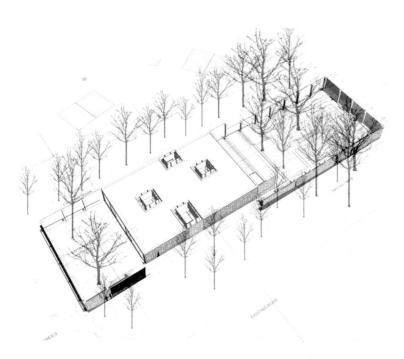

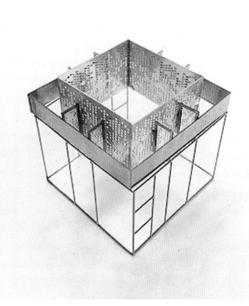

LIGHT INSPIRATIONS

Maggie's Lanarkshire demonstrates that health and well-being can be fostered through tangible design strategies, including physical connections to nature; strategic views and visual relief; quiet material qualities; integration of art; and by enabling users to interact with and adjust space and light. Reiach and Hall worked intimately with the clients to develop the healing character and type of spaces that best support the day-to-day activities and changing needs of the center's staff and visitors. While the overall building form and section are shaped to admit daylight throughout the year, luminous and spatial flexibility are ensured by furniture, drapes, and electric lighting that can be adjusted to create individual atmospheric qualities that support different activities and desired moods. A restrained form, elegantly modest structure, and refined materials and details result in a simple yet healing environment that provides a place of rest and renewal, supported by nature and the changing moods of Scottish light.

▽ The changing forces of nature, light, and time are woven into the healing design concepts of the building and landscape design. Detail of the glazed Danish brick wall and exterior landscape terrace on the east.

DESIGN PROFILE

1. Building Profile
Project: Maggie's Centre, Lanarkshire
Location: Airdrie, Scotland, UK
Architect: Reiach and Hall Architects
Client: Maggie Keswick Jencks Cancer Caring Centres Trust
Building Type: Healthcare
Square Footage: 300 sq m (3,229 sq ft)
Completion: 2014
Estimated Cost: £1.8m

2. Professional Team
Architect: Neil Gillespie
General Contractor: John Dennis
Structural Engineer: SKM
Engineering: KJ Tait
Lighting Design: Speirs + Major
Light-catchers: Jonathan Speirs
Quantity Surveyor: CBA
Landscape Architect: Rankin Fraser Landscape Architecture
CDM Coordinator: Alexander Project Management

3. Climate Profile
Climate (Köppen-Geiger Climate Classification System): Cfb: maritime temperate climate
Latitude: 55.9° north latitude
Solar Angles: Noon
June 21: 57.6°
March/September 21: 34.1°
December 21: 10.6°
Length of Day: Approximate Hours of Daylight from Sunrise to Sunset
June 21: 17h 35m
March/September 21: 12h 15m
December 21: 6h 59m
Heating Degree Days: 3398 heating degree days °C (6331 heating degree days °F) (18°C and 65°F base temperature) [44]
Cooling Degree Days: 16 cooling degree days °C (24 cooling degree days °F) (18°C and 65°F base temperature) [45]

4. Design Strategies
Daylighting Strategies:
1) Sidelighting: east and west floor-to-ceiling glazing; sidelit interior light courts; borrowed sidelighting throughout interior, and 2) Toplighting: four interior toplit light courts with borrowed sidelighting to interior spaces.
Sustainable Design and High-Performance Strategies:
High-performance envelope, glazing, mechanical systems, and electric lighting.
Renewable Energy Strategies:
None.

Reiach and Hall: Structure and Materials

The exploded diagram illustrates the tripartite scheme with the building wrapped by a perforated brick wall and bracketed on the west and east by gardens. The post-and-beam structure is open to sidelighting on the east and west and punctured with four courtyards to bring light to the heart and boundaries of the building.

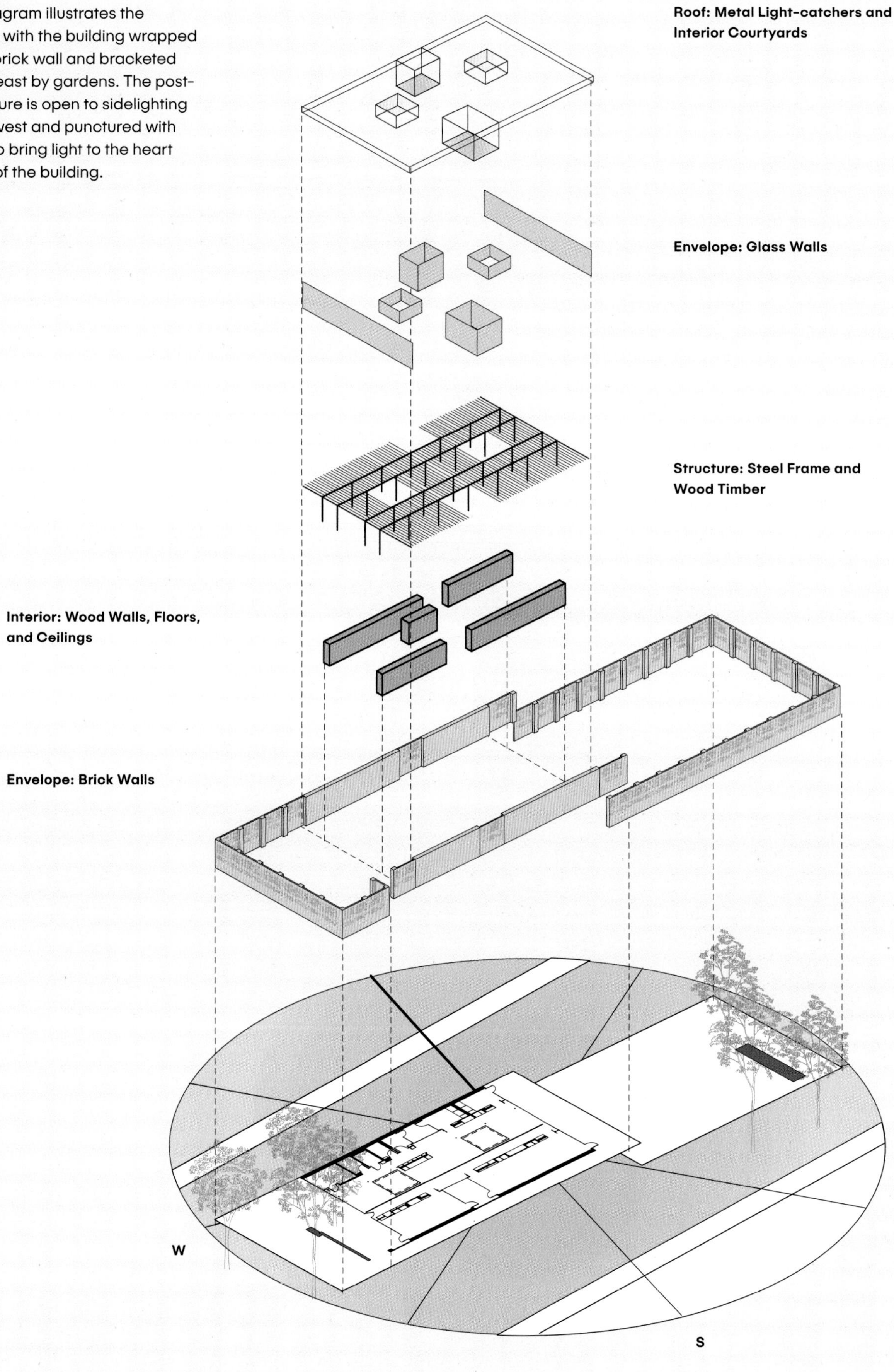

Roof: Metal Light-catchers and Interior Courtyards

Envelope: Glass Walls

Structure: Steel Frame and Wood Timber

Interior: Wood Walls, Floors, and Ceilings

Envelope: Brick Walls

W

S

The upper diagram illustrates the visual transparency of the building, with long views from the west entry through the building to the east garden. Glazed walls and openings allow diagonal interior views, while courtyards provide views of the sky and surrounding site. The lower diagram illustrates the integration of east and west sidelighting with toplighting in the courtyards.

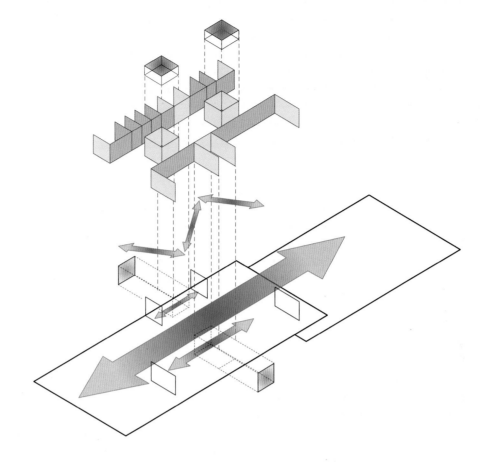

Enclosure and Gardens

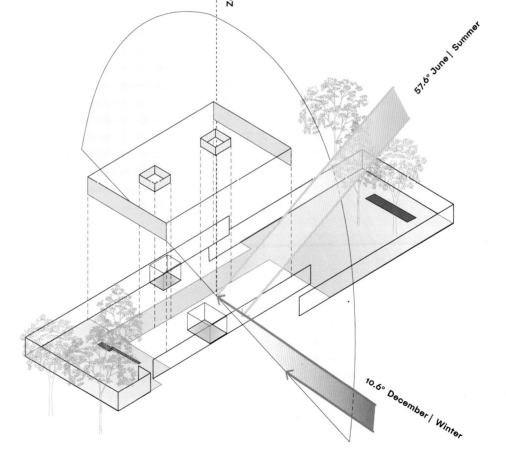

Daylight Analysis: Seasonal Plans

Illuminance studies (in lux) illustrate the seasonal and diurnal light levels and distribution. Sidelighting is provided by the floor-to-ceiling glazing on the west and east façades. Toplighting enters through the four interior courtyards. Daylight changes dramatically on a seasonal basis due to latitude (57.6° north latitude) and varying length of day (17h 35m on June 21 and 6h 59m on December 21).

Sunny Sky Illuminance (Lux)

——————	1000
——————	875
——————	750
——————	625
——————	500
——————	376
——————	251
——————	126

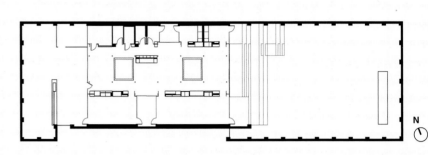

N

December 21

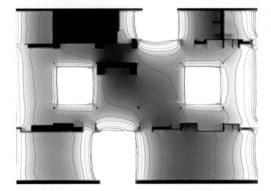

9:00 am

March/September 21

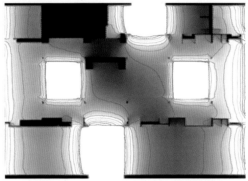

June 21

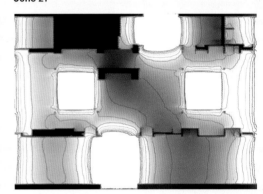

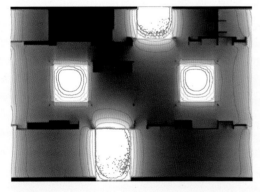

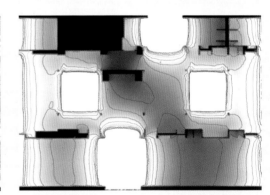

12:00 pm

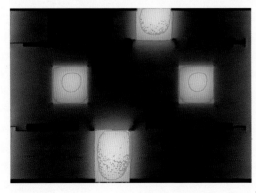

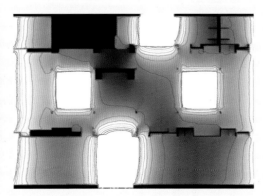

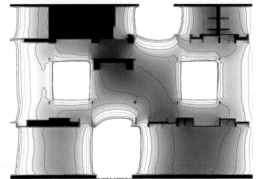

3:00 pm

Seasonal Perspectives_Looking West

Seasonal perspective renderings illustrate the visual quality of daylight and the movement of sunlight within the building on the solstices and equinoxes. Toplighting from the courtyards balances sidelighting from the west and east façades

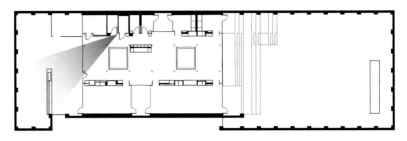

N

December 21

March/September 21

June 21

9:00 am

12:00 pm

3:00 pm

Equinox Walk-Through

Perspective renderings and luminance studies (in candela/square meter; cd/m2) illustrate the visual quality of daylight and contrast ratios from four view locations within the building during the equinoxes (March/September 21 at noon). Light-reflecting finishes, glazed façades, and courtyards ensure a relatively uniform surface brightness throughout the building, with the highest contrast located in direct sunlight and at the window wall. Interior shading controls visual comfort, glare, direct sunlight, and solar gains on a seasonal basis.

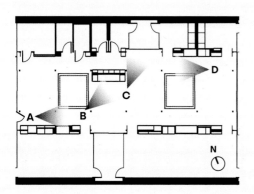

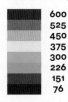

Sunny Sky
Luminance (Cd/m²)

	600
	525
	450
	375
	300
	226
	151
	76

View A: March/September 21 at 12:00 pm

View A: March/September 21 at 12:00 pm

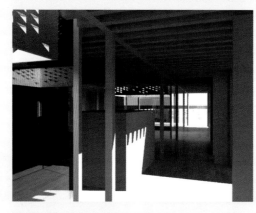

View B: March/September 21 at 12:00 pm

View B: March/September 21 at 12:00 pm

View C: March/September 21 at 12:00 pm

View C: March/September 21 at 12:00 pm

View D: March/September 21 at 12:00 pm

View D: March/September 21 at 12:00 pm

Chapter 5: endnotes

Introduction

1 Henry Plummer, *The Architecture of Natural Light*, New York: The Monacelli Press, 2009, 218.

2 Peter Zumthor, *Peter Zumthor Atmospheres: Architectural Environments—Surrounding Objects*, Basel: Birkhäuser, 2012, 22.

3 Mies van der Rohe, "Ludwig Mies van der Rohe Quotes," *Art Quotes*, http://www.art-quotes.com/auth_search.php?authid=6340#.V5thGugrIps.

Chapter 5.1

4 "The Architecture," Clyfford Still Museum, https://clyffordstillmuseum.org/architecture.

5 Brad Cloepfil, Founding Principal, Allied Works Architecture, telephone interview with author, recorded July 29, 2015.

6 "Average Weather for Aurora, Colorado, USA," WeatherSpark.com, https://weatherspark.com/averages/29768/Aurora-Colorado-United-States.

7 Brad Cloepfil.

8 "Clyfford Still Museum," Allied Works Architecture, http://www.alliedworks.com/projects/clyfford-still-museum/.

9 "About the Museum," Clyfford Still Museum, https://clyffordstillmuseum.org/about-the-museum/.

10 Christopher Rush, Senior Lighting Designer, Arup, telephone interview with author, recorded February 4, 2016.

11 Brad Cloepfil.

12 Ibid.

13 Ibid.

14 Stuart Horodner, "Brad Cloepfil," *Bomb Magazine*, Spring 2005, http://bombmagazine.org/article/2731/brad-cloepfil.

15 Brad Cloepfil.

16 Ibid.

17 Aidan Chopra, "A Conversation with Allied Works," SketchUp (blog), posted by "Aidan Chopra," February 22, 2012, https://blog.sketchup.com/sketchupdate/conversation-allied-works.

18 Christopher Rush.

19 Erin McConahey, Christopher Rush, and Brian Stacy, "The Clyfford Still Museum," *The Arup Journal*, Issue 1, 2013, 18.

20 Deane Madsen, "2013 AL Design Awards: Clyfford Still Museum, Denver," *Architectural Lighting*, August 1, 2013, http://www.archlighting.com/design-awards/2013-al-design-awards-clyfford-still-museum-denver_o.

21 Erin McConahey, Christopher Rush, and Brian Stacy, "The Clyfford Still Museum," 16.

22 Aidan Chopra, "A Conversation with Allied Works."

23 Brad Cloepfil.

24 "Degree Days: Energy Data for Professionals," Degreedays.net: Weather Underground, http://www.degreedays.net/#generate.

25 Ibid.

26 Deane Madsen, "2013 AL Design Awards: Clyfford Still Museum."

27 Ibid.

Chapter 5.2

28 Neil Gillespie, Architect, Reiach and Hall, telephone interview with author, recorded August 21, 2015.

29 "Climate: Airdrie," Climate-data.org, http://en.climate-data.org/location/8993/.

30 Neil Gillespie.

31 Charles Jencks and Edwin Heathcote, *Architecture of Hope*, London: Francis Lincoln Limited, 2010, 8.

32 "Maggie's Centre Lanarkshire Project Profile," Reiach and Hall Architects, 2014, 8.

33 Laura Kinnaird, Architect, Reiach and Hall, telephone interview with author, recorded August 11, 2015.

34 Neil Gillespie.

35 Ibid.

36 "Vote for Maggie's Lanarkshire – RIBA Stirling Prize," Maggie's Centre Lanarkshire, https://www.maggiescentres.org/our-centres/maggies-lanarkshire/news/article/vote-for-maggies-lanarkshire-stirling-prize-2015/?page=1.

37 Neil Gillespie.

38 Ibid.

39 Laura Kinnaird.

40 Neil Gillespie.

41 Laura Kinnaird.

42 Neil Gillespie.

43 Ibid.

44 "Degree Days: Energy Data for Professionals," Degreedays.net: Weather Underground, http://www.degreedays.net/#generate.

45 Ibid.

Chapter 6
Integrated Light

6.1 Stacking Green House
6.2 Piano Pavilion, Kimbell Art Museum

"In order to successfully integrate ecology and design, we must mirror nature's deep interconnections in our own epistemology of design. We are still trapped in worn-out mechanical metaphors. It is time to stop designing in the image of the machine and start designing in a way that honors the complexity and diversity of life itself."[1]

Sim Van der Ryn and Stuart Cohen, Architects

An integrated approach to architectural design (also known as integrated design, integrative design, whole building design, and systems thinking) combines diverse yet related design strategies for the benefit of ecological systems at all scales. Bill Reed, an architect and ecological design visionary, describes the intentions of integrative design: "The design process should begin by determining, as best as possible, how to increase the beneficial interrelationships between human, biotic, technical, and earth systems. This understanding becomes the foundation for any design aimed at saving resources, restoring the health and benefits of natural system processes."[2]

Focusing on the increasing complexity of architectural design and practice, architect Kiel Moe elaborates on related considerations in his book *Integrated Design in Contemporary Architecture*: "Any building project is contingent upon an idiosyncratic assemblage of theoretical, practical, ecological, economical, political, social, and cultural parameters that presuppose the design and performance of architecture. Reflexively, architecture in turn affects these parameters. ... The real complexity of architecture is in the cogent organization and integration of the multivariate parameters, directing its potential effects toward some larger end through an architectural agenda."[3]

While daylighting is just one dimension of integrated design, its influence extends broadly across all aspects of building design, including the synthesis of daylighting with climate, program, structure, construction methods, comfort, health, energy, performance, technical systems, and aesthetics. Foremost, however, daylighting guides the giving of form in architectural design. Daylight is most effectively addressed through the configuration of the building massing, section, and spatial organization. It intersects with comfort in the design of the building envelope and spatial planning to enhance natural ventilation and passive heating and cooling. The structure and characteristics of materials (including surface reflectance, value, texture, and hue) impact the quality, mood, and atmosphere

▷ Expansive translucent skylights with exterior shading louvers capture north light and provide an even distribution of daylight in the entry lobby. Piano Pavilion, Kimbell Art Museum, Fort Worth, Texas, USA; Renzo Piano, Renzo Piano Building Workshop.

"We have the opportunity and imperative to evolve our thinking and practice in a way that can contribute to regenerating our planet. Slowing down the processes of degradation, while essential, is insufficient; regenerating the evolving resiliency and matrix of life in each place is the other half of achieving a sustainable condition. … This nature of work will require us to think more and more like living systems and embrace a whole systems mind and design process in order to wholly participate in the system of life."[4]

Bill Reed, Integrative Design Collaborative

created by daylight. Integration of daylight with electric lighting, mechanical systems, and renewable energy systems is critical in achieving low- to net-positive energy goals. The integrated design process invites designers to explore how daylighting can be addressed from many perspectives, across a wide variety of scales.

In the following studies of works by Vo Trong Nghia Architects (VTNA) and Renzo Piano Building Workshop (RPBW), daylight integration is approached from two distinct perspectives, one that —at first glance—may seem very low-tech and the other very high-tech. Yet, in essence, both firms rely on simple daylighting strategies that give form to the building massing, section, and detailing while simultaneously addressing ecological concerns such as energy, performance, and comfort.

First is the Stacking Green House in Ho Chi Minh City, Vietnam, by VTNA, which is shaped in massing, plan, and section by the interrelationships between light and air. Located in a hot–humid climate, this prototype house responds to the constraints of a narrow urban infill site and integrates passive design strategies for solar control, natural ventilation, and indirect daylighting. The Stacking Green House is a reinterpretation of the traditional Vietnamese courtyard house in which VTNA incorporated vertical zoning, interior and boundary courtyards, and double envelopes with vertical gardens to minimize energy consumption, reduce the need for air conditioning, diffuse direct sunlight, and enhance biodiversity within the city. This "passive house" requires "active participation" from the occupants, who are invited to tune the building envelope to admit or block light and air based on outside temperatures and weather conditions.

Next is the Piano Pavilion in Fort Worth, Texas, by RPBW, which, because of their integral relationship, is discussed in concert with the 1972 Kimbell Art Museum by Louis Kahn. The two projects illustrate a forty-year evolution of integrated design thinking by two master architects. The differing approaches of Kahn and Piano are most elegantly revealed in their synthesis of daylight, structure,

and technological systems within the galleries themselves. In the Kimbell, the room sections, proportions, structure, skylight, and interior reflector are designed to transform a small slice of direct sunlight into soft ambient illumination through reflection from multiple surfaces.

A contrasting approach to daylighting in the Piano Pavilion uses large expansive skylights covering the entire roof. The skylights are shaded by a series of parallel exterior photovoltaic louvers that are adjustable to gather variable amounts of indirect light from the north while generating electricity from the southern

▷ Interior view looking northeast toward the exterior courtyard and 'stacking green' planter boxes. The double envelope controls direct solar gain while admitting indirect daylight and natural ventilation to create a cool refuge from the tropical climate. Stacking Green House, Ho Chi Minh City, Vietnam; Vo Trong Nghia, Vo Trong Nghia Architects.

△ The narrow linear skylight and perforated aluminum reflector transform direct sunlight into ambient daylight through multiple ceiling and room reflections. Kimbell Art Museum, Fort Worth, Texas, USA; Louis Kahn.

sunlight. An interior scrim is integrated beneath the roof structure. Sidelighting is introduced for direct visual connections to the site and to minimize the boundaries between inside and outside. An even distribution of light is created with a layered roof system that can be configured to provide flexible and varied lighting zones within the galleries. Design elements are brought together to serve multiple functions, including daylight collection, solar control, light diffusion, electric energy generation, spatial flexibility, and adjustability. Innovative design, construction, and technological systems afforded an estimated 50 percent increase in energy performance and carbon reductions at the Piano Pavilion when compared to the Kimbell. [5]

While accommodating very different climates, cultures, and programs, both Vo Trong Nghia and Renzo Piano skillfully address the integration of daylighting with program, performance, construction methods, technological systems, aesthetics, and atmospheric experiences. The projects reveal the tremendous potential of daylighting design in elevating sustainable design goals and achieving significant ecological benefits.

◁ The southwest façade shelters the interior rooms from direct sunlight by a series of "stacking green" double façades with vertical planter boxes, a ventilation gap, and large areas of operable glazing. The green façade integrates daylight, natural ventilation, and passive cooling, while providing privacy.

Case study 6.1

Stacking Green House

Ho Chi Minh City, Vietnam

Vo Trong Nghia, Vo Trong Nghia Architects

"Green architecture helps people live harmoniously with nature and elevates human life by embracing the powers of sun, wind, and water into living spaces. If the current way of thinking does not change, sooner or later, citizens will actually live in concrete jungles. For a modern architect the most important mission is to bring green spaces back to the earth." [6]

Vo Trong Nghia, Vo Trong Nghia Architects

△ The ground-floor entry can double as a street-level garden terrace or a parking garage.

LIGHT AND THE QUALITY OF PLACE

Ho Chi Minh City

Located east of the Mekong Delta on the Saigon River, Ho Chi Minh City is roughly 50 kilometers (30 miles) from the China South Sea and only 19 meters (62 feet) above sea level. Climate change, increased flooding, and rising sea levels inspire design priorities that focus on low-energy architecture and the integration of climate-responsive and passive design solutions. Ho Chi Minh City is the most densely populated area in Vietnam, with more than 10 million people inhabiting the metropolitan region. As the population continues to increase, there are corresponding challenges of housing, employment, transportation, congestion, noise, access to green spaces, air pollution, and related issues of health and well-being. Architect Vo Trong Nghia, of Vo Trong Nghia Architects (VTNA), is the designer of the Stacking Green House, a prototype home in Ho Chi Minh City. He explains his commitment to reintroducing nature, climate response, and the tropical beauty of Vietnam into the urban context: "I'm working to bring nature back to the city. ... My goal is to solve these problems through sustainable, long-term and affordable architecture. ... [On] a typical city street ... you can see heavy traffic with lots of motorbikes. You can hear the city noise. There are rows of terraces [houses]. There's not enough light, and people are suffering from all kinds of pollution. ... People utilize every inch for construction, leaving no space for plants. Because of this the city has almost no greenery." [7]

Climate, Site, and Light

Ho Chi Minh City is in a hot–humid tropical climate, with a rainy season from May to October, and a dry season from December to April. The city experiences an average of 1,868 millimeters (73.5 inches) of annual rainfall, and an average relative humidity of 78–82 percent. [8] Temperatures are very uniform, ranging from an average low of 25.9°C (78.6°F) in December to an average high of 29.5°C (85.1°F) in April. [9] Located at 10.5° north latitude, the length of day varies little throughout the year, with approximately 13 and 11.5 hours of daylight on the summer and winter solstices. Given the

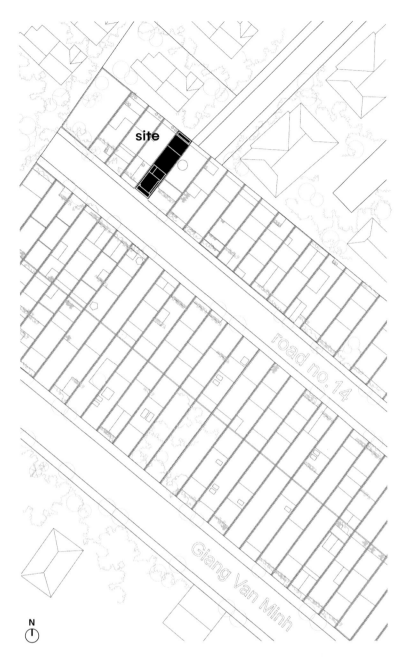

N

△ ▷ The linear urban site led to the "tube house" floor plan. An exterior courtyard is located on each end of the house, while double envelopes enclose the open ends of upper floors. A skylight and light well bring daylight to the center of the house.

proximity to the equator, the sun altitude is consistently high in the sky throughout the year. The sun reaches the highest noon altitude of 103° (13° north of the zenith) in June (when the apparent position of the sun flips to the north side of the house), and the lowest noon altitude of 56° in December. The quality of light in Ho Chi Minh City varies seasonally with the rainy and dry seasons as the skies shift from overcast to clear. The rainy season, from May to October, brings predominantly overcast skies (58–78 percent), frequent precipitation, and thunderstorms. Prevailing winds are from the southeast, south, and southwest. Given the persistently hot and humid conditions throughout the year, cooling is the primary design concern for human comfort and energy savings.

LIGHT AND THE DESIGN INTENTIONS

Stacking Green Program

The Stacking Green House is a climate-responsive and low-energy housing prototype that can be replicated throughout the city and other tropical regions. Given the lack of gardens, parks, and green spaces in Ho Chi Minh City, the prototype house is designed to reintroduce nature into the urban environment, one house at a time. Vo Trong Nghia explains the concept of the house and its distinctive vertical green façades: "There is an interesting custom among the people in Ho Chi Minh City: They love their life with a large variety of tropical plants and flowers around the streets. Even in the modernized city, people unconsciously desire the substitute of lush tropical forest. 'Stacking Green' architecturalized this custom into a façade composed of planters like horizontal louvers." [10]

The house, located on an urban infill lot, was designed for a family of four: a couple, a grandmother, and a child. The program activities are vertically organized on four floors. On the ground level are a carport, bedroom, and courtyard with open stairs; the first floor has living and kitchen spaces; the second floor holds the master bedroom and bath; and a small study/child's room and meditation space with exterior garden and green roof are on the third floor. The narrow southwest and northeast ends of the house contain "stacking green" double-façades with planter boxes. VTNA is currently designing and constructing larger housing projects in the city and surrounding region to introduce the climate-responsive and ecological design principles of the Stacking Green House at multi-family and neighborhood scales.

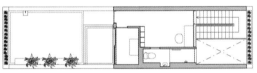

Third floor

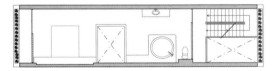

Second floor

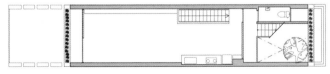

First floor

Ground floor

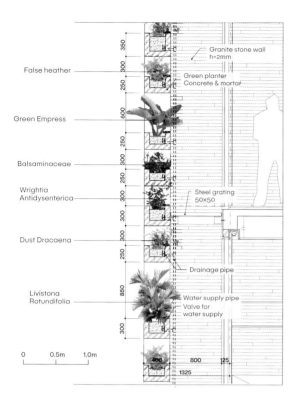

False heather

Green Empress

Balsaminaceae

Wrightia
Antidysenterica

Dust Dracaena

Livistona
Rotundifolia

Granite stone wall
h=2mm

Green planter
Concrete & mortar

Steel grating
50x50

Drainage pipe

Water supply pipe
Valve for
water supply

0   0.5m   1.0m

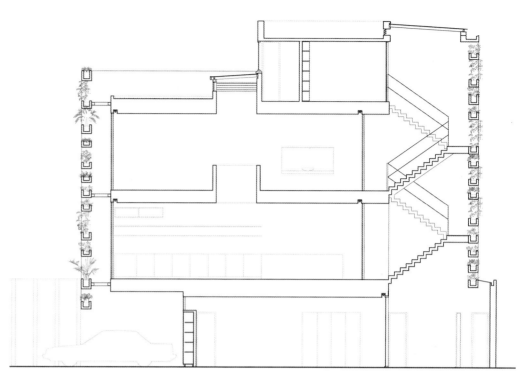

△ A construction detail of the southwest façade
illustrates the layering of the double envelope
with exterior planting boxes, air gap, and interior
operable glazing.

△ ▽ The building massing, section, and detailing
effectively integrate passive design strategies for
lighting, ventilation, and cooling with visual and
thermal comfort, privacy, and sustainability while
fostering a connection to nature.

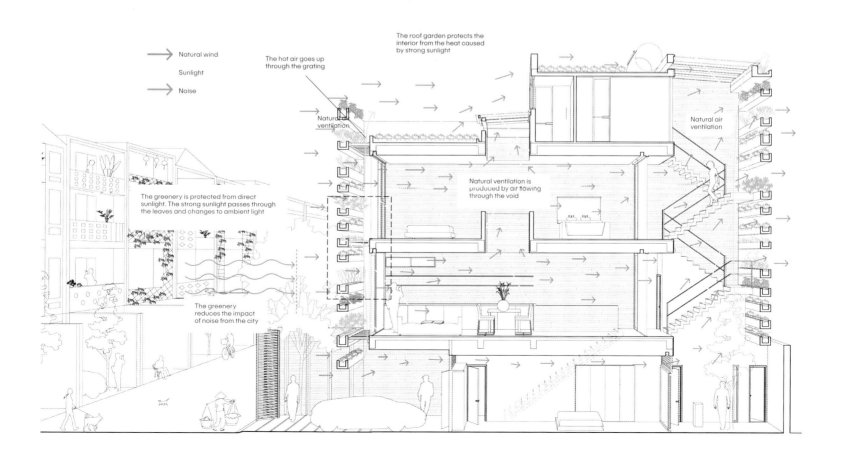

Natural wind

Sunlight

Noise

The hot air goes up
through the grating

The roof garden protects the
interior from the heat caused
by strong sunlight

Natural air
ventilation

Natural air
ventilation

The greenery is protected from direct
sunlight. The strong sunlight passes through
the leaves and changes to ambient light

Natural ventilation is
produced by air flowing
through the void

The greenery
reduces the impact
of noise from the city

Shaped by Site, Climate, and Nature

This prototype house is designed in plan, section, and massing to reintroduce nature to the city, mitigate climate change, and reduce the need for air conditioning and electricity. The house is based on the typical "tube house" precedent, which is a common infill-housing type in Ho Chi Minh City. Given the linear site, the dimensions are 4 by 20 meters (13 by 65.6 feet), with neighbors on both sides. Only the narrow ends of the house and rooftop are exposed to light and air, while the long concrete side walls are solid with no windows. The house is designed to provide year-round shelter from the tropical heat and sun, and to optimize air flow, solar control, and indirect daylight.

The design of the section is key to the integrated cooling, natural ventilation, and daylighting strategies. The rooms are vertically stacked with open floor plans, carefully designed spaces between floors, and high ceilings to optimize airflow and light. The living spaces are recessed from the narrow ends of the site and buffered from the street by vertical gardens and courtyard spaces, which effectively reduce the depth of the floor plan in the living spaces to facilitate air flow and deeper daylight penetration. Living spaces are located behind the carport or elevated from the ground floor to enhance cooling and privacy.

The narrow southwest and northeast façades are constructed with a double envelope composed of vertically stacked planter boxes, behind which is located an air space (in the form of either an open shaft on the south or a tall vertical courtyard on the north) and operable glass windows. Diffused sidelighting is admitted from the narrow end walls. Fresh air flows through cross- and stack-ventilation systems fostered by operable façades and vented skylights at the center of the house and over the courtyard. Daylight admitted through the central skylight reflects from the stone surfaces of the interior walls to provide soft indirect light deep in the lower-level floors. The green roof and courtyard provide private exterior green spaces.

▽ Details of the rooftop garden, glazed air shaft, skylight, and fourth-floor living space.

▷ A skylight and asymmetric light well admit toplighting to the center of the long linear house. Double envelopes with vertical planting boxes, ventilation slot, and interior glazing provide sidelighting at the perimeter.

LIGHT AND THE DESIGN STRATEGIES

Passive Design and Thermal Comfort

Vo Trong Nghia explains that many buildings in Vietnam are constructed using European models that do not account for the tropical climate and persistent heat, humidity, and cooling loads: "The climate is totally different in Europe. ... In Ho Chi Minh City we just have hot summer [all year]. ... We have many problems with energy and electricity. It can stop anytime in the day. So we design our house for a tropical climate. We [make a] shadow and invite the wind into the house. And we use the sunlight instead of the [electric] lighting so we can reduce electricity."[11]

The Stacking Green House is designed to run on nature rather than electricity. Traditional bioclimatic principles are reinterpreted, as VTNA explains: "The green façade and roof top garden protect its inhabitants from the direct sunlight, street noise and pollution. Natural ventilation through the façades and two toplights allow this house to save energy in a harsh climate. ... We referred to the bioclimatic principles of a traditional Vietnamese courtyard house.[12]

To provide thermal and luminous comfort, the house needs to be "tuned" to the outside temperature, relative humidity, and dew points. Occupants open and close the house during the day and night to optimize natural ventilation as needed. Given the year-round cooling load, diurnal temperature variations determine when

passive strategies for natural ventilation, shading, and daylight are effective and when the house must rely on mechanical air conditioning. The house envelope is monitored and adjusted for light and air throughout the day and evening. Passive strategies for cross- and stack-ventilation are most effective in the morning, evening, and nighttime. During the mid-day temperature peak, or when air temperatures exceed the occupants' comfort zone, the house can be closed and cooled, as needed, with air conditioning.

Post-occupancy evaluations confirmed the effectiveness of the integrated passive strategies in reducing cooling and electric lighting loads and minimizing the need for air conditioning, as VTNA explain: "According to the post-occupancy measurement of the indoor environment, wind flows throughout the house thanks to the porous façades and two skylights. This result was already proven by the behavior of the inhabitants; they scarcely use the air conditioner even in the tropical climate, their electricity fees are just $25 USD [US dollars] per month, thanks to the wind flow and other passive design methods."[13]

Double Green Envelope

In an interview with *Dezeen* editor-in-chief Marcus Fairs, Vo Trong Nghia clarifies his reinterpretation of the double envelope for a tropical climate: "We make the double skin, not by glass and glass; but by green [plants] and glass."[14] The exterior layer of the double envelope is composed of vertically stacked planter boxes. There are 25 planter boxes, with 12 on the southwest façade and 13 on the northeast. The depth and spacing of the boxes both optimizes shading and nurtures the plants, which include fan palm, false heather, dust dracaena, and other ornamental tropical species. Irrigation and drainage are integrated in the planter boxes for ease of maintenance.

Air spaces between the exterior vertical gardens and the interior glass envelopes are critical in controlling solar gains and direct sunlight. On the southwest façade, a three-story-tall open air shaft 1,355 millimeters (53 inches) in width, is located between the exterior planter boxes and the interior operable glass façade. In contrast, on the northeast façade, a four-story skylit vertical courtyard is positioned between the exterior planter boxes and the interior glass façade. The inner glass walls are designed with elegant floor-to-ceiling folding wood and glass doors that have operable upper and lower windows to allow varied configurations and degrees of openness, air flow, and acoustic privacy. During the rainy season from May to October, the layering of the double envelope and operable glass walls admits air but prevents rain from entering the house, as Vo Trong Nghia explained in his interview with Marcus Fairs: "We have a lot of rain in Ho Chi Minh City. We have one layer outside with green [plants]; one layer with air [a vertical shaft or courtyard], and one layer with glass. If you invite wind through

△ Detail of the central skylight with vents and shutters to mediate direct sunlight and provide natural ventilation. The skylight, positioned adjacent to a granite-clad concrete wall and light well, reflects daylight to a lower level.

▷ A four-story skylit courtyard is positioned between the exterior planter boxes and the interior glazing on the northeast façade. The four-story stairway is suspended between the planting boxes and interior landing.

△ The ground-level entry doubles as a garden terrace or garage. Horizontal louvered doors provide privacy and security while admitting daylight and air.

▷ Tall folding glass windows open at the upper and lower levels to adjust the degree of air, privacy, and enclosure.

the house, you just open the window … even when it's raining you can open the window." [15]

LIGHT AND THE ART OF MAKING

Materials and Thermal and Luminous Comfort

Luminous and thermal comfort are inseparable in the Stacking Green House, with the strategies to admit light and air integrated into the architectural form and considered in the choices of structure and materials. The house was constructed using a reinforced concrete frame, with vertically stacked concrete planter boxes cantilevered from the two side walls to span the 4-meter (13-foot) width of the house. Concrete walls are finished on the interior with thin, 2-centimeter-thick (0.79-inch) gray horizontal granite tiles harvested from the waste byproducts of stone cutting. Granite is used to clad the interior concrete walls on all levels of the house, even the ground-level carport, which can double as an outdoor courtyard with a large horizontally louvered door and an interior tree. On the opposite side of the ground level, the north courtyard is similarly finished with granite to provide a cool visual counterpoint to the lush vertical green façade, white ceilings, and wood floors, cabinets, and shelving.

Direct sunlight is filtered through the green façades to create a dappled play of light and shadow. Skylights have vents and shutters that can be adjusted to admit or block sunlight and air on the upper floors. Visual delight and changing luminous effects are created by the combined side and toplighting, as VTNA explains: "During the day we get the varying light with the time of day [animated] by the toplight in the center. In the morning and the afternoon, the sunlight enters through the … leaves on both façades, creating beautiful shadow effects on the granite walls." [16] Interior wall partitions are kept to a minimum to enhance air flow and to provide long views to

the green plants on the building envelope. The upper floors have high ceilings to bring diffuse sidelight more deeply into the floor plan and to enhance air circulation.

Design Integration

Vertical gardens, double envelopes, skylights, and courtyards foster cross- and stack-ventilation and provide indirect illumination while creating private outdoor rooms and green spaces. Green roofs introduce garden spaces, views of the city, and rainwater harvesting. The simplicity of strategies and their integrated functions resulted in a construction cost of $480 US dollars per square meter ($42 per square foot) and reduced need for electricity for cooling. [17] The average electricity cost is $25 per month, with an estimated reduction of 30–50 percent over typical houses in Ho Chi Minh City. [18]

LIGHT INSPIRATIONS

The Stacking Green House, as a prototype, demonstrates that the integration of vertical gardens with passive strategies can effectively reduce energy consumption and minimize related environmental impacts. Traditional strategies for solar control, passive cooling, natural ventilation, and filtered daylight are coupled with a contemporary approach to vertical gardens and double envelopes to create a shaded refuge from the hot–humid climate, while reinterpreting the beautiful dappled light of the lush tropical forests

△ View of the second-floor bedroom and bath reveals the integration of sidelighting and toplighting to provide natural light throughout the depth of the house.

of Vietnam. Vo Trong Nghia emphasizes that the benefits of these integrated design strategies help people "to live harmoniously with nature and elevate human lives."[19]

VTNA is slowly, one project at a time, greening Ho Chi Minh City and beyond. Vo Trong Nghia suggests that reconnecting to nature is a key to ecological transformation of the urban environment: "If people can develop a sense of treasuring nature, their way of urban planning and construction will become more ecologically friendly. Then Ho Chi Minh City and other cities in Vietnam will become better."[20]

While constructed as a single-family home, when replicated at the neighborhood scale (as several current projects by VTNA are exploring) the benefits to the owners, neighborhood, and city could significantly reduce energy and climate impacts, foster passive independence from the unstable electrical grid, and create a more beautiful and livable urban environment.

◁ Large operable doors and windows adjust airflow, privacy, and acoustic connections to the urban site.

DESIGN PROFILE

1. Building Profile
Project: Stacking Green House
Location: Ho Chi Minh City (Saigon), Vietnam
Architect: Vo Trong Nghia Architects
Client: Individual
Building Type: Residential
Square Footage: 215 sq m (2,314 sq ft)
Estimated Cost: $480 per sq m ($42 per sq ft)
Completion: 2011

2. Professional Team
Architect: Vo Trong Nghia
Partners: Vo Trong Nghia, Daisuke Sanuki, Shunri Nishizawa
General Contractor: Wind and Water House JSC
Photographs: Hiroyuki Oki

3. Climate Profile
Climate (Köppen-Geiger Climate Classification System): Aw: tropical climate
Latitude: 10.5° north latitude
Solar Angles: Noon
June 21: 103° (13° north of zenith)
March/September 21: 79.5°
December 21: 56°
Length of Day: Approximate Hours of Daylight from Sunrise to Sunset
June 21: 12h 45m
March/September 21: 12h 07m
December 21: 11h 29m
Heating Degree Days: 0 heating degree days °C (0 heating degree days °F) (18°C and 65°F base temperature)[21]
Cooling Degree Days: 3966 cooling degree days °C (6918 cooling degree days °F) (18°C and 65°F base temperature)[22]

4. Design Strategies
Daylighting Strategies: 1) Sidelighting: bilateral sidelighting on southwest and northeast façades; layered envelope with exterior shading (vertically stacked planter boxes); air space or courtyard between exterior façades; operable windows and doors, and 2) Toplighting: open toplit air shaft on the south; central skylight with lightwell; and skylight above courtyard on the north.
Sustainable Design and High-Performance Strategies: Daylighting and natural ventilation throughout the house; solar control; and three-dimensional layered envelope.
Renewable Energy Strategies: None.

Vo Trong Nghia: Structure and Materials

The exploded diagram illustrates the layered
envelope and the integration of sidelighting and
toplighting. The "stacking green" façades on the
southwest and northeast diffuse direct sunlight and
block heat gains through double envelopes, which
includes exterior planting boxes, air space, and
operable glass on the interior. A skylight and light
shaft admit daylight to the heart of the building.

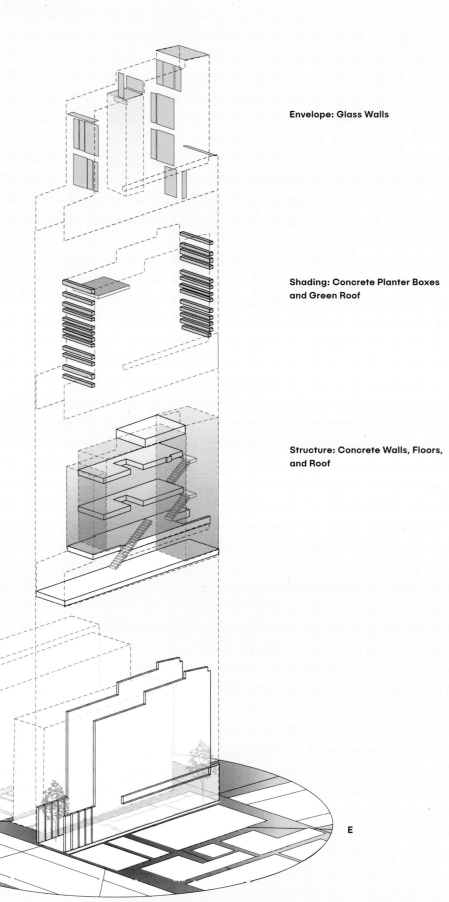

Envelope: Glass Walls

**Shading: Concrete Planter Boxes
and Green Roof**

**Structure: Concrete Walls, Floors,
and Roof**

W

E

S

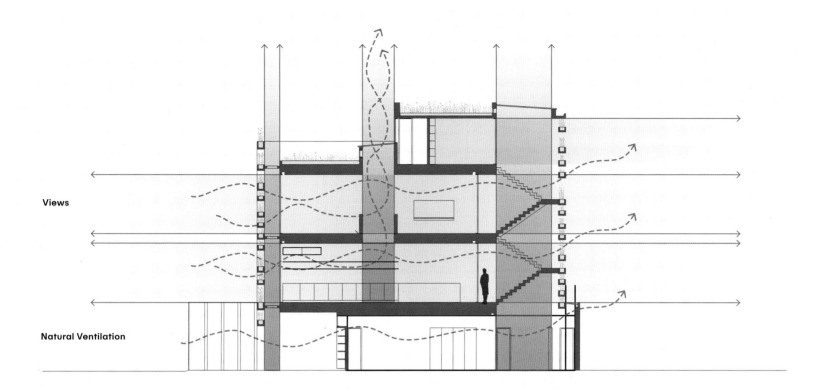

Views

Natural Ventilation

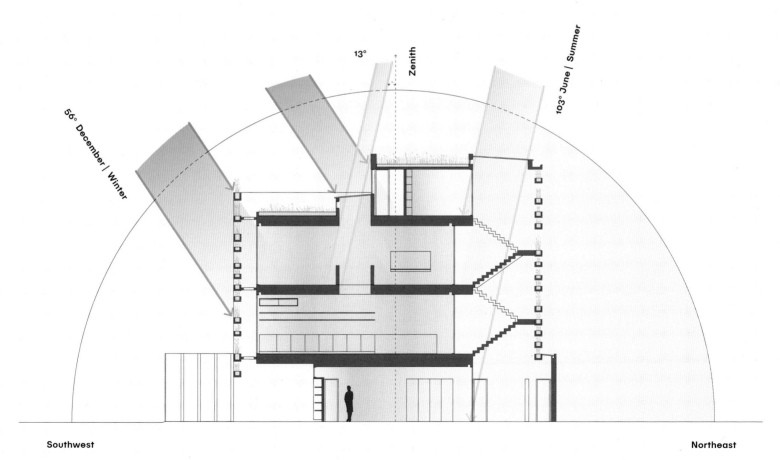

13°

Zenith

56° December / Winter

103° June / Summer

Southwest

Northeast

The upper southwest–northeast section illustrates the ventilation strategies of the air gap on the southwest façade, central light well, and northeast courtyard. The lower section illustrates the movement of the sun from the south to the north façades during the winter and summer given the proximity to the equator (10.5° north latitude).

Daylight Analysis: Seasonal Plans

Illuminance studies (in lux) illustrate the relatively uniform seasonal and diurnal light levels and distribution given the proximity to the equator (10.5° north latitude) and relatively consistent length of day (12h 45m on June 21 and 11h 29m on December 21).

N

December 21 at 12:00 pm

Fourth foor

Third floor

Second floor

First floor

June 21 at 12:00 pm

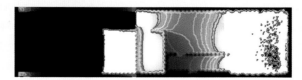

Overcast Skies
Illuminance (Lux)

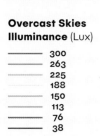

- 300
- 263
- 225
- 188
- 150
- 113
- 76
- 38

Seasonal Sections_Looking Northwest

Section studies illustrate how the double façade and floor-to-ceiling glazing admit sidelighting, while the skylight and light well provide daylight to the center of the house.

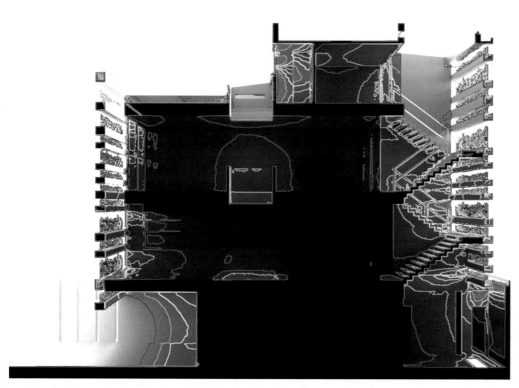

June 21 at 12:00 pm

Overcast Skies
Illuminance (Lux)

———	300
———	263
··········	225
	188
———	150
———	113
———	76
———	38

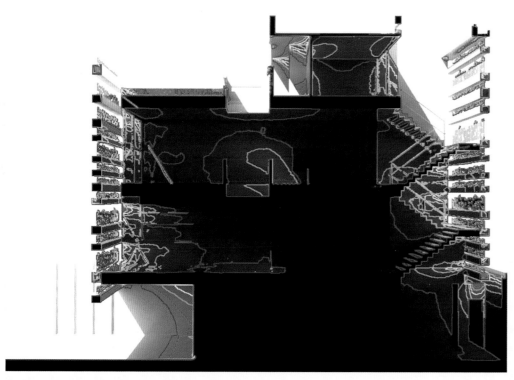

December 21 at 12:00 pm

Seasonal Perspectives_Second Floor_Looking Southwest

Seasonal perspective renderings illustrate the visual quality of daylight and the movement of sunlight within the building on the solstices and equinoxes. The double envelope controls direct sunlight and heat gain, while shading controls direct sunlight from the skylight as needed.

December 21

March/September 21

June 21

9:00 am

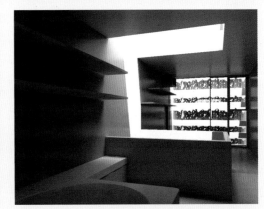

12:00 pm

3:00 pm

Seasonal Perspectives_Second Floor_Looking Northeast

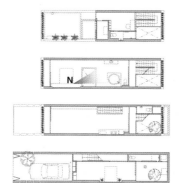

December 21

March/September 21

June 21

9:00 am

12:00 pm

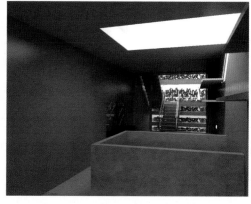

3:00 pm

Equinox Walk-through

Perspective renderings and luminance studies (in candela/square meter; cd/m2) illustrate the visual quality of daylight and contrast ratios from four view locations within the house during the equinoxes (March/September 21 at noon). The highest contrast occurs in direct sunlight and at the window wall or skylight. The house remains in relative darkness as a refuge from the heat and high humidity of the climate. Natural ventilation enters through the double envelope and vents through the skylights.

**Sunny Sky
Luminance** (Cd/m²)

100
88
75
63
50
38
26
13

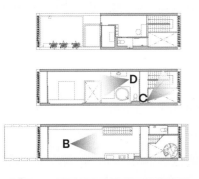

N

View A: March/September 21 at 12:00 pm

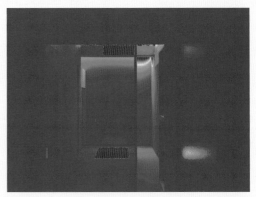

View A: March/September 21 at 12:00 pm

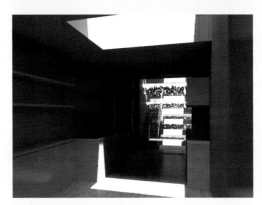

View B: March/September 21 at 12:00 pm

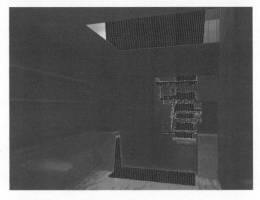

View B: March/September 21 at 12:00 pm

View C: March/September 21 at 12:00 pm

View C: March/September 21 at 12:00 pm

View D: March/September 21 at 12:00 pm

View D: March/September 21 at 12:00 pm

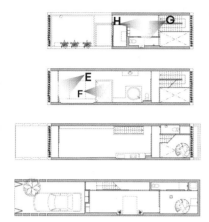

N

View E: March/September 21 at 12:00 pm

View E: March/September 21 at 12:00 pm

View F: March/September 21 at 12:00 pm

View F: March/September 21 at 12:00 pm

View G: March/September 21 at 12:00 pm

View G: March/September 21 at 12:00 pm

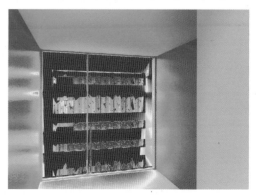

View H: March/September 21 at 12:00 pm

View H: March/September 21 at 12:00 pm

Case study 6.2

Piano Pavilion, Kimbell Art Museum

Fort Worth, Texas, USA

Renzo Piano, Renzo Piano Building Workshop

"It's about respecting what is there, but telling your story. ... I love that building from Kahn. ... Of course what Kahn did is fantastic. He actually brought light inside to give life to the silky surface of the vault, the concrete vault. ... But the way we put light on the new pavilion at the Kimbell is a different one. First we changed the quantity of light inside by having louvers on the roof. And they can open so they can tune the quantity of light." [23]

Renzo Piano, Renzo Piano Building Workshop

△ An aerial view of the site reveals a sympathetic response in scale, form, and massing. The daylit galleries are located above ground, with an electrically-illuminated gallery, auditorium, support spaces, and parking beneath green roofs or underground.

◁ The Piano Pavilion by Renzo Piano establishes a respectful relationship with the legendary Kimbell Art Museum by the modern Master Louis Kahn. Piano employs design and technological strategies that respond to the new challenges of museums while harmonizing with the historic Kimbell. South and east façades of the Piano Pavilion juxtaposed to the south and west façades of the Kimbell Art Museum.

LIGHT AND THE QUALITY OF PLACE

A Conversation Between Masters

Louis Kahn's 1972 Kimbell Art Museum in Fort Worth, Texas—one of the greatest modern architectural masterpieces—is renowned for the exquisite qualities of its light, space, and construction. Renzo Piano, principal of Renzo Piano Building Workshop (RPBW), worked for Louis Kahn from 1965 to 1970, during which time Kahn received the commission for the Kimbell. In 2007, Piano was commissioned to design the museum expansion. The resulting Piano Pavilion closes the circle in this decades-long conversation between master architects.

Piano understood that his charge was to have a respectful conversation with Kahn, while remaining faithful to his own approach to design: "Competing with a masterpiece is stupid. It's also wrong. I love that building from Kahn since the beginning. ... This is a kind of seminal building ... unpretentious, deep, profound, a kind of masterpiece. So the idea here was to put the building across the lawn at the right distance and to tell a different story." [24]

Separated in time by more than forty years, the program goals and cultural forces shaping the museum today are distinct from those facing Louis Kahn in the early 1970s, as Piano explains: "The problem here was not really to become bigger but to complement what was already there. ... So the story we're going to tell with the new building was a story of openness, accessibility, urbanity. ... The idea is that instead of competing it's more about trying to put in the campus what was a necessity and probably missing. This is the real essence of what we tried to do." [25]

Texas Light

The tallgrass prairies, rangeland, and farms of North Central Texas lie within the southern reaches of the Great Plains, which stretch from Alberta, Canada, to northern Mexico. This vast and open horizontal landscape celebrates a connection to the sky and dynamic weather conditions characteristic of the humid subtropical climate. The clear and sunny Texas days are offset by brief periods of overcast skies and often-volatile thunderstorms and precipitation in the form of rain, hail, and rare snowfall. Temperatures range from an average low of 7°C (44°F) in January, to the average high of 29°C (84°F) in August. [26] Located at 32.7° north latitude, the length of day varies from approximately 14 hours on the summer solstice to 10 hours on the winter solstice. Sun angles at noon reach a maximum altitude of 80.8° in the summer and a low of 33.8° in winter. The predominance of clear skies and high sun angles throughout the year underscores the need to provide a sheltering roof that mediates solar gains, temperatures, and light levels. Despite so many days of sunlight, there remains a monthly rhythm of clear and overcast skies, including an average of six to seven overcast days per month (with the exception of July and August, which average four to five overcast days). [27]

LIGHT AND THE DESIGN INTENTIONS

Daylight and the Museum Program

The goals of the museum expansion were to honor Kahn's beloved building and create a worthy architectural companion. While retaining daylight as a design priority, the new museum was to be physically minimal, open, and distinct from the internally focused and sheltering enclosure of the Kimbell. The program, which aspired to set new standards for the integration of daylight and electric lighting while supporting the museum's requirements for the conservation and exhibition of art, included the following criteria: 1) To provide a condition where daylight is the primary source of light for the display of art; 2) to have the ability to tune daylight

transmission, and therefore change the mix of daylight and electric light within the gallery; 3) to be able to reduce daylight levels within the gallery to allow the display of sensitive objects requiring 4.64 footcandles (50 lux) or less; and 4) to reduce daylight in the galleries to a minimum when the museum is closed. [28] Achieving new standards of energy performance, reduced carbon emissions, and sustainability were related performance goals.

Onur Teke, Associate Architect at RPBW, summarized additional qualitative and experiential daylighting goals for the expansion: "It's a different time and different society. We were trying to achieve the feeling like taking a shower of light. You're washed with light from the sky, with as much light as possible." [29] Teke further explained that they also sought a direct visual relationship to the site: "There is always a connection between outside and inside. You can see people on bicycles while looking at a Caravaggio. ... You're not in a closed box. The most important thing for Renzo's architecture is the transparency and openness. You see the roof structure and light. It takes you outside." [30]

RPBW sought to minimize the visual distinctions between inside and outside and to foster an open, expansive sense of space, as Piano explains in an interview with critic Jerome Weeks: "It's fundamentally a roof flying above the ground, open, accessible, visible, transparent. ... The two buildings work in a complementary way. Kahn is more introverted, and the pavilion is more extroverted." [31] Piano emphasized the importance of the dynamics and the ever-changing qualities of natural light: "You notice that natural light is never the same. You have clouds passing by and

▷ The site plan illustrates the respectful distance between the two buildings as well as the rooftop gardens and a new walkway lined with elm trees. To the west is the Amon Carter Museum by Philip Johnson, and to the east the Modern Art Museum of Fort Worth by Tadao Ando.

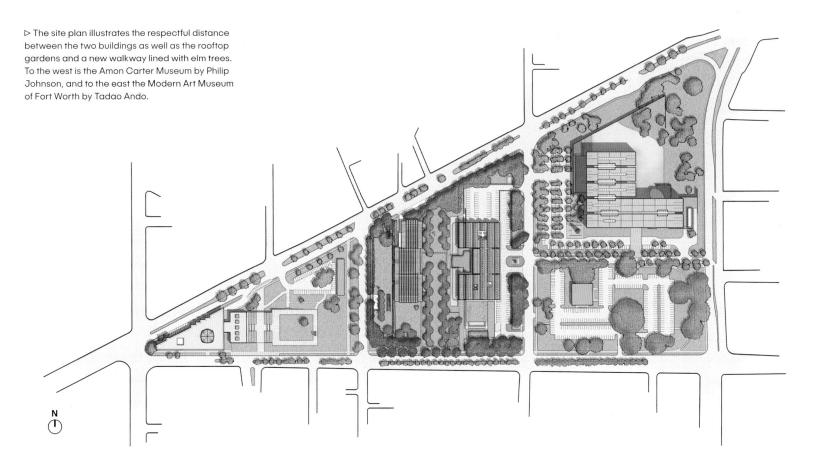

N

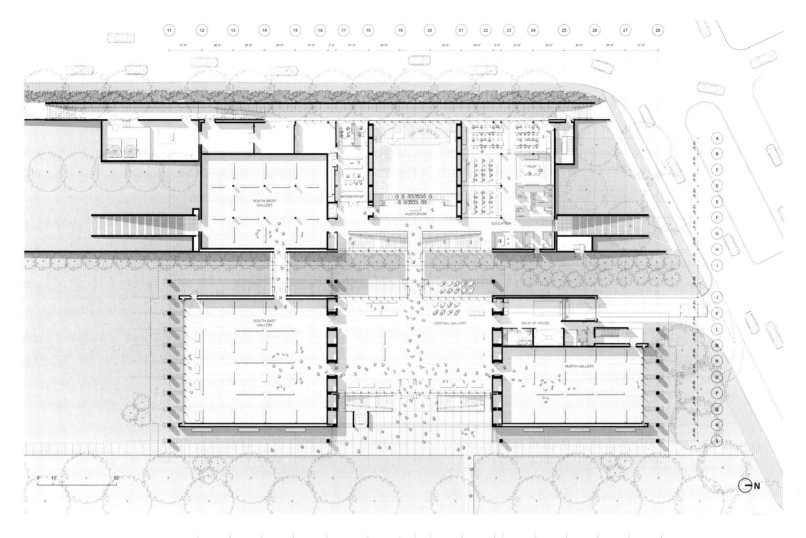

△▷The ground- and basement-level plans show how the gallery spaces are organized into two zones. The gallery spaces are located to the east, while the electrically-illuminated gallery, auditorium, and various classrooms and support spaces are located to the west and beneath an expansive green roof.

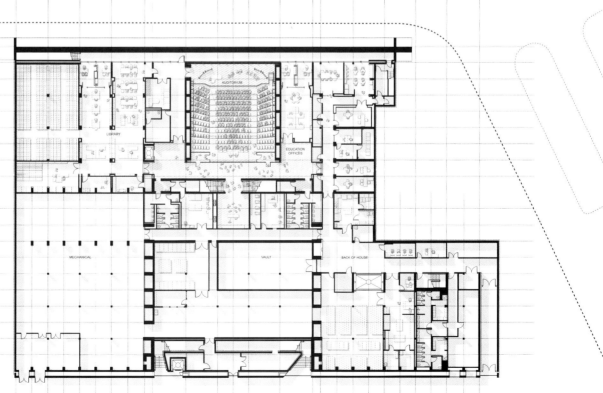

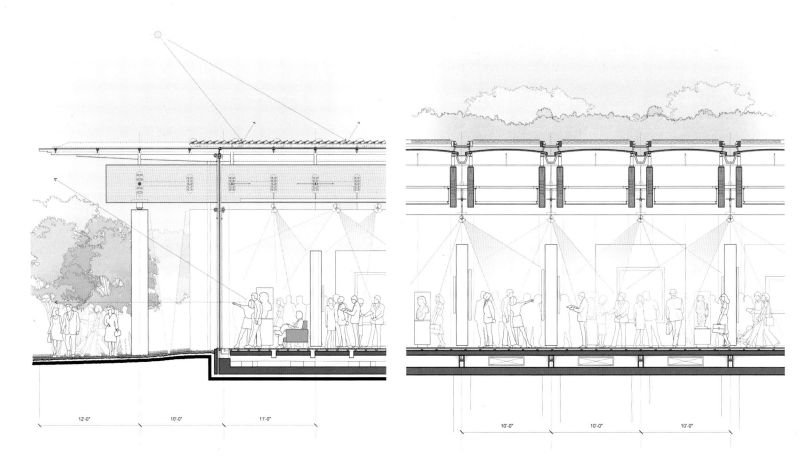

△ A south–north section detail illustrates the integration of toplighting and sidelighting in the pavilion galleries. Translucent overhangs extend beyond the glass façade to shade direct solar gains. Horizontal louvers with south-facing photovoltaic cells run east–west above the roof skylights to capture indirect north daylight while generating electricity. Large expanses of glazing allow direct views to the site. Vertical shading and adjustable rooftop louvers mediate the amount and distribution of daylight.

△ A west–east section detail of the skylights illustrates the exterior rooftop louvers, translucent glazing, and interior fabric scrims that diffuse daylight before entering the gallery below.

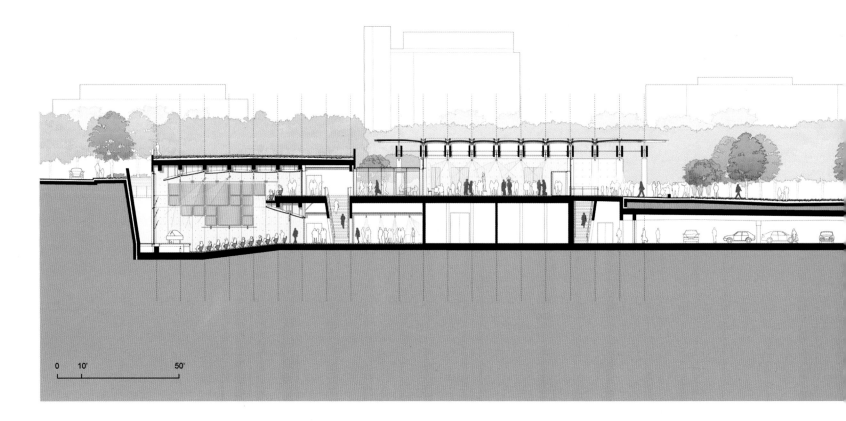

0   10'   50'

◁ View of the south façade of the Piano Pavilion and the west façade of the Kimbell Art Museum in the distance. Piano chose a quiet palette of concrete, wood, glass, and steel to complement Kahn's use of concrete, travertine, glass, and steel.

▽ The site/building sections illustrate the way in which Piano located much of the expanded program in the addition beneath a green roof or below ground to preserve a scale and massing appropriate for the Kimbell Museum.

you feel [the clouds]. You feel the beginning of the day. You feel the end of the day. You feel the difference. And artificial light is perfect, it's too perfect. It's too flat." [32]

Site Relationship

The 9.5-acre (3.8-hectare) site is bracketed to the west by the Amon Carter Museum by Philip Johnson, and to the east by the Modern Art Museum of Fort Worth by Tadao Ando. In his original site design, Kahn planned that visitors would enter the museum through the west entry, embarking on a choreographed journey that traversed the southern boundary of a sunken sculpture garden, passed through an elevated and shaded portico featuring linear pools of water, and entered a court with the dappled light

of yaupon holly trees, before finally reaching the soft reflected light of the west lobby. The west entry sequence was never fully realized, however, since Kahn did not know that most visitors arriving by automobile would enter directly into the lower level of the museum from the east parking lots.

The Piano Pavilion, a rectilinear building similar in scale and height to the Kimbell, reorients the arrival sequence, with the first view of the site directed toward the west façade of Kahn's museum and the garden space between the two buildings, as Teke explained: "[The new west] parking is underground and full of light. When you park your car you have no idea what's above ground. The glass elevator very slowly rises above ground facing toward Kahn, slowly

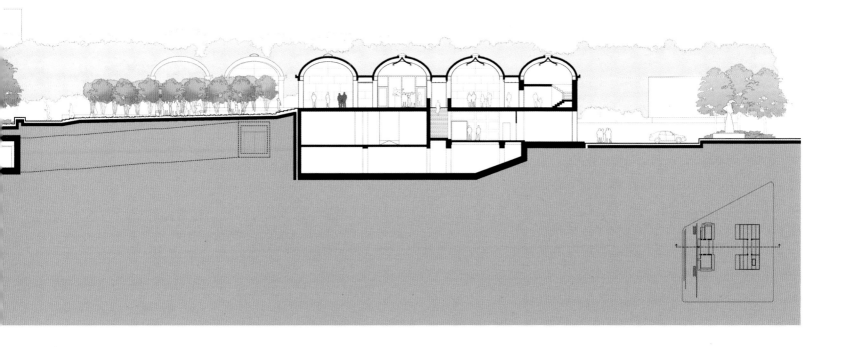

moving towards the light. You see the columns, water, and elm trees. You realize you have a beautiful day outside. We frame the Kahn building. You see the beautiful masterpiece behind the trees. You turn left to see the new building, which is open and transparent." [33]

The site design maintains a respectful distance of 49 meters (160 feet) between the Kimbell and the new pavilion, as Piano explained: "When we have a dialogue between two persons ... you put yourself the right distance. ... It's the same thing for a building. ... When the visitor comes up and the door opens; you have in front Kahn." [34]

The park-like site design includes a green roof on the western portion of the expansion, more than 320 new trees, and an allée of elms between the two buildings.

LIGHT AND THE DESIGN STRATEGIES

Kahn and Piano Building Forms

Kahn's Kimbell Art Museum is composed of 16 linear galleries organized on a tartan grid that is elongated on the north–south axis. This orientation ensures an even distribution of natural light throughout the day as the sun moves from east to west. The tripartite plan was designed to be entered on the west through the sheltering portico and grove of trees into the central zone, which contains the lobby, shop, and information desk. Stairs provide a link to the lower-level gallery and east entry. The north zone contains two galleries, a restaurant, and an auditorium. Located in the south zone are a series of five parallel galleries. The building plan features three internal light courts. Each court has a distinct luminous quality, including the Blue Court, which celebrates the sky and water; the Yellow Court, filled with sunlight; and the soft, sheltering Green

△ Stairs from the lower level and east parking provide access to the ground-floor lobby and art galleries at Kahn's Kimbell Art Museum.

Court, integrating gardens and sculptures. [35] Introverted in plan and section, indirect diagonal views are provided through openings between the intimate galleries and contrasted by direct views into the glazed courtyards. Visual access to the site is limited to the west entry lobby and portico. The architecture creates protective and sheltering contemplative spaces for artwork. A sense of place and time is experienced through subtle diurnal and seasonal changes of the diffuse, reflected, and filtered daylight in galleries and courtyards.

◁ View of the west lobby of Kimbell reveals the use of sidelighting at the entry, with an adjacent entry garden and loggia. North–south skylights and perforated aluminum reflectors provide ambient toplighting throughout the galleries.

above-ground portion of the light-filled and seemingly delicate east wing "pavilion" creates a respectful, even humble, relationship to Kahn's museum.

Kahn and Piano Galleries

In the Kimbell's 1972 film on the museum, Kahn explains his desire to create a quiet and contemplative sanctuary in which to experience the beauty and mystery of art in natural light: "Every work of architecture should be in natural light. And this [the Kimbell] in particular because you are seeing works of art that are really poetry."[36] Kahn further explained that each room has a particular quality of light and relationship to the sun: "An architect is a composer; truly his greatest act is that of composing and not designing. ... Steven Douglas' inspired statement about architecture ... said 'What slice of the sun does your building have?' and I added, 'What slice of the sun enters your room?'"[37]

Kahn allowed a very specific "slice of the sun" to enter his galleries, all of which measure 30 by 7 meters (100 by 23 feet) and are oriented on the north–south axis. Sunlight enters a 0.9-meter-wide (3-foot) Plexiglas skylight and strikes a perforated aluminum reflector, which reflects diffuse light onto the silvery concrete cycloid vaults and then back to the travertine-clad side walls. Indirect light is also diffused through the perforated reflector to the space below. The room itself becomes a light fixture, with direct sunlight from the skylight interacting with the reflector, ceiling, walls, and space. Adjustable track lighting is integrated into the reflector design, while mechanical and electrical systems are concealed in the ceiling channels in the lower volume between galleries. The room proportions, skylight, and reflector designs were carefully tuned by Kahn and lighting designer Richard Kelly to achieve the desired quantities of light.

Sited west of the Kimbell, the Piano Pavilion comprises two wings linked by glass passageways. The east wing (known as the "pavilion") is light-filled, open, and minimal in structure and detailing. In contrast, the west wing is earth-sheltered and internally focused, containing the west gallery (for light-sensitive work), the auditorium, and educational spaces. In the large daylit galleries of the "pavilion," direct views to the site are provided through shaded glass walls on the south and north, and indirect views of the sky through the translucent luminous ceilings. Glazed lobbies in both wings provide visual and physical connections between the two wings. Since much of the expansion is hidden below ground, the modest scale of the

△ View of the west zone of the Piano Pavilion, which houses the auditorium and educational activities. A glazed corridor passes through a narrow landscape between the east and west sides of the pavilion. South glazing admits abundant daylight to the stairs leading to the lower-level auditorium and support spaces.

▷ Daylit galleries in the east zone include adjustable walls that mediate light and views. Informal gathering spaces along the perimeter of the glazed façades provide direct visual connection to the site. Exterior overhangs and supplemental shading provide solar and daylighting control at the window wall.

Some forty years later, Piano took a decidedly different approach by using indirect north daylight rather than direct sunlight. The atmospheric qualities of Piano's expansively glazed toplit galleries are reminiscent of the vast horizontal landscape and sky found in this region of Texas. In his interview with Jerome Weeks, Piano describes Texas as "a place of big skies and brilliant light."[38] In contrast to the intimate silvery light and shadow of the Kahn galleries, Piano exposes the volume of the gallery space to the spacious overhead sky. Where Kahn admits a "slice of the sun," Piano admits multiple "slices of the sky." Where Kahn created a series of intimate galleries, Piano provided two large daylight galleries, also 30 meters (100 feet) in length but of differing widths—approximately 21 by 30 meters (70 by 100 feet) and 13 by 30 meters (43 by 100 feet) to the south and north. Toplighting and sidelighting are combined in both galleries, along with direct views and connections to the site. A translucent glass roof spans the entire gallery, above which is located a series of shading louvers oriented on the east–west axis and open to the north. Piano created a series of parallel views to the north, or "slices of the sky," through which indirect light enters the gallery. North daylight is further diffused as it passes through a translucent glass roof, the void created by the depth of the beams, and a translucent scrim before reaching the concrete walls and gallery space. Piano's layered luminous ceiling acts like a parasol that protects against the direct sun and transmits soft, diffuse light. The end wall of each gallery

has floor-to-ceiling glazing that is shaded by exterior overhangs to provide views of the site and changing weather and seasons.

LIGHT AND THE ART OF MAKING

Design Process

Louis Kahn and lighting designer Richard Kelly developed and refined the contemplative quality of daylight at the Kimbell through iterative refinement and testing of more than 100 daylighting variations using drawings, scale models, and full-scale mock-ups; refinements to the skylight reflector were further evaluated by computer analyst Isaac Goodbar from Edison Price Lighting.[39] The Piano Pavilion was designed with the same spirit of iterative exploration, testing, and integration. The collaboration included initial studies of Kahn's museum, multiple design scenarios, qualitative and quantitative analyses, and prototype testing throughout the design and construction phases. RPBW focused on design and Arup oversaw analyses of daylighting and artificial lighting. Underscoring the importance of physical models, Onur Teke estimates that 150–200 physical models were used to explore and test design ideas, as well as five full-scale mock-ups to study the quality of light, measure daylight performance, and test construction methods and detailing.

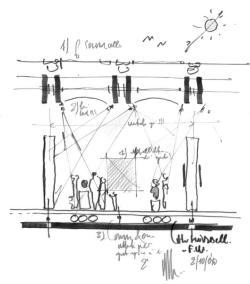

△ Piano's expansive skylights and multi-layered ceiling admits diffuse daylight throughout the gallery. Toplighting and sidelighting combine to provide an even distribution of light with direct views to the site. With direct visual and physical connection to the site, the pavilion defines a new relationship to the community that encourages accessibility, transparency, and openness.

◁ Kahn's inwardly focused galleries celebrate a mysterious play of light and shadow. The thin north–south skylight captures direct sunlight to redistribute it from the perforated aluminum reflector to the concrete ceiling to the gallery below. View of a south gallery.

◁ View of the east façade reveals the translucent shading that extends beyond the building façade to control direct sunlight and solar gains while creating a sheltered pathway along the building perimeter.

△ Detail of a full-scale mock-up used to study the integration of design strategies, materials, structure, and systems.

Arfon Davies explained that Arup was intimately involved with the design and testing from the onset, which was key to their successful collaboration. Davies clarified that the entire team was engaged in understanding the client brief, climate, history, and context. Arup helped develop and assess early conceptual schemes, including the study of issues such as solar geometry, daylight availability, and diurnal and seasonal movements of the sun, using simple methods such as sketching and physical models. As the project developed, design assessments and analyses shifted to studying shapes and geometry, and the progression of the design scenarios to support daylighting goals. Early quantitative analyses included computer and physical modeling to fine-tune and develop the geometry, transmission of light, and potential glazing systems and diffusion elements in the gallery. [40]

In the later stages of design development, full-scale mock-ups of building elements were tested in Italy in order to assess design and detailing of elements such as the skylight, roof assembly, photovoltaic louvers, and construction system. Two 6 by 6-meter (20 by 20-foot) gallery mock-ups were also built in Texas to evaluate the daylighting design in real time and under real sky conditions, as Davies explained: "Mock-ups are very useful from a lighting perspective. We can really assess how much light there is present in the room, and also understand the distribution. This allows the client to go into the room and experience the

daylight conditions. It allows the architect to experiment with finishes and how they impact the quality of light and the conservation aspects." [41]

Piano Pavilion Integrated Design

In the Piano Pavilion, rigorous design integration resulted in clarity and simplicity, with each layer of the gallery roof serving multiple purposes, as Onur Teke explains: "The main difference with this building compared to other Renzo roofs, is that with this roof there is a single layer with different functions." [42]

For example, the photovoltaic louvers on the exterior serve multiple purposes, including shading and solar control, adjustment of daylight levels and distribution (depending on the louver position from closed to open 45 degrees to the north), generation of

◁ △ Full-scale construction details and room mock-ups were essential to develop, refine, and test the integration of design strategies, construction and material detailing, and systems performance.

electricity, and hail protection (when rotated 180 degrees). The second layer of the glass roof combines varied glazing attributes, including krypton-filled polyvinyl butyral (PVB) glazing with a low-emissivity coating and an acid-etched frit, to effectively address the diffusion of direct sunlight, control of heat gain and loss, mediation of ultraviolet radiation, and safety performance. The third and final layer is the interior scrim, fabricated using a Trevira Comfort and Safety flame-retardant yarn that provides diffusion of daylight and sufficient transparency to see the structure, skylight aperture, and sky through the louvers. [43]

Daylight combined with LED electric lighting reduces energy consumption for lighting by 75 percent compared to the Kimbell. [44] Photovoltaic cells generate sufficient electricity to offset up to 70 percent of the carbon emissions from the electric lighting and control systems. [45] The expansion minimizes external heat loss and gains as well as stormwater runoff by locating two-thirds of the building below ground and beneath a green roof. The pavilion also employs 36 geothermal wells to harvest groundwater for heating and cooling, which combine with a displacement air system from the "breathing floor" to optimize energy performance and comfort. On the topic of sustainability and energy performance, Piano muses, "In Texas that

is the kingdom of oil, we can prove you can make a building that doesn't throw oil out of the window." [46]

Piano clarified that integration of design and technology allowed the team to achieve a high level of performance while maintaining design excellence: "It is the overall design, as well as the solar technology built into the roof system, that yields important energy savings. This is the way it should be: designing for energy savings is not an 'add on,' but, rather, the proper way to build." [47] Arup and RPBW estimate that daylighting, LED electric lighting, control systems, photovoltaic cells, and the geothermal system reduce overall energy consumption and carbon emissions by 50 percent compared to the Kimbell. [48]

Daylight Analyses

Kahn and Piano approached the daylight levels, light distribution, and illumination of the artwork from distinct perspectives. In both projects, the conservation of artwork was a primary concern, with daylight and electric lighting controlled to meet the daily and annual illuminance requirements within each gallery, depending upon the light sensitivity of the medium. Studies of the Kimbell by Arfon Davies and colleagues at Arup suggest that Kahn's approach to daylight is most effective for ambient illumination. In an interview with *Mondo*arc*, Davies described daylight studies of the Kimbell conducted prior to design of the Piano Pavilion: "Interior illuminance levels were logged and High Dynamic Range (HDR) imaging was used to capture daylight conditions at different times of the day, and under different sky conditions. It quickly became apparent that the quantity of daylight within the Kahn galleries was much lower than was expected; the presence of artificial light in the space is much more. Further study and discussion with the museum also showed that there was a preference for a mix of light, the use of both electric light and daylight at all times, something that low levels of daylight can accommodate." [49]

In contrast, goals for the Piano Pavilion included utilizing daylight to illuminate the artwork and to reduce the electric lighting load and related energy and carbon emissions, as Arfon Davies clarified: "A low carbon strategy encourages the use of daylight over electric light, which leads to a regime where, for much of the year, the art is displayed under natural light alone, and electric light is used only in the winter and towards the end of the day when daylight levels fall. This approach was somewhat different to the existing Kahn building, with relatively low levels of daylight and electric light used during all museum open hours."[50]

The new pavilion had additional daylight priorities, including: 1) using daylight as the primary source of light; 2) the ability to tune daylight transmission; 3) the ability to reduce light levels to 4.64 footcandles (50 lux) or less; and 4) minimizing daylight when the museum is closed.[51] Iterative quantitative analyses were conducted by Arup to evaluate and refine the daylight strategies, roof system, structure and construction detailing, and systems integration to achieve the daylighting goals.

One example of the highly detailed daylight analysis is Arup's transmission simulation, used to assess the effect of the skylight louver "tilt position." Various louver settings were studied using 5-10-15-20 degrees (open to the north) to evaluate the resulting illuminance levels and uniformity of the light distribution on the vertical wall. The simulations studied "average" annual conditions at noon on the spring/fall equinox under sunny sky conditions. Illuminance levels were estimated in footcandles on the vertical gallery walls, with values ranging from a minimum of 6 footcandles (64.5 lux) with the louvers opened 5 degrees, to a maximum of 40 footcandles (430.5 lux) with the louvers opened 20 degrees.[52] Additional types of daylight assessments were used throughout all design phases to evaluate and refine the project, meet the program goals, and to integrate supplemental electric lighting and control systems.

LIGHT INSPIRATIONS

The museums of Louis Kahn and Renzo Piano use daylight to different ends. Kahn's daylighting design is renowned for its elegant construction, awe-inspiring qualities of light and shadow, and graceful design resolution. The architecture of the Kimbell is artfully illuminated by indirect and ambient light, while the artwork is highlighted with electric lighting. For Piano, there was an expanded daylight program, with the goal of illuminating the artwork with natural light, fostering direct connections to the site, along with integrating new construction methods, technologies, and sustainable design strategies. Each building stands on its own merits, reflecting the visions of two very different master architects and their respective eras. Despite the same client and site, Louis Kahn and Renzo Piano use daylighting to create distinctive architectural vocabularies and programmatic responses. Against the backdrop of the Kimbell, one of Louis Kahn's greatest architectural legacies, Renzo Piano achieves a respectful and elegant luminous conversation across the decades while creating his own masterful language of light.

DESIGN PROFILE

1. Building Profile
Project: Piano Pavilion, Kimbell Art Museum
Location: Fort Worth, Texas, USA
Architect: Renzo Piano Building Workshop
Client: Kimbell Art Foundation
Building Type: Museum
Square Footage: 9,395 sq m (101,130 sq ft)
Estimated Cost: $135m
Completion: 2013

2. Professional Team
Design Architect: Renzo Piano, Renzo Piano Building Workshop (Genoa, Italy) in collaboration with Kendall/Heaton Associates, Inc. (Houston, Texas)
Design team: M. Carroll (partner in charge), O. Teke with S. Ishida (partner), S. Ishida, M. Orlandi, S. Polotti, D. Hammerman, F. Spadini, E. Moore, A. Morselli, S. Ishida, D. Piano, D. Reimers, E. Santiago; F. Cappellini, F. Terranova (models)
Executive Architect: Kendall/Heaton Associates Inc., Houston, TX
Project Manager: Paratus Group, New York, NY
Executive Committee Advisor: Bill Lacy, FAIA, December 2006–June 2010
Construction Manager: The Beck Group, Dallas/Fort Worth, TX
Structural Engineer: Guy Nordenson and Associates, New York, NY, and Brockette, Davis, Drake, Inc., Dallas, TX (consultant to construction manager)
Lighting: Arup Lighting, London, Great Britain
MEP Engineers: Arup, London, UK, with Summit Consultants, Fort Worth, TX
Civil Engineer: Huitt-Zollars, Fort Worth, TX
Façade Consultant: Front, New York, NY
Landscape Architect: Michael Morgan Landscape Architecture and Pond & Company, Atlanta, GA
Concrete Consultants: Dottor Group, Venice, Italy; Reg Hough, Rhinebeck, NY; Capform, Carrollton, TX
Cost Consultant: Stuart-Lynn Company
Acoustical/Audiovisual: Harvey Marshall Berling Associates Inc., New York, NY
Geotechnical: Henley-Johnston Associates, Dallas, TX
Wind Engineering: Rowan Williams Davies & Irwin, Guelph, Ontario, Canada
Security: Architects Security Group, Ormand Beach, FL

3. Climate Profile
Climate (Köppen-Geiger Climate Classification System): Cfa: humid subtropical climate
Latitude: 32.7° north latitude
Solar Angles: Noon
June 21: 80.8°
March/September 21: 57.3°
December 21: 33.8°
Length of Day: Approximate Hours of Daylight from Sunrise to Sunset
June 21: 14h 18m
March/September 21: 12h 9m
December 21: 9h 58m
Heating Degree Days: 1339 heating degree days °C (2343 heating degree days °F) (18°C and 65°F base temperature)[53]
Cooling Degree Days: 1726 cooling degree days °C (2760 cooling degree days °F) (18°C and 65°F base temperature)[54]

4. Design Strategies
Daylighting Strategies: 1) Sidelighting: end walls with floor-to-ceiling glazing, exterior shading, and interior shades, and 2) Toplighting: exterior photovoltaic shading louvers open to the north, translucent skylights, and interior fabric scrim.
Sustainable Design and High-Performance Strategies: Daylighting with solar shading throughout; high-performance glazing; low-energy LED lighting; air displacement supply system; fresh air processed through a central unit to efficiently recover energy and moisture; breathable floor in the galleries with low-velocity air; high-efficiency bathroom fixtures; green roof; photovoltaic cells; and 36 140-meter (460-foot) geothermal wells to store energy and provide low-carbon heating and cooling.
Renewable Energy Strategies: Photovoltaic electric energy generation, geothermal heating and cooling system.
Energy: Uses 50 percent of the amount of energy per square foot required by Kahn's Kimbell Art Museum.[55]
Carbon: Photovoltaic cells will replace 80 tonnes (90 tons) of carbon dioxide production annually, or about 20 percent of the annual carbon emissions of the new building.[56]

Piano: Structure and Materials

The exploded diagrams illustrate the relationship between the Piano Pavilion by Renzo Piano and the Kimbell Art Museum by Louis Kahn. The diagram of the Piano Pavilion reveals a similar scale and massing to the Kimbell Museum. Organized on a north–south axis, the concrete walls enclose galleries on the east and west, while large floor-to-ceiling glass façades open to the south and north. The extension of the roof provides solar control and shading for the façades. A layered translucent ceiling admits filtered toplighting throughout the galleries. The skylights include rooftop louvers, translucent glazing, and interior fabric scrims. Louis Kahn's concrete structure admits a small slice of direct sunlight into thin linear skylights. Direct sunlight reflects from a perforated aluminum reflector beneath the skylight to the concrete ceiling vault and space below. Three courtyards provide diffuse sidelighting and interior views that contrast with the toplit galleries.

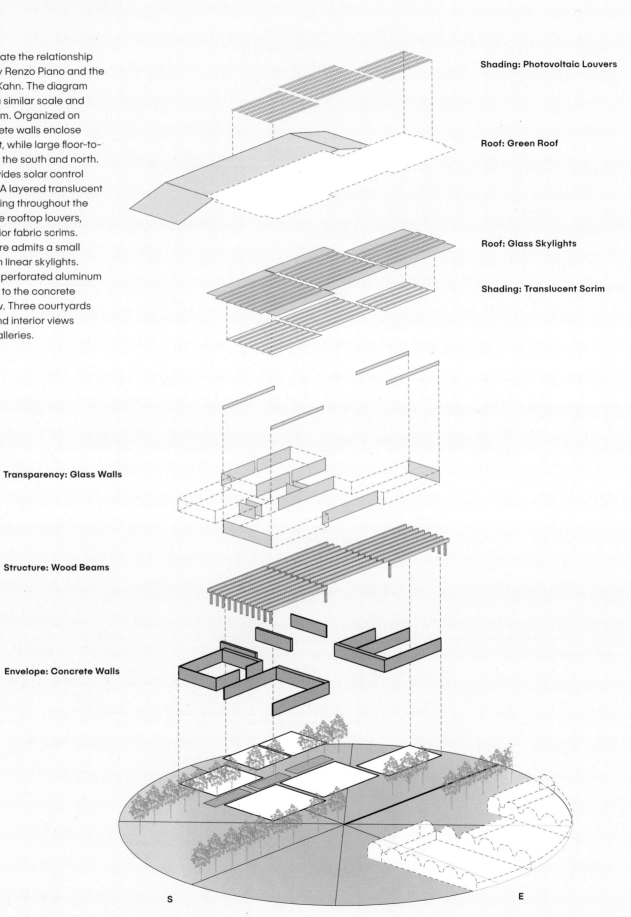

Shading: Photovoltaic Louvers

Roof: Green Roof

Roof: Glass Skylights

Shading: Translucent Scrim

Transparency: Glass Walls

Structure: Wood Beams

Envelope: Concrete Walls

S   E

Kahn: Structure and Materials

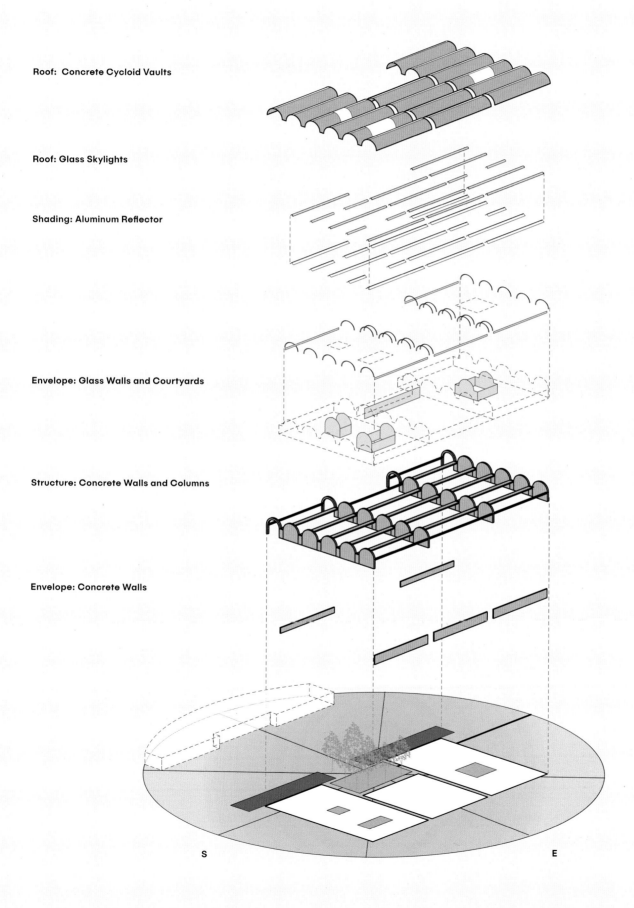

Roof: Concrete Cycloid Vaults

Roof: Glass Skylights

Shading: Aluminum Reflector

Envelope: Glass Walls and Courtyards

Structure: Concrete Walls and Columns

Envelope: Concrete Walls

S

E

Views, Massing, and Site

Plan diagrams illustrate the visual and physical relationships between the two buildings. Direct views are provided across a newly landscaped site. The Piano Pavilion celebrates direct views to the landscape while the Kimbell Museum provides interior views to the courtyards.

(Opposite page) The upper section illustrates Louis Kahn's toplit gallery, which gathers a small slice of sunlight through a linear north–south skylight. An aluminum reflector bounces daylight to the concrete ceiling vault and gently to the space below. The lower section illustrates Renzo Piano's toplit gallery, which employs operable exterior louvers to capture north light while generating electricity with south-facing photovoltaic cells. Translucent glazing and a fabric scrim further diffuse daylight before entering the gallery below. Floor-to-ceiling glazing with interior shading and exterior translucent overhangs admit diffuse sidelighting.

Views

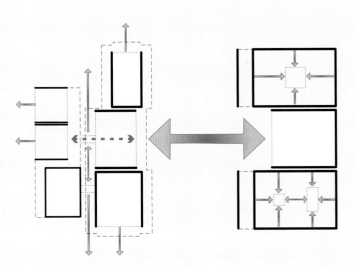

Massing

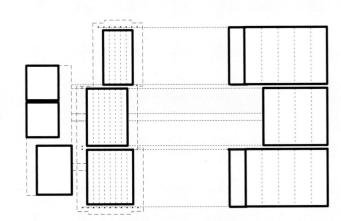

Site

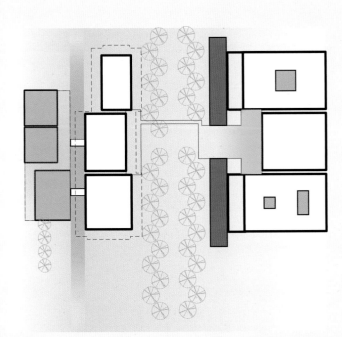

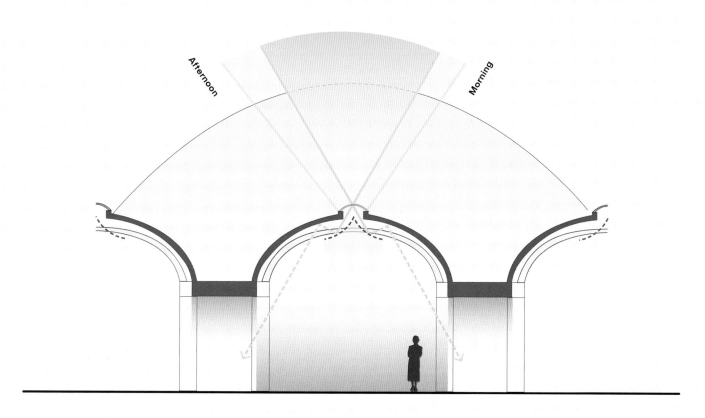

West

East

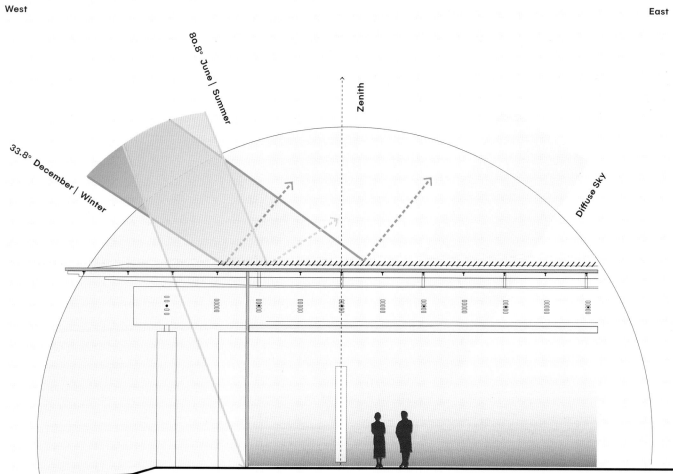

South

North

Arup Daylight Analysis: Illuminance

Lighting consultants at Arup worked with architects to develop design concepts, evaluate strategies, optimize the performance, and to test computer simulations, physical models, and full-scale mock-ups for the climate and geographic location (37.2° north latitude). A transmission analysis of a gallery, using Radiance software, evaluated the effect of the system tilt angle of the rooftop louvers on the light levels and daylight distribution on the gallery walls for the equinox (March 21 at noon). Adjustable louvers enable light levels and distribution to vary based on exhibition needs and performance goals.

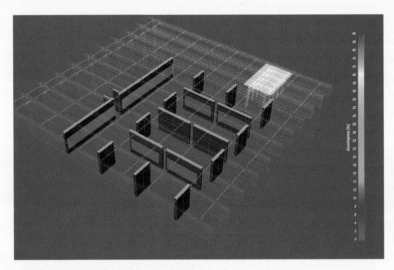

Transmission Analysis: System Tilt Angle:
5°, March 21, 12:00 pm, sunny sky (fc)

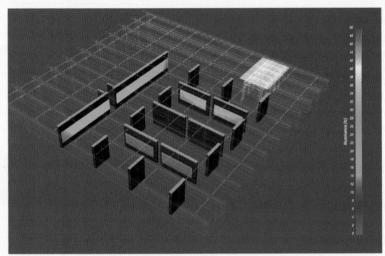

Transmission Analysis: System Tilt Angle:
10°, March 21, 12:00 pm, sunny sky (fc)

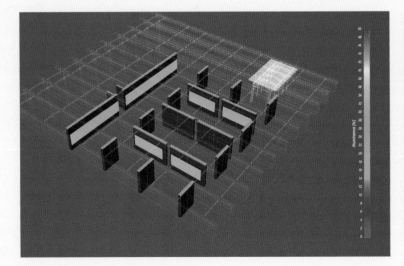

Transmission Analysis: System Tilt Angle:
15°, March 21, 12:00 pm, sunny sky (fc)

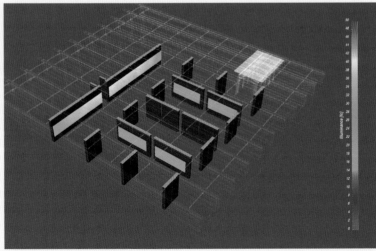

Transmission Analysis: System Tilt Angle:
20°, March 21, 12:00 pm, sunny sky (fc)

Chapter 6: endnotes

Introduction

1 Sim Van der Ryn and Stuart Cohen, *Ecological Design: Tenth Anniversary Edition*, Washington: Island Press, 2007, ix–x.

2 Bill Reed, "A Living Systems Approach to Design," American Institute of Architects National Convention Keynote Address, May 2007, http://www.integrativedesign.net/images/Living_System_Design.pdf.

3 Kiel Moe, *Integrated Design in Contemporary Architecture*, New York: Princeton Architectural Press, 2008, 6.

4 Bill Reed, "Whole Systems Integration Process," *Integrative Design Collaborative*, http://www.integrativedesign.net/integrative.htm.

5 "Architectural Fact Sheet: Renzo Piano Pavilion," Renzo Piano Building Workshop and Kendall Heaton Associates, 4.

Chapter 6.1

6 "Architecture Rebel," YouTube video, 23:38, posted September 9, 2014, https://www.youtube.com/watch?v=bgQoVbEX8-A.

7 Ibid., 8:50 and 23:38.

8 "Climate: Ho Chi Minh City," Climate-data.org, http://en.climate-data.org/location/4235/.

9 "Average Weather for Ho Chi Minh City, Vietnam," WeatherSpark.com, https://weatherspark.com/averages/33994/Ho-Chi-Minh-City-Ho-Chi-Minh-Vietnam.

10 "Stacking Green House Project Profile," Vo Trong Nghia, 1.

11 Dezeen, "WAF 2012: Vo Trong Nghia/Stacking Green," YouTube video, 2:19, posted by Ashui.com, January 7, 2013, https://www.youtube.com/watch?v=kzXD5cNDiGg.

12 "Stacking Green," *Divisare,* http://divisare.com/projects/212110-vo-trong-nghia-architects-stacking-green.

13 "Stacking Green House Project Profile," 1.

14 Dezeen, "WAF 2012: Vo Trong Nghia/Binh Duong School," YouTube video, 2:18, posted by *Ashui.com,* January 7, 2013, https://www.youtube.com/watch?v=o5a7UkiEluA.

15 Dezeen, "WAF 2012: Vo Trong Nghia/Stacking Green," 5:17.

16 "Stacking Green," *Divisare.*

17 "Stacking Green House Project Profile," 1.

18 Vo Trong Nghia Architects, email with author, July 28, 2016.

19 "Architecture Rebel," 23:38.

20 Ibid.

21 "Degree Days: Energy Data for Professionals," Degreedays.net: Weather Underground, http://www.degreedays.net/#generate.

22 Ibid.

Chapter 6.2

23 Kimbell Art Museum, "A Conversation with Renzo Piano – Kimbell Art Museum," YouTube video, 8:50, posted by the "Kimbell Art Museum," November 19, 2013, https://www.youtube.com/watch?v=LvZlN1YqeXs.

24 Ibid., 9:10.

25 Ibid., 10:21.

26 "Average Weather for Fort Worth, Texas," WeatherSparks.com, https://weatherspark.com/averages/30313/Fort-Worth-Texas-United-States.

27 "Dallas/Fort Worth Climatology," National Oceanic and Atmospheric Administration, http://www.srh.noaa.gov/fwd/?n=dfwclimo.

28 "Renzo Piano Pavilion, Kimbell Art Museum," *Mondo*arc*, Issue 78 (April/May 2014), 56, https://issuu.com/mondiale/docs/ma78_digi_lr.

29 Onur Teke, Associate Architect, Renzo Piano Building Workshop, telephone interview with author, recorded August 1, 2015.

30 Ibid.

31 Kimbell Art Museum, "A Conversation with Renzo Piano," 10:47.

32 Ibid., 9:10.

33 Onur Teke.

34 Kimbell Art Foundation, "Kahn: Piano—The Piano Pavilion at the Kimbell Art Museum," YouTube video, 3:08, posted by the Kimbell Art Museum, November 26, 2013, https://www.youtube.com/watch?v=tx6R_4zCTUU.

35 Kimbell Art Museum, "Kahn Building," https://www.kimbellart.org/architecture/kahn-building.

36 Paul Falkenberg, "Louis Kahn, architect," *Archivio Nazionale Cinema d'Impresa,* YouTube archival footage from 1972, Published on December 4, 2013, 10:54, https://www.youtube.com/watch?v=ZbE3rmh62x4.

37 Ibid.

38 Kimbell Art Museum, "A Conversation with Renzo Piano," 22:02.

39 Aaron Seward, "A Luminous History," *Architectural Lighting,* November 21, 2011, http://www.archlighting.com/projects/a-luminous-history_o?o=7.

40 Arfon Davies, Associate Director of Lighting, Arup, telephone interview with author, recorded January 12, 2016.

41 Ibid.

42 Onur Teke.

43 "Renzo Piano Pavilion," *Mondo*arc,* 52–54.

44 Ibid., 58.

45 Ibid., 52.

46 Jerome Weeks, "Renzo Piano and the New Kimbell Annex," *Art and Seek,* May 27, 2010, http://artandseek.net/2010/05/27/renzo-piano-and-the-new-kimbell-annex/.

47 Ibid.

48 "Architectural Fact Sheet: Renzo Piano Pavilion," *RPBW*, 4.

49 "Renzo Piano Pavilion, Kimbell Art Museum," *Mondo*arc*, 54.

50 Ibid., 56.

51 Arfon Davies.

52 Arfon Davies, email communication with author, "Analysis of daylight illuminance within the gallery at various louver tilt angles," September 25, 2015.

53 "Degree Days: Energy Data for Professionals," *Degreedays.net: Weather Underground*, http://www.degreedays.net/#generate.

54 Ibid.

55 "Architectural Fact Sheet: Renzo Piano Pavilion," *Renzo Piano Building Workshop and Kendall Heaton Associates*, 1.

56 Ibid.

RESOURCES

Bibliography

Acuweather. "Weather Data Depot." *EnergyCap Inc.* **http://www.weatherdatadepot.com.**

"Architecture Rebel." YouTube video. Posted by "Al Jazeera English," September 9, 2014. **https://www.youtube.com/watch?v=bgQoVbEX8-A.**

"ARPAE Project Profile." *Italy: Mario Cucinella Architects*, 2015.

"Architectural Fact Sheet: Renzo Piano Pavilion." *Renzo Piano Building Workshop and Kendall Heaton Associates.*

"Art Museum Naoshima Project Brief." *Tadao Ando Architect & Associates.*

"Atmospheres by Peter Zumthor." *Arcspace.com: Danish Architecture Centre*, July 19, 2006. **http://www.arcspace.com/bookcase/atmosphere-/.**

Auping, Michael. *Seven Interviews with Tadao Ando.* Texas: Modern Art Museum of Fort Worth, 2002.

Baker, N.V., A. Fanchiotti, and K. Steemers, editors. *Daylighting in Architecture: A European Reference Book.* London: James & James, 2001.

Ballesteros, Mario. "The Museum as Platform." *Domus*, December 3, 2013. **http://www.domusweb.it/en/architecture/2013/12/03/the_museum_as_platform.html.**

Birch, Amanda. "Serpentine Pavilion 2011." *bdonline.co.uk*, June 27, 2011. **http://www.bdonline.co.uk/serpentine-gallery-pavilion-by-peter-zumthor/5020460.article.**

Blackwood, Michael. *Tadao Ando.* 1989. Michael Blackwood Production Inc. YouTube video. June 28, 2015. **https://www.youtube.com/watch?v=61g14g6hF7c.**

Blaser, Werner. *Tadao Ando: Sunken Courts.* Zürith: Verlag Niggli AG, 2007.

Böhme, Gernot. "Encountering Atmospheres: A Reflection on the Concept of Atmosphere in the Work of Juhani Pallasmaa and Peter Zumthor." *OASE,* no 91 (2013): 93-100.

Bullock, Kathern. "Serpentine Pavilion 2011 by Peter Zumthor." YouTube video. Posted by Kathern Bullock, April 20, 2015. **http://www.dailymotion.com/video/x2oludh.**

"Capilla del Retiro: Undurraga Devés Arquitectos." *ArchDaily*, April 2, 2012. **http://www.archdaily.com/221334/capilla-del-retiro-undurraga-deves-arquitectos/.**

Cather, Christine. "First Writing Group at Maggie's Lanarkshire." *Wee Read* (blog), June 12, 2015. **http://www.weeread.scot/first-writing-group-at-maggies-lanarkshire.**

Chopra, Aidan. "A Conversation with Allied Works." SketchUp (blog). Posted by Aidan Chopra, February 22, 2012. **https://blog.sketchup.com/sketchupdate/conversation-allied-works.**

"Climate Data for Cities Worldwide." *Climate-Data.Org.* **http://en.climate-data.org.**

"Clyfford Still Museum." *Allied Works Architecture.* **http://www.alliedworks.com/projects/clyfford-still-museum/.**

"Clyfford Still Museum, Allied Works Architecture." *Arcspace.com: Danish Architecture Centre*, March 5, 2012. **http://www.arcspace.com/features/allied-works-architecture/clyfford-still-museum/.**

Corrodi, Michelle and Klaus Spechtenhauser. *Illuminating.* Basel: Birkhäuser Publishers, 2008.

Corkill, Edan. "Icon and iconoclast Tadao Ando's architectural vision goes way beyond buildings: interview with Japan Times." *Japan Times Ltd.*, December 28, 2008. Accessed November 8, 2015. **http://www.japantimes.co.jp/life/2008/12/07/style/icon-and-iconoclast/#.VkD_RVWrS1t.**

Cucinella, Mario. "Beyond Zero Housing." *University of Nottingham.* SlideShare, PowerPoint Presentation. Posted by "Creative Energy Homes," October 24, 2012. **http://www.slideshare.net/CreativeEnergyHomes/bzch-mario-cucinella.**

Cuttle, Christopher. *Lighting by Design, second edition.* Amsterdam: Elsevier, 2008.

Dezeen. "WAF 2012: Vo Trong Nghia/Binh Duong School." Youtube video. Posted by Ashui.com, January 7, 2013. **https://www.youtube.com/watch?v=o5a7UkiEluA.**

Dezeen. "WAF 2012: Vo Trong Nghia/Stacking Green." YouTube video. Posted by Ashui.com, January 7, 2013. **https://www.youtube.com/watch?v=kzXD5cNDiGg.**

"Degree Days: Energy Data for Professionals." *Weather Underground.* **http://www.degreedays.net/#generate.**

Descottes, Hervé with Cecilia E. Ramos. *Architectural Lighting: Designing with Light and Space.* New York: Princeton Architectural Press, 2011.

Deutsches Architektur Museum, editor. *The Secret of the Shadow: Light and Shadow in Architecture.* Germany: DAM, 2002.

Fjeld, Per Olaf. *Architect Sverre Fehn: Intuition – Reflection – Construction.* Helsinki: Museum of Finnish Architecture, 2009. **http://www.e-architect.co.uk/finland/sverre-fehn-architecture-exhibition.**

Frick, Mathias. "Tadao Ando, From Emptiness to Infinity." *A Design Film Festival 2014.* YouTube video. 2014. **http://designfilmfestival.com/2014/tadao-ando.**

"Future of the GSA." *The Flow*, no. 14 (2011): 8-9. Accessed January 13, 2016. **http://www.gsa.ac.uk/media/455325/gsa_flowissue14_a4.pdf.**

Gannon, Todd, editor. *The Light Construction Reader.* New York: The Monacelli Press, 2002.

Glancey, Jonathan. "Peter Zumthor Unveils Secret Garden for Serpentine Pavilion." *The Guardian*, April, 4, 2011. **http://www.theguardian.com/artanddesign/2011/apr/04/peter-zumthor-serpentine-gallery-pavilion.**

Guzowski, Mary. *Towards Zero Energy Architecture: New Solar Design.* London: Laurence King, 2010.

Guzowski, Mary. *Daylighting for Sustainable Design.* New York: McGraw-Hill, 2000.

Helsing Almaas, Ingerid. "People have to be strong to cope with good architecture: *An interview with Sverre Fehn.* Arkitektur N*, May 10, 2010. **http://architecturenorway.no/stories/people-stories/fehn-97/.**

Heathcote, Edwin. "Museo Jumex." *Architectural Record*, May 16, 2014. **http://www.architecturalrecord.com/articles/7976-museo-jumex.**

Heathcote, Edwin. "Mexico City's Jumex Museum." *Visual Arts*, November 22, 2013. **http://www.ft.com/cms/s/2/5bfc3cc4-51cf-11e3-8c42-00144feabdc0.html.**

Hegger, Manfred, Matthias Fuchs, Thomas Stark, and Martin Zeumer. *Energy Manual: Sustainable Architecture.* Basel: Birkhäuser Publishers, 2008.

Hildebrand, Grant. *Origins of Architectural Pleasure.* Berkeley: University of California Press, 1999.

Hodson, Chris. "Copper Awards: Winner, Chapel of St. Lawrence, Vantaa, Finland, Avanto Arkkitehdit." *Architectural Review*, November 1, 2011. **http://www.architectural-review.com/copper-awards-winner/8621684.article.**

Horodner, Brad. "Brad Cloepfil." *Bomb Magazine*, Spring 2005. **http://bombmagazine.org/article/2731/brad-cloepfil.**

Huxtable, Ada Louise. " The Pritzker Architecture Prize Essay: The Paradox of Sverre Fehn." *The Pritzker Architecture Prize.* Hyatt Foundation, 1997. **http://www.pritzkerprize. com/1997/essay.**

Illuminating Engineering Society of North America (IESNA). *The IESNA Lighting Handbook, 10th edition.* New York: IESNA, 2011.

Jencks, Charles and Edwin Heathcote. *Architecture of Hope.* London: Frances Lincoln Limited, 2010.

Jodidio, Philip. *Tadao Ando at Naoshima: Art Architecture Nature.* New York: Rizzoli, 2006.

Kelly, Richard. "Lighting as an Integral Part of Architecture." *College Art Journal,* vol. 12, no. 1: Autumn, 1952. Accessed April 25, 2016. **http://www.jstor.org/stable/773361.**

Keswick Jencks, Maggie. *A View from the Front Line.* Edinburgh: Maggie Keswick and Charles Jencks, 1995. **https://www.maggiescentres.org/ media/uploads/file_upload_plugin/view-from- the-front-line/view-from-the-front-line_1.pdf.**

Kimbell Art Foundation. "Kahn : Piano – The Piano Pavilion at the Kimbell Museum." YouTube video. Posted by the Kimbell Art Museum, November 26, 2013. **https://www.youtube.com/ watch?v=tx6R_4zCTUU.**

Kimbell Art Museum. "A Conversation with Renzo Piano – Kimbell Art Museum." YouTube video. Posted by the Kimbell Art Museum, November 19, 2013. **https://www.youtube.com/ watch?v=LvZIN1YqeXs.**

Knowles, Ralph. *Ritual House.* Washington: Island Press, 2006.

Köster, Helmut. *Dynamic Daylighting Architecture Basics, Systems, Projects.* Basel: Birkhäuser Publishers, 2006.

Licht, Ulrike Brandi. *Lighting Design: Principles, Implementation, Case Studies.* Basel: Birkhäuser Publishers, 2006.

Lie, Tanja. "The Word Thief: *An interview with Per Olaf Fjeld on the words of Sverre Fehn." Arkitektur N,* November 5, 2009. **http://architecturenorway. no/stories/people-stories/fjeld-on-fehn-09/.**

Lobell, John. *Between Silence and Light: Spirit in the Architecture of Lois I. Kahn.* Boston: Shambhala Publications, Inc., 1979.

Lopez, Barry. *Arctic Dreams: Imagination and Desire in a Northern Landscape.* Toronto: Bantam Books, 1987.

Lovell, Jenny. *Building Envelopes: An Integrated Approach.* New York: Princeton Architectural Press, 2010.

Lyle, John Tillman. *Regenerative Design for Sustainable Development.* New York: John Wiley & Sons, 1994.

Madsen, Deane. "2013 AL Design Awards: Clyfford Still Museum, Denver." *Architectural Lighting,* August 1, 2013. **http://www.archlighting. com/design-awards/2013-al-design-awards- clyfford-still-museum-denver_o.**

"Maggie's Centre Lanarkshire Project Profile." *Reiach and Hall Architects,* 2014.

Major, Mark, Jonathan Speirs, and Anthony Tischhauser. *Made of Light: The Art of Light and Architecture.* Basel: Birkhäuser Publishers, 2005.

Malin, Nadav. "Strategies for Succeeding with Integrated Design." *Environmental Building News.* **https://www2.buildinggreen.com/article/ integrated-design-0.**

McConahey, Erin, Christopher Rush, and Brian Stacy. "The Clyfford Still Museum." *The Arup Journal.* Issue 1, 2013, 16.

McKeown, Henry. "Glasgow School of Art." *Glasgow School of Art Research Excellence Framework 2014,* 2014. **http://radar.gsa. ac.uk/3148/14/McKeown131115JR.pdf.**

Meek, Christopher and Kevin Van Den Wymelenberg. *Daylighting and Integrated Lighting Design.* New York: Routledge, 2015.

Merin, Gili. "Peter Zumthor: Seven Personal Observations on Presence in Architecture." *ArchDaily,* December 3, 2013. **http://www. archdaily.com/452513/peter-zumthor-seven- personal-observations-on-presence-in- architecture.**

Meyers, Victoria. *Designing with Light.* New York: Abbeville Press Publishers, 2006.

Millet, Marietta. *Light Revealing Architecture.* New York: Van Nostrand Reinhold, 1996.

Moe, Kiel. *Integrated Design in Contemporary Architecture.* New York: Princeton Architectural Press, 2008.

Murray, Christine. "AJ editor Christine Murray talks to Peter Zumthor." *Architects' Journal,* June 2, 2011. **http://www.architectsjournal.co.uk/news/ daily-news/peter-zumthor-my-work-is-not- about-design/8615593.article.**

"Museo Jumex Complete – David Chipperfield Interview." *Designboom,* November 18, 2013. **http://www.designboom.com/art/ museo-jumex-complete-david-chipperfield- interview-11-18-2013/.**

MX-LAB. "Museo Jumex by David Chipperfield Architects." YouTube video. Posted by MX-LAB, October 25, 2013. **https://www.youtube.com/ watch?v=vVAnD1vGJGw.**

Norwegian Ministry of Foreign Affairs. "The Architecture Behind Nordic Modernism." *The Royal Norwegian Embassy,* Slovakia. **http://www.norway.sk/travel/sports/Sverre_ Fehn_architect/#.Vnm2wsYrK1s.**

National Oceanic and Atmospheric Administration. "Climate," *U.S. Department of Commerce.* **http://www.noaa.gov/index.html.**

Neumann, Dietrich. *The Structure of Light: Richard Kelly and the Illumination of Modern Architecture.* New Haven: Yale University Press, 2010.

"Nobel Center, David Chipperfield." *Stockholm Association of Architects.* YouTube video. Posted by the Nobel Center, April 4, 2014. **https://www. youtube.com/watch?v=ceSKkeLD7Dg.**

Pallasmaas, Juhani. *The Eyes of the Skin: Architecture and Polemics.* New York: John Wiley & Sons, 2012.

"Peter Zumthor's Serpentine Gallery Pavilion." *The Telegraph.* YouTube video. Posted by *The Telegraph,* June 27, 2011. **http://www.telegraph. co.uk/culture/art/architecture/8601393/Peter- Zumthors-Serpentine-Gallery-Pavilion.html.**

Phillips, Derek. *Daylighting: Natural Light in Architecture.* London: Architectural Press, 2004.

Plummer, Henry. *The Architecture of Natural Light.* New York: The Monacelli Press, 2009.

Plummer, Henry. *Nordic Light: Modern Scandinavian Architecture.* New York: Thames & Hudson, 2012.

"Pritzker Architecture Prize." *Hyatt Foundation.* **http://www.pritzkerprize.com.**

Puustinen, Anu and Ville Hara. *Chapel of St. Lawrence Project Profile.* Helsinki: Avanto Architects, 2010.

Rao, Joe. "Summer Skywatching: July's Twilight Nights." *Space.com,* June 30, 2014. **http://www.space.com/26402-summer- solstice-twilight-july-skywatching.html.**

Reed, Bill. "Whole Systems Integration Process." *Integrative Design Collaborative.* **http://www. integrativedesign.net/integrative.htm.**

Reed, Bill. "A Living Systems Approach to Design." *American Institute of Architects National Convention Keynote Address*, May 2007. **http://www.integrativedesign.net/images/Living_System_Design.pdf.**

Reinhart, Christoph. *Daylighting Handbook I: Fundamentals Designing with the Sun.* USA: Christoph Reinhart, 2014.

"Renzo Piano Pavilion, Kimbell Art Museum, Fort Worth, Texas." *Mondo*arc.* Issue 78: April/May 2014. **http://www.mondoarc.com/projects/retail/2334939/renzo_piano_pavilion_kimbell_art_museum_fort_worth_texas.html.**

Richards, Brent. *New Glass Architecture.* New Haven: Yale University Press, 2006.

"Royal Gold Metal Lecture 2013 – Peter Zumthor." *Royal Institute of British Architects*, YouTube video. Posted by Royal Institute of British Architects, February 2013. **https://vimeo.com/60017470.**

Russell, Sage. *The Architecture of Light.* La Jolla CA: Conceptnine, 2008.

Ruusuvuori, Aarno, Göran Schildt, and J.M. Richards. *Alvar Aalto: 1898-1976.* Helsinki: The Museum of Finnish Architecture, 1978.

Ryan, Raymund. "Museo Jumex in Mexico City by David Chipperfield Architects." *The Architectural Review*, February 11, 2014. **http://www.architectural-review.com/today/museo-jumex-in-mexico-city-by-david-chipperfield-architects/8658048.fullarticle.**

Seppänen, Antti T. "AVANTO: Chapel of St. Lawrence." Vimeo video. Posted by Antti T Seppänen - Oiva-Filmi. **https://vimeo.com/33339110.**

Schildt, Goran. *Alvar Aalto: The Mature Years.* New York: Rizzoli, 1989.

Schittich, Christian, editor. *inDETAIL: Solar Architecture.* Basel: Birkhäuser Publishers, 2003.

"Serpentine Gallery 2011." *Arcspace.com: Danish Architecture Centre*, May 2011. **http://www.arcspace.com/features/atelier-peter-zumthor/serpentine-gallery-pavilion-2011/.**

"Serpentine Gallery Park Nights 2011: Peter Zumthor and Piet Oudolf with Fritz Hauser and Peter Conradin Zumthor." YouTube video. Posted by Serpentine Galleries, 2011. **https://vimeo.com/92263112.**

Seward, Aaron. "A Luminous History." *Architectural Lighting*, November 21, 2011. **http://www.archlighting.com/projects/a-luminous-history_o?o=7.**

Spirit of Space. "Reid Building at The Glasgow School of Art, A Conversation with Steven Holl & Chris McVoy." New York: Steven Holl Architects. Vimeo video. Posted by Steven Holl Architects, July 22, 2014. **http://www.stevenholl.com/videos/101410201.**

"Stacking Green." *Divisare.* **http://divisare.com/projects/212110-vo-trong-nghia-architects-stacking-green.**

Stasthaki, Ellie. "Steven Holl completes the Reid Building." *Wallpaper*, February 26, 2014. **http://www.wallpaper.com/architecture/steven-holl-completes-the-reid-building-the-latest-addition-to-the-glasgow-school-of-art-campus.**

Steane, Mary Ann. *The Architecture of Light: Recent Approaches to Designing with Natural Light.* London: Routledge, 2011.

Steffy, Gary. *Architectural Lighting Design, third edition.* New York: John Wiley & Sons, 2008.

Steven Holl Architects. *Green Sheet: Seona Reid Building, Glasgow School of Art.* New York: Steven Holl Architects.

Sullivan, Louis. "The Tall Office Building Artistically Considered." *Lippincott's Monthly Magazine*, March 1896.

Tanizaki, Jun'ichirō. *In Praise of Shadows.* New Haven: Leete's Island Books, Inc., 1997.

Thaureau, Vanessa. *Ultimate Lighting Design.* New York: teNeues, 2005.

"The Architecture." *Clyfford Still Museum.* **https://clyffordstillmuseum.org/architecture.**

Torres, Elias. *Zenithal Light.* Barcelona: School of Barcelona (ETSAB), 2004.

Tregena, Peter and Michael Wilson. *Daylighting: Architecture and Lighting Design.* London: Routledge, 2011.

Twombly, Robert. *Louis Kahn: Essential Texts.* New York: W. W. Norton & Company, 2003.

Van der Ryn, Sim and Stuart Cohen. *Ecological Design: Tenth Anniversary Edition.* Washington: Island Press, 2007.

"Vote for Maggie's Lanarkshire – RIBA Stirling Prize." *Maggie's Centre Lanarkshire.* **https://www.maggiescentres.org/our-centres/maggies-lanarkshire/news/article/vote-for-maggies-lanarkshire-stirling-prize-2015/?page=1.**

Wachtmeister, Jesper. *Kochuu: Japanese Architecture/Influence & Origin.* 2003. Sweden: Solaris Filmproduktio. DVD.

"Weather Graphs and Maps." *Weatherspark.com.* **https://weatherspark.com.**

"Degree Days: Energy Data for Professionals." *Degreedays.net: Weather Underground.* **http://www.degreedays.net/#generate.**

"Weather Almanac." *Weather Underground.* **http://www.wunderground.com.**

Winchip, Susan. *Fundamentals of Lighting, second edition.* CA: Fairfield Publishing, 2011.

Zumthor, Peter. *Peter Zumthor Atmospheres: Architectural Environments – Surrounding Objects.* Basel: Birkhäuser, 2012.

Index   page numbers in italics refer to illustrations.

Credits

CHAPTER 1:
CHOREOGRAPHED LIGHT

**Chapel of St. Lawrence
(Pyhän Laurin Kappeli), Vantaa, Finland**

Anu Puustinen and Ville Hara,
Avanto Architects

Architect: Avanto Architects

Architectural Drawings and Models:
Avanto Architects

Photographs:
Pyhan Laurin Kappeli 10
Kuvio 14, 16 (bottom), 21
Tuomas Uusheimo 15, 16 (top), 18, 19, 20
Avanto Architects Ltd. 22

Concept Diagrams: Fiona Wholey
(drawings after Avanto Architects)

Daylight Analysis: Tim Mayer, School
of Architecture University of Minnesota
(using Velux Daylight Visualizer)

**Reid Building, Glasgow School of Art,
Glasgow, Scotland, UK**

Steven Holl Architects

Architect: Steven Holl, Steven Holl Architects

Architectural Drawings and Models:
Steven Holl Architects 40, 45
JM Architects 43

Photographs:
Chris McVoy 11, 39 (top)
Alan McAteer 13, 34, 40
Iwan Baan 35, 36, 37, 38, 39 (bottom), 41, 42
JM Architects 43

Concept Diagrams: Fiona Wholey
(drawings after Steven Holl Architects)

Daylight Analysis: Tim Mayer, School
of Architecture University of Minnesota
(using Velux Daylight Visualizer)

CHAPTER 2:
ATMOSPHERIC LIGHT

ANDO MUSEUM, Naoshima, Kagawa, Japan

Tadao Ando, Tadao Ando Architect & Associates

Architect: Tadao Ando Architect & Associates

Architectural Drawings: Tadao Ando Architect
& Associates

Photographs: Yoshihiro Asada

Concept Diagrams: Fiona Wholey (drawings
after Tadao Ando Architect & Associates)

Daylight Analysis: Yixuan Cheng, School
of Architecture University of Minnesota
(using Velux Daylight Visualizer)

**Serpentine Gallery 2011, Kensington
Gardens, Hyde Park, London, England, UK**

Peter Zumthor, Atelier Peter Zumthor
(architecture), Piet Oudolf (garden design)

Architect: Atelier Peter Zumthor

Watercolor: Serpentine Gallery Pavilion 2011,
Designed by Peter Zumthor, Watercolor on
paper © Peter Zumthor

Structural Section illustration: Ed Clark,
Arup London

Photographs:
Daniel Imade, Arup London 57, 76, 77
  Serpentine Galleries:
Serpentine Gallery Pavilion 2011, Designed
  by Peter Zumthor, Photograph © 2011
  John Offenbach 73
Serpentine Gallery Pavilion 2011, Designed
  by Peter Zumthor, Photographs © 2011
  Walter Herfst 72, 75 (left)
Construction Images – Serpentine Galleries
  74, 78
Urszula Maj 75 (right) © 2011 Hufton & Crow/
  VIEW 79

Concept Diagrams: Fiona Wholey
(drawings after Atelier Peter Zumthor)

Daylight Analysis: Nicole Kiel, School
of Architecture University of Minnesota
(using Velux Daylight Visualizer)

CHAPTER 3:
SCULPTED LIGHT

**Jumex Museum (Museo Jumex),
Mexico City, Mexico**

David Chipperfield, David Chipperfield
Architects

Architect: David Chipperfield Architects

Sketches: David Chipperfield

Architectural Drawings: David Chipperfield
Architects

Photographs:
Simon Menges 87, 93, 94, 95, 96
Iwan Bann 91, 92

Concept Diagrams: Fiona Wholey and
Rebecca Nash (drawings after
David Chipperfield Architects)

Daylight Analysis: Arup London (using Radiance)

**ARPAE Headquarters: Regional Agency
for Environmental Protection and Energy
(Agenzia Regionale per la Prevenzione,
Ambiente ed Energia), Ferrara, Italy**

Mario Cucinella, Mario Cucinella Architects

Architect: Mario Cucinella Architects

Architectural Drawings and Study Models:
Mario Cucinella Architects

Photographs: Moreno Maggi

Concept Diagrams: Fional Wholey and Rebecca
Nash (drawings after Mario Cucinella Architects)

Bioclimatic Study: Manens-Tifs SpA (Roberto
Zecchin, Adileno Boeche, Andrea Fornasiero)

CHAPTER 4:
STRUCTURED LIGHT

Ulltveit-Moe Pavilion, National Museum – Architecture (Nasjonalmuseet Arkitektur), Oslo, Norway

Sverre Fehn

Architect: Sverre Fehn and Martin Dietrichson

Architectural Drawings and Models: Kima Arkitektur

Exhibition Pavilion Plan: © National Museum of Art, Architecture and Design

Sverre Fehn: 1970 Osaka Pavilion Proposal: Drawings and Models

Study Model: Therese Husby and National Museum

Concept Sketches: Andreas Harvik © National Museum of Art, Architecture and Design

Photographs:
Thomas Meyer 119, 122, 127 (top), 128
Børre Høstland © National Museum of Art, Architecture and Design 123
Morten Thorkildsen © National Museum of Art, Architecture and Design 125, 126, 127(bottom), 129 (bottom)
Knut Øystein Nerdrum © National Museum of Art, Architecture and Design 129 (top), 130
Annar Bjørgli, Manthey Kula: 2015 "Ode to Osaka" Installation © National Museum of Art, Architecture and Design 131

Concept Diagrams: Fiona Wholey (drawings after Sverre Fehn and Martin Dietrichson)

Daylight Analysis: Tianwei Gu, School of Architecture University of Minnesota (using Velux Daylight Visualizer)

Chapel of Retreat (Capilla del Retiro) Sanctuary of Auco, Calle Larga, Los Andes Valley, Valparaíso, Chile

Cristián Undurraga, Undurraga Devés Architects

Architect: Undurraga Devés Architects

Architectural Drawings: Undurraga Devés Architects

Photographs: Sergio Pirrone

Concept Diagrams: Fiona Wholey (drawings after Undurraga Devés Architects)

Daylight Analysis: Chenxuan He, School of Architecture University of Minnesota (using Velux Daylight Visualizer)

CHAPTER 5:
MATERIAL LIGHT

Clyfford Still Museum, Denver, Colorado, USA

Brad Cloepfil, Allied Works Architecture

Architect: Allied Works Architecture

Architectural Drawings and Models: Allied Works Architecture

Photographs: Jeremy Bittermann

Concept Diagrams: Fiona Wholey (drawings after Allied Works Architecture)

Daylight Analysis: Arup New York (using Radiance)

Maggie's Centre, Lanarkshire, Airdrie, North Lanarkshire, Scotland, UK

Neil Gillespie, Reiach and Hall Architects

Architect: Reiach and Hall Architects

Architectural Drawings and Models: Reiach and Hall Architects

Photographs: David Grandorge

Concept Diagrams: Fiona Wholey (drawings after Reiach and Hall Architects)

Daylight Analysis: Tianwei Gu, School of Architecture University of Minnesota (using Velux Daylight Visualizer)

CHAPTER 6:
INTEGRATED LIGHT

Stacking Green House, Ho Chi Minh City, Vietnam

Vo Trong Nghia, Vo Trong Nghia Architects

Architect: Vo Trong Nghia Architects

Architectural Drawings: Vo Trong Nghia Architects

Photographs: Hiroyuki Oki

Concept Diagrams: Fiona Wholey (drawings after Vo Trong Nghia Architects)

Daylight Analysis: Tianwei Gu, School of Architecture University of Minnesota (using Velux Daylight Visualizer)

Kimbell Art Museum and Piano Pavilion, Fort Worth, Texas, USA

Kimbell Art Museum, Louis Kahn

Piano Pavilion, Renzo Piano, Renzo Piano Building Workshop

Kimbell Art Museum

Architect: Louis Kahn

Photographs:
212 (bottom) View from the southwest with Henry Moore's Figure in a Shelter (1983), Louis I. Kahn (1901–1974), architect. Photograph: Robert LaPrelle © 2013 Kimbell Art Museum, Fort Worth, Texas.
218 West lobby, Louis I. Kahn (1901–1974), architect. Photograph: Robert LaPrelle © 2013 Kimbell Art Museum, Fort Worth, Texas.
220 (top) South galleries, Louis I. Kahn (1901–1974), architect. Photograph: Robert LaPrelle © 2013 Kimbell Art Museum, Fort Worth, Texas.

Concept Diagrams: Fiona Wholey (drawings after Kimbell Art Museum)

Piano Pavilion

Architect: Renzo Piano Building Workshop

Architectural Drawings and Models: Renzo Piano Building Workshop

Photographs:
212 (top) South view, Renzo Piano Pavilion. Photo By Robert Laprelle. © 2013 Kimbell Art Museum, Fort Worth, Texas.
213 Aerial Photography Inc.
217 South view, Renzo Piano Pavilion. Photograph: Robert Laprelle. © 2013 Kimbell Art Museum, Fort Worth, Texas.
219 Nic Lehoux
220 (bottom) Nic Lehoux
221 (left) Nic Lehoux
221 (right) Photograph: Stefano Goldberg, Publifoto © Renzo Piano Building Workshop
222 Photograph: Onur Teke © Renzo Piano Building Workshop

Concept Diagrams: Fiona Wholey (drawings after Renzo Piano Building Workshop)

Daylight Analysis: Arfon Davies, Associate Director, Arup London (using Radiance)